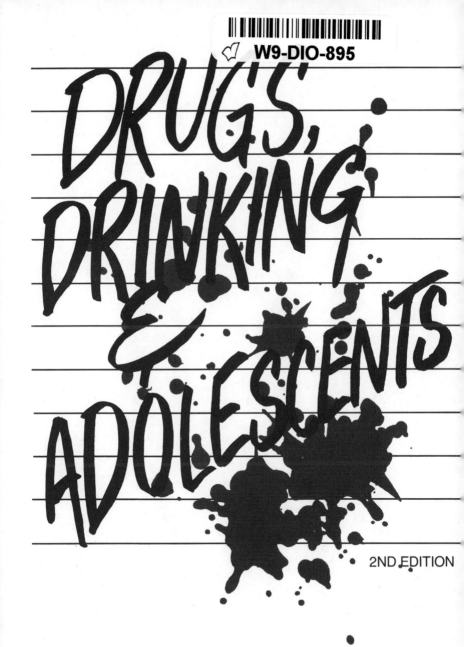

DRUGS,
DRINKING
&
ADOLESCENTS

2ND EDITION

Drugs, Drinking and Adolescents

Second Edition

DONALD IAN MACDONALD, M.D.

Clinical Professor of Pediatrics
University of South Florida
Tampa, Florida
Deputy Assistant to the President
Director, Drug Abuse Policy Office
The White House
Washington, D.C.

YEAR BOOK MEDICAL PUBLISHERS, INC.

CHICAGO • LONDON • BOCA RATON

Library of Congress Cataloging-in-Publication Data

Macdonald, Donald Ian.
    Drugs, drinking, and adolescents.

    Includes bibliographies and index.
        1. Youth—United States—Drug use.   2.   Drug abuse—
Treatment—United States.   3.   Youth—United States—
Alcohol use.   4.   Alcoholism—Treatment—United States.
I. Title. [DNLM: 1.   Substance Abuse—in adolescence.
WM 270 M478d]
HV5824.Y68M35   1989   362.2'93'088055   89-5527
ISBN 0-8151-5993-5

        1   2   3   4   5   6   7   8   9   0   MG   93   92   91   90   89

Sponsoring Editor: Nancy E. Chorpenning
Developmental Editor: Craig A. Pugh
Assistant Director, Manuscript Services: Frances M. Perveiler
Production Project Manager: Gayle Paprocki
Proofroom Manager: Shirley E. Taylor

To Andy and his family,
who contributed the most and, in
the process, gained the most.

PUBLISHER'S NOTE

Dr. Macdonald joined the White House staff in Washington, D.C., in February, 1987, as the Director of the Drug Abuse Policy Office. He is the President's advisor for drug abuse policy and provides advice and assistance regarding AIDS and the human immunodeficiency virus (HIV) epidemic.

Dr. Macdonald first wrote this book in 1984, prior to joining the Administration, based on his experience as a practicing pediatrician in Clearwater, Florida, and as a national leader in the parents' movement against drug abuse.

FOREWORD TO THE FIRST EDITION

During the decades of the 1960s and 1970s, an unprecedented and tragic increase in the use and abuse of psychoactive drugs occurred in this country. Its most dangerous impact was on young people, particularly teenagers. In earlier decades, though many adolescents smoked cigarettes and often began to experiment with alcohol, they were essentially drug-free so far as illicit drugs were concerned. By 1982, however, the percentage of high school seniors who had had some experience with illicit drugs climbed from essentially zero to over 65%.

American Society in general and the American medical profession in particular were slow to recognize the danger and importance of this drastic change in drug use patterns. Only in the 1980s did organized medicine begin to take note that the one population subgroup in this country which was showing a decrease rather than an increase in life expectancy was American teenagers; and that the major causes of death among our teenagers, including accidents and violence, very often were related to high levels of drug and alcohol use.

Much of this delayed recognition resulted from a prolonged national debate concerning the true nature of the American drug problem. Until the end of the 1970s, many American professionals, particularly those in academia and the prestige media, tended to see society's *reaction* to drug use, rather than the rapidly accelerating levels of drug use themselves, as our major legitimate national concern. One example was the very title of the final report of President Nixon's Shaffer Commission report: "Marijuana: A Signal of Misunderstanding." A second was the report prepared by the Task Force on Drug Abuse of the 1978 President's Commission on Mental Health. This review of the American drug scene paid essentially no attention to the tremendous increase in national and particularly adolescent drug use which was well-documented by that time. It devoted the bulk of its attention and concern to questions concerning decriminalization not only of marijuana, but other psychoactive drugs as well, and how to identify levels of illicit drug use which were safe and acceptable for America's teenagers. In this connection, it went so far as to express uncertainty that levels of marijuana use by adolescents, as high as daily, were necessarily undesirable or dangerous. In view of the fact that such attitudes were widespread until recent years, it is quite understandable why drug use patterns continued to increase as long as they did.

In contrast, Dr. Ian Macdonald has consistently attempted to increase both the medical profession's and the public's informed awareness of the extent and seriousness of the drug problem in this country, and to sustain constructive initiatives for dealing with it at a professional and personal level. This book is but one of many such activities on his part. His book makes a substantial contribution toward rectifying a gap in the medical literature and the priorities of medical training. Though the addictive disorders have been described as this nation's number one health problem because of their combined mortality, morbidity, economic and social destructiveness, they continue to receive a very low percentage of classroom time in medical schools—less than 0.6%—and in the attention they receive in the medical literature and medical meetings. This volume constitutes a significant effort to redress that unacceptable imbalance.

WILLIAM POLLIN, M.D.
Director
National Institute on Drug Abuse

PREFACE TO THE SECOND EDITION

In the years since this book was first published, there have been many changes that impact upon substance abuse in teens which were not anticipated as I wrote the first edition in 1983. Some of the news has been good, but many of the changes have produced tragic consequences.

The good news has been the increased awareness of the dangers of drug use, along with a shift in attitude away from acceptability of use. What was "cool" in the late 1970s is no longer acceptable behavior, as measured by responses to the High School Senior Drug Abuse Survey (page 4). Of even greater significance is the behavioral change marked by a downward trend in the number of high school seniors using drugs (in all categories), including, for the first time in 1987, cocaine.

Two important events in the "bad news" category are the emergence of free-base cocaine (particularly "crack") and the spread of human immunodeficiency virus (HIV) and acquired immune deficiency syndrome (AIDS). "Crack" cocaine, which began to appear widely in the mid-1980s, increased cocaine's potential for toxicity and dependence. It also became increasingly attractive to younger and younger users as its cost dropped. HIV infection and AIDS are particularly relevant because 25% of all HIV-infected individuals admit to intravenous drug use. Additionally, many others who are infected are regular users of intoxicants which have negative effects on judgment and inhibition. Of major concern is the fact that over two thirds of infants with HIV infection have at least one parent who has been a user of intravenous drugs.

Year Book Medical Publishers arranged for another health care professional in the field of substance abuse to consult on this second edition, in view of my changed commitments since first writing this book. I thank Dr. Ruth R. Wharton, former chairman of the Illinois State Medical Society Committee on Alcoholism and Drug Abuse, and currently treating physician for alcoholism and substance abuse programs, for her careful review of the first edition and her thoughtful recommendations of editorial changes and updating of data to reflect some of the events of the past five years.

DONALD IAN MACDONALD, M.D.

Contents

1

The Drug Epidemic

Adolescent drug abuse is a major disease seen regularly by pediatricians, but diagnosed infrequently. The reasons for missing the diagnosis are multiple, but for the affected teenager and his family, such error may be disastrous. Suspecting the diagnosis but delaying therapy or referring for ineffective treatment is a common and serious problem. In a country with an estimated 3 million adolescent alcoholics,[1] all pediatricians are, almost certainly, seeing at least a few.

The teenager who comes to a pediatric office because of fatigue, cough, sore throat, red eyes, chest pain, or other unexplained symptoms may have a drug problem. It is no longer adequate to do laboratory work for infectious mononucleosis, anemia, and hepatitis and not consider drugs as a possible cause of fatigue. If the child's lethargy is too quickly blamed on insufficient sleep, an overly busy schedule, or mild adolescent withdrawal, the real cause of the problem may be missed.

When adolescents are brought to a pediatric office with cough, sore throat, red eyes, and other upper respiratory complaints, smoking should be considered a possible cause. Ordering complete blood counts, throat cultures, nasal smears for eosinophils, and chest and sinus x-rays without considering smoking as an etiologic agent is an inadequate diagnostic workup. Before prescribing various antihistamine-decongestant medications, the physician should consider the child's behavior and look for clues that he or she may be smoking tobacco or marijuana.

Adolescent drug abuse, a disease of epidemic proportions, presents as a recognizable syndrome closely related to a wide variety of other teenage problems. This book will look at the characteristics of this syndrome as well as the stages of chemical dependency.

1

Probable causes of the problem (the best solution to which is prevention) will also be discussed.

The patterns of use and abuse of chemicals in adolescents have changed remarkably in recent years and continue to change. The chemicals presently in use are varied, stronger, and more readily available than they were only 5 years ago. Not only are more children presently involved, but involvement is heavier and occurring at younger ages.

THE EPIDEMIC

A sharp upswing in adolescent drug use began in the mid 1970s, preceded by a marked increase of usage by college students about 10 years earlier. Drugs had always been available, but never were they used in such quantity by such young people. Never had use been so socially acceptable nor the myth of harmlessness so widely believed. Previously, illicit drug use in our culture was typically a condition of people in economic or personal distress. The heroin addict of the ghetto was the prototype. The drugs abused prior to 1960 were most often the opiates well known for their ability to relieve pain. The typical adolescent drug abuser in the 1980s does not fit the picture of the 1940 drug abuser. His socioeconomic status and his drug choices have changed markedly.

Harvard professor Timothy Leary became a guru of a new psychedelic age when he propounded the use of lysergic acid diethylamide (LSD) to "expand one's consciousness." Psychiatrists in training took the drug to understand the deeper recesses of their minds. Priests took it to establish a closer relationship with God. Major newspapers carried enthusiastic reports from users of this new drug, and the epidemic was on.

University students adopted LSD, marijuana, and a host of other psychedelics as their drugs, and their illegality was accepted as a part of a general youth protest against such things as "the establishment," "unjust war," and "environmental rape." The risks of LSD were soon apparent, and although this drug slipped from its earlier promise, the popularity of the milder psychedelics continued to grow, and by the mid 1970s, marijuana was being strongly urged as a candidate for legalization. Piggybacking the civil rights movement, originally aimed at promoting rights and opportunities for blacks, came a distorted movement seeking the legal right to the intoxicant of one's choice. Adults declared opposition to drug use by adolescents, but few could deny that such use was escalating.

Many Americans who had no real involvement in the youth or civil rights movements of the 1960s were also on the road to chemical dependency. These people, also, were dealing with life chemically, but their chemicals were the legal tranquilizers and sedatives prescribed by their physicians for stress and anxiety. It was a frequent occurrence in the early 1970s for pediatricians to see in their offices glassy-eyed and tranquilized mothers of young children. These were respectable middle-class housewives, women whose physicians had prescribed diazepam (Valium) or chlordiazepoxide (Librium) to help them cope with the stresses of their everyday lives. Along with these and other exciting and less legal new drugs, the acceptability and use of alcohol continued to escalate. The hope of better living through chemistry seemed to have arrived.

By the mid 1970s, increasing numbers of younger children were being swept into this chemophilic society. Between the years of 1975 and 1978, the number of high school seniors who smoked pot (marijuana) daily jumped from 6.0% to 10.7%, with the typical daily user consuming 3.5 joints per day (Table 1–1). Even more alarming, perhaps, was the escalation in the numbers of youngsters who had begun their marijuana smoking by the ninth grade. The senior class of 1975 had had only 17% of its members initiated by the time they were freshmen. In startling contrast 34.1% of freshmen in 1975 had already tried pot. Of these, 16.2% had begun by the eighth grade.[2]

The Johnston-Bachman-O'Malley figures, which have been most useful for monitoring trends, are from a report commissioned by a federal agency, the National Institute on Drug Abuse (NIDA). Beginning in 1975, researchers have performed an annual survey of high school drug use. Each year, 15,000 to 19,000 students have been chosen from small schools, large schools, rural areas, inner cities, East and West, North and South. Figures for drug use have been surprisingly homogeneous for a diversity of demographic pop-

TABLE 1–1.   High School Seniors Drug Abuse*

Drug	1975 (%)	1978 (%)	1980 (%)	1982 (%)	1984 (%)	1986 (%)
Marijuana						
Ever used	47	59	60	59	55	51
Used in past month	27	37	34	28	26	21
Use daily	6	10.7	9.1	6.3	5.0	3.3
Used by ninth grade	17	27	31	35		25.2
Alcohol						
Daily	5.7	5.7	6	5.7	4.8	4.8
In past month	68	72	72	70	67	67
Cigarettes–daily	27	28	21	25		
Stimulants (other than cocaine)– past month	8.5	8.7	12.1	13.7	8.3	5.2
Cocaine–ever used	9	12.9	15.7	16		
Perceive great risk (in regular use)						
Marijuana	43	35	50	60	67	74
Tobacco	51	59	64	60.5	64	69
Friends disapprove of regular use						
Marijuana	75	NA	72	75	79	83
Tobacco	64	NA	74	70	74	74

* Adapted from Johnston L.D., Bachman J.G., O'Malley P.M.: *Student Drug Use, Attitudes, and Beliefs: National Trends 1975-1987*. Rockville, Md., NIDA, 1987 (available from the National Institute on Drug Abuse, Division of Research, 5600 Fishers Lane, Rockville, MD 20857).[2]
Note: NA = question not asked.

ulations. Some increased use was noted in large cities when compared with rural areas, and some increased use was reported in the Northeast and West when compared with the South. More significantly all areas and populations showed substantial increases in use, and the trend has been toward similar usage patterns in all groups.

One notable exception to the uniformity of utilization is that the number of black male seniors using marijuana daily in 1978 remained at 5.7%, while 13.7% of their white male classmates were involved. This emphasizes again that it is a misconception to view

TABLE 1–2. Alcohol Use Among High School Seniors in 1979[3]

	%
Drink daily	6
Five or more drinks in a row in last 2 wk	
One occasion	
Boys	52
Girls	31
Three or more occasions	
Boys	26
Girls	12

drug use as only a black or inner city problem. Instead it would appear that marijuana use is at least as big a problem for affluent suburbia.

The Michigan State University researchers who compiled these figures also considered alcohol.[3] Small comfort may be gained from noting that the number of seniors who drink daily has remained unchanged since 1975. When biweekly use was examined in 1979, 52% of high school senior males admitted to consuming five or more alcoholic drinks at one sitting (Table 1–2) within the previous 2 weeks. This quantity of alcohol consumed over a 1- to 2-hour period is sufficient to produce legal intoxication in a high percentage of young people. Perhaps even more startling was that 26% of male seniors admitted to having five or more drinks on three or more occasions within the previous 2 weeks.

The marijuana and alcohol usage patterns for girls have been somewhat milder than those of their male counterparts. Marijuana was used daily by approximately 4% of senior girls in the class of 1982, compared with 8% of their male counterparts. The percentage of daily alcohol users among girls in the same class was 3.5%, compared with 7.5% of the boys. Cigarette use was a different matter. In 1977, female high school seniors equalled males at the half-a-pack-a-day smoking level (17%). By 1977 they had taken a lead that they continue to hold. At lower levels of smoking, there are even larger sex-related differences, with more females than males numbered as occasional smokers.[2] Nearly 320,000 Americans died in

1987 as a result of cigarette smoking, and the American Cancer Society estimated that lung cancer will be the leading cause of cancer deaths in American women.

It would not be unfair to say that intoxication has become a normal behavior pattern for high school senior boys if "normal" is defined as the behavior of over 50% of the population. On the other hand, to call intoxication normal, especially in childhood, distorts the use of a word that to some is synonymous with "acceptable" and "healthy."

Following a seminar during which the Johnston-Bachman-O'Malley senior statistics were given, a young man commented to me that he believed the usage numbers were all too low. He had been smoking pot daily when he was a high school freshman, and it was his observation that he was the only one of his pot-smoking group who had made it to the senior year. His comment raises the question of drug use as a cause of high school dropout. The U.S. Bureau of the Census has estimated that approximately 15% of our children never graduate from high school.[4] Even higher dropout rates are reported by the National Center for Educational Statistics, which estimated that in 1981, 27.9% of children who were ninth graders 3 years earlier did not graduate with their class.[5] In other words, the Johnston-Bachman-O'Malley usage numbers quoted earlier may not measure the rates of use among our most seriously troubled young people, but instead may look at the more "normal" population. Drug-abuse concerns and strategy need to focus on this new epidemic, which involves large numbers of otherwise normal children. For the more than 20% of young people who drop out of school the prognosis is probably worse. For them, different approaches to prevention and treatment are perhaps needed. The solutions to their personal and social problems may be beyond the limits of this book, which has been written for those less troubled children whose major problems are immaturity and the use of psychoactive chemicals.

Since 1978 there have been encouraging decreases in daily usage rates for marijuana and tobacco. Monthly usage rates have also fallen, but less dramatically. These decreases may reflect increasing concern among teenagers about the dangers of such use. In 1982, 60% of high school seniors saw regular marijuana use as harmful, compared with only 35% of the class of 1978 (Table 1–1). Also noted in the survey was increasing disapproval by teenagers of the practice of regular and frequent use of marijuana. In 1987, 83% of seniors thought their friends would disapprove of such use, compared with 69% in 1977.[2] Changes in attitudes about alcohol or drinking have been slower to change but in the class of 1987 the use of illicit drugs turned downward. Unfortunately, the levels are still high and the chemophilia continues.

A LOOK AT ALCOHOL

Considerable confusion exists among adults, physicians as well as others, about the relationship of juvenile drinking and drug abuse. Children have been quick to point out that adult society consumes much alcohol in various forms, and adolescents see it as more dangerous than their drug, marijuana. Adults who say that they are glad that their child uses no drugs, although well aware of his alcohol use, need to develop a better understanding of the relationship of drugs to alcohol. Any person who consumes enough alcohol on weekends to cause even occasional problems with driving or social situations has a drug problem.

In truth the use of marijuana and alcohol are very closely related for the adolescent. In a number of surveys, marijuana use and drinking go hand in hand. I asked 104 children at Straight, Inc., an adolescent treatment program in St. Petersburg, Fla., about their patterns of drug and alcohol use. Of these, 103 said they smoked pot regularly, and 103 said they drank alcohol regularly. In terms of their drug of choice, approximately one third of these preferred alcohol, and two thirds preferred marijuana. Both groups agreed they would take either or both if that was what they thought it would take to make them high. If only one of the two were available, they would take it. This does not contradict surveys reporting that ''only'' 59.5% of high school seniors have tried marijuana and 92.6% have tried alcohol,[2] and it reinforces early studies demonstrating that preference relates to availability.[6]

This book may single out marijuana and other drugs, but it should be understood that, when speaking about adolescent drug abuse, alcohol is definitely included.

ADOLESCENT MORTALITY

Talking about young people and drugs often tends to take on a moral tone. Morality is relevant, but the emphasis here is health and the related issues of mortality, morbidity, and failure to achieve full adult maturational development. In the 15- to 24-year age range, the leading causes of death are accidents, homicides, and suicides. All have a strong correlation with drug and alcohol use. Marvelous technical and medical advances in our society have produced declining death rates for all ages with each passing decade in this century, with one exception. Mortality rates in the 15- to 24-year age range have risen significantly in the last 20 years.[7] Pediatricians need to take note.

The American Safety Council estimates that over 50% of all accidental deaths in this country are related to alcohol or other drug abuse. Approximately 50,000 people die on the highways of this country every year. In 1981, young drivers (aged 16 to 24 years) constituting 17% of the U.S. population were involved in accidents resulting in 48% of the fatalities. A total of 21,431 young drivers accounted for crashes resulting in 23,690 deaths, and 9,834 of these drivers themselves were killed.[8] It is not only the drunken driver who suffers, but his passengers, occupants of other cars, and pedestrians who are unfortunate enough to be in his way.

Homicide, another drug-related disease, is also on the upswing, particularly in areas where drug trafficking and use are heavy. Unfortunately, innocent bystanders are often killed in incidents that have become all too common in these drug centers.

DRUG ABUSE: A NATIONAL DISASTER

The effect of drugs on the nonusing population cuts much deeper than the mortality figures. Perhaps most important is the weakening of our national fiber in a number of measurable and fairly obvious ways. Areas affected include scholastic performance, work performance, family relationships, military readiness, the cost of goods and services, the crime rate, and the filling of our mental-health institutions.

Scholastic aptitude test (SAT) scores in this country fell for 18 straight years following 1964, when less than 2% of the population had ever tried pot. Performance scores improved slightly in 1982, correlating well with the decreased daily use of marijuana recorded among high school seniors in that year. Despite this fairly obvious correlation, little is said about the relationship of drugs to school performance in SAT reports. Drug use is related to truancy, sleeping in school, change in short-term memory, and attention abilities. A number of factors may underly both an increase in drug use and a decrease in overall school testing performance, but the possibility of a cause-and-effect relationship should not be ignored.

Our military performance also suffers. From the classes of 1978 and 1979, where daily marijuana use among high school seniors reached an all-time high, came many of the servicemen now serving us overseas. Unfortunately, the military got more than its proportionate share of troubled young people from these classes. Many young people are in military service because their parents had difficulties with them and perceived military life as a way of helping them learn discipline and "get their acts together." This use of the military service is helpful for some, but when drugs or alcohol are the problem, it is not of any great value to either the young people or the military. Drug and alcohol rehabilitation centers at military installations across the country are bursting at the seams. Unfortunately they are unable to help most of these unfortunate young people, and the number of medical discharges is rising.

On-duty use of marijuana on the naval carrier Midway was estimated to be 60% in 1982. A survey run at Norfolk and San Diego Naval Stations in December 1980 asked returning seamen to submit urine samples for examination. These seamen were assured there would be no prosecution or notation in their record about what might be found in their specimens. At both installations a marijuana screen was positive in 48% of approximately 1,000 recruits. In a Department of Defense survey that same year, in which anonymity was guaranteed, 27% admitted to illicit drug use within the previous 30 days. Thanks to an extensive program of education and testing that number has continued to fall, most recently to 5.5%. Similarly, the survey showed a drop in self-reported heavy drinkers from 12% to 9%.

United States military leaders are not alone in their concern about the relationship of marijuana use to performance. Airlines have requested permission to check pilots for marijuana. The National Football League, with its recent cocaine scandals, recognizes the need for closer supervision of athletes and for monitoring their performance. Alcohol and drug use are blamed for the majority of absenteeism in the auto industry. The National Institute on Alcohol Abuse and Alcoholism estimated that in 1984, alcohol-related industry losses were $117 billion.[11]

The chairman of the National Transportation Safety Board has expressed his concern about alcohol and drug use in the railroad industry.[12] In 18 recently investigated cases involving alcohol and drug use, 25 railroad employees were killed, another 13 were injured, and property damage in excess of $25 million was reported. A crash in Livingston, La., on Sept. 28, 1982, involved the derailment of 43 cars, 14 of which contained toxic material. Property damage from this incident was estimated at $10 million, and approximately 3,000 people were evacuated from their homes for as long as 2 weeks. Investigation revealed that the locomotive crew members had consumed alcoholic beverages immediately before reporting for duty and probably while on duty. Less than a week later, an engineer and head brakeman were killed in a crash near Newport, Ark., where property damage was estimated at $1 million. The engineer had a blood alcohol level of 0.04 mg percent plus additional unabsorbed alcohol in his stomach.

It is a long-standing joke that buying a car produced on a Monday is not a good idea. Those cars produced on "hangover day" are most apt to be "lemons" and are sensibly avoided. In recent years there has been a more general decline in the quality of American workmanship, which many believe is related to the close proximity of marijuana to the assembly line.

Pediatricians have become increasingly concerned about child abuse and its disastrous effects on young people and families. They should also be aware that more and more of the abused young people have parents who are chemically dependent. An 8-month-old child was brought to my office with two broken legs and a broken skull produced when the parents were unable to get the baby's feet into his shoes. Both parents, age 18, were chemically dependent, immature, and lacking in the parenting and life skills to cope with their roles as parents and marriage partners. This sort of story is becoming increasingly common.

A survey by an Oklahoma legislator[13] revealed that 62% of all prisoners in that state were incarcerated for crimes directly related to alcohol and/or drug use. Of those in the Oklahoma mental health system, 42% had alcohol- or drug-related problems.

Virtually all alcoholics and drug addicts begin their use as adolescents. Pediatricians and parents have reason to be alarmed and to take action.

2

The Stages of Drug Use

Many believe that drug use does not become a problem until one passes over a line into an area called "drug abuse." An article that appeared in a Sunday newspaper supplement a few years ago entitled "Are you an Alcoholic?" illustrates this belief. Readers were asked to give themselves points for positive answers to questions such as "Do you ever drink alone?" and "Do you ever drink in the morning?" If you reached a total of 70 points, you were declared alcoholic, which allowed the reader to assume that a score of 69 was safe. Similar assumptions have been made about adolescent drinking and drug use.

The Second Report of the National Commission on Marijuana and Drug Abuse[14] identified and defined five patterns of marijuana use. These five, (1) experimental drug use, (2) social or recreational use, (3) circumstantial or situational drug use, (4) intensified drug use, and (5) compulsive drug use, are much like those described in this chapter in four stages. An important point of difference is that in this chapter these patterns should be seen as stages of a progressive disease, and not as isolated entities.

The AMA divides patterns of drug use into categories but also fails to refer to them as parts of a progressive process. The AMA divisions are (1) drug experimentation, (2) drug use (which is subdivided into a recreational category and a regular use category), (3) drug abuse, and (4) drug dependency.[15]

A description of the natural history of cocaine dependency by Nizama comes closer to the staging employed here. He divides the syndrome into 11 stages considered to be part of a progressive process.[16] These stages are (1) curiosity, (2) initiation, (3) pleasure, (4) group identification, (5) group prestige, (6) family isolation, (7) psychopathic behavior, (8) ritualistic behavior, (9) dependency and tolerance, (10) general physical deterioration, and (11) severe sociopathic personality destruction.

Drug and alcohol users do not begin with the goal of becoming addicted or alcoholic. When they begin to use drugs, they embark on a course that for many is a downward trail. With progression the user passes through recognizable stages where typical behaviors are noted. The staging used here[17,18] is a modification for adolescents of the Johnson Institute Model,[19] which so well describes the progression of the adult alcoholic.

The stages of drug use are as follows: 0, curiosity in a "do-drug" world; 1, learning the mood swing; 2, seeking the mood swing; 3, preoccupation with the mood swing; and 4, "doing drugs to feel okay" (Table $2-1$).[15] It should be noted that acute reactions to drug use can and do occur in all except stage 0, regardless of level or pattern of use.

Entry into each stage is preceded by a harmful decision made by the drug user. The most conscious decision is the one leading him to experiment. His later evaluations and decisions are less under his control and may be seen as situational appraisals colored by problems that the drugs have created. It is important in prevention and therapy to stress the concept that although the child may blame his parents, school, or environment for his drug use, it is he who opened his mouth and took the drug.

STAGE 0: CURIOSITY IN A "DO-DRUG" WORLD

Stage 0 corresponds roughly with Nizama's stage of curiosity,[16] a stage that is omitted from the other systems of staging. For the pediatrician interested in prevention, it may be the most important stage.

We live in a world that abounds with inducements to use drugs, legally and otherwise. In such a world, we are all made more susceptible. The role of this "do-drug" environment is covered in Chapter 5. The teenager is additionally at risk because of his normally

TABLE 2 – 1. **Stages of Drug Abuse**[15]

Stage	Mood Alteration	Feelings	Drugs
1: Learning the mood swing	Euphoria Normal Pain	Feel good Few consequences	Tobacco Marijuana Alcohol
2: Seeking the mood swing	Euphoria Normal Pain	Excitement Early guilt	All of the above plus: Inhalants Hash oil, hashish "Ups" "Downs" Prescriptions Cocaine / "crack"
3: Preoccupation with the mood swing	Euphoria Normal Pain	Euphoric highs Doubts including: Severe shame and guilt Depression Suicidal thoughts	All of the above plus: Mushrooms PCP LSD
4: Using drugs to feel normal	Euphoria Normal Pain	Chronic Guilt Shame Remorse Depression	Whatever is available

Sources	Behavior	Frequency
"Friends"	Little detectable change Moderate "after the fact" lying	Progresses to weekend usage
Buying	Dropping extracurricular activities and hobbies Mixed friends (straight and druggie) Dress changing Erratic school performance and "skipping" Unpredictable mood and attitude swings "Conning" behavior	Weekend use progressing to 4-5 times per week Some solo use
Selling	"Cool" appearance Straight friends dropped Family fights (verbal and physical) Stealing—police incidents Pathologic lying School failure, skipping, expulsion, jobs lost	Daily Frequent solo use
Any way possible	Physical deterioration (weight loss, chronic cough) Severe mental deterioration (memory loss and flashbacks) Paranoia, volcanic anger, and aggression School dropout Frequent overdosing	All day every day

curious nature, his willingness to take risks, and his desire to be accepted by his peers. Chapter 6 explores this peer pressure and the particular susceptibility of the immature child. His susceptibility is further enhanced by the easy availability of drugs, which is discussed in Chapter 10.

A combination of environmental and personal forces coupled with easy access to drugs eventually leads most children to the question, "Will it hurt to try one?" Experimental drug use is often motivated by curiosity or the desire to experience new feelings or mood states. The fear of being called "chicken" often provides the final push to "give it a try." We know that adolescents learn by experiment, but the odds involved in making this experiment are unreasonably high. In Russian roulette the odds are one to five in the experimenter's favor. For the middle school child who experiments with tobacco, the odds are considerably more hazardous, being closer to one to three. This means that for every four children who try tobacco, 20 years later one will still be trying to kick the habit. With alcohol, 10% of adult users are problem drinkers. For those who begin at 12.6 years (now the average age of the first drink), there are greatly increased risks. Experimentation may indeed be very dangerous. The correct answer to the question, "Will it hurt to try one?" is, "There's a very good chance one will hurt you." No one can predict for sure who will get hooked except to say the nonuser never will.

STAGE 1: LEARNING THE MOOD SWING

The drugs used in this stage are tobacco, alcohol, and marijuana. For many, tobacco is the first, although tobacco is often not considered a "real" drug; the child who smokes cigarettes does so hoping to fulfill some need.

Children do not believe tobacco makes for better smelling breath or better athletic performance, both of which are important to them. Nor do they believe it makes them live longer or that it is approved by their parents. Most know it is illegal for minors, but large numbers continue to get hooked. Something in what they see in their environment or in advertisements must suggest to them that smokers are macho men on horses or desirable girls at the net in tennis. The pediatrician has a real diagnostic clue if a child admits cigarette smoking. Helpful, also, is the information that the child's friends smoke even if the child himself denies use.

Alcohol use often begins at the family bar. Many children begin with hard liquor, often in the company of a peer or sibling. Euphoria and overdosing may both occur on the first try. The negative aftereffects of nausea, hangover, and parental discovery may postpone subsequent use, but the euphoria and exciting comradery of the experience will be remembered.

Many children approach marijuana as a "no-no" and refuse the first few times it is offered to them. When they finally do accept, it is not from a pusher in the usual sense, but most often from an older sibling or a friend who wants to share an exciting experience. This is an important epidemiologic point. Many times the decision to experiment is not made in response to a question asking whether the teenager is a user, but comes in the form of being handed a joint. To refuse may imply immaturity or cowardice.

The first marijuana smoke may not produce a high. The novice will often accept a joint and take only a token puff, inhaling none, hoping to prove he is not "square." Subsequent use and practice eventually lead to feelings of excitement and pleasure with little if any aftereffects. The child has entered a world where drug use is accepted and where new and interesting experiences are frequent. Excitement accompanies education about paraphernalia such as rolling papers, bongs, and "power hitters," and drug varieties such as sinsemilla may now be a part of his world.

Pleasurable experimentation leads to so-called recreational use in which weekend social life is built around "partying." Teenagers increasingly use the verb "to party" to mean getting high or stoned. For the 70% of high school seniors who drink and the 28.5% who smoke marijuana every month,[2] life is made more exciting by their chemicals. Use tends to occur in social settings among friends or acquaintances who desire to share an experience perceived by them as acceptable and pleasurable. Social events where kegs are on tap are particularly attractive. In many communities, invitations, guest lists, and introduction of guests to parents have become a thing of the past. Teenagers talk of comparing notes prior to weekends to find which homes are having social functions. From this list they decide which need to be "checked out" or "crashed."

The most significant part of this stage is learning how easy it is to feel good. It is this feeling of euphoria (see arrow, Table 2–1) that leads to progressive use. The power of pleasure to shape future behavior should not be underestimated. There are few, if any, consequences noted by the user, except perhaps for some mild guilt. Knowledge of peers who may be having difficulty does not affect the teenager who feels comfortable about his own ability to control use. Some would call this the stage of "moderate" use, a word which implies harmlessness and seems inappropriate in light of the facts of progressive adolescent drug use. Others who would call this the stage of "responsible" use should be reminded that indulging in illegal activity should never be considered responsible.

Regular pot smokers at UCLA were asked why they smoked.[20] The two most common reasons were to "feel good" and because pot was a part of the social scene at school. Both of these are stage 1 reasons, but the third most common answer, "to help me relax," is a sign of progression. When one decides to get high as a goal rather than using drugs as an accompaniment to social occasions, he enters stage 2. The next question is, "Will it hurt if I take one to relax?" The answer is, "Very possibly."

STAGE 2: SEEKING THE MOOD SWING

No longer content to wait for someone to offer him a joint or a beer, it is now important to have one's own supply or ready access. A new status is achieved by the owner of joints or a bag of pot. Midweek use may begin. Taboos against drug use may be believed to be adult vs. youth issues or a violation of his constitutional rights and tend to concern him less and less.

At first stage 2 use may be motivated by a perceived need or desire to cope with a specific situation or condition. The situation may be related to studies, athletic performance, or stress at home. An example of such use is the athlete who takes amphetamines hoping to improve his competitive edge. Later his usage pattern may become more diffuse, and drugs may be taken to deal with a variety of circumstances.

Perceiving no negative consequences of the marijuana he had been told was evil and dangerous, the youth, adventuresome by nature, is apt to move on and experiment with other drugs. Prescription drugs found in the home medicine chest such as tranquilizers, sedatives, and amphetamines may be tried along with stronger cousins of marijuana such as hashish and hash oil. When "head shops" were flourishing, inhalants with names such as "Rush" and "Lockerroom" became popular for the sudden stimulation they produced. A variety of compounds may be tried, but alcohol and/or marijuana remain the chief drugs of most young users.

Behavior changes, often subtle at first, may begin to appear. Marijuana has been called "galloping lethargy," referring to characteristic changes noted in the adolescent user's behavior. An "amotivational syndrome of pot" has been described in which goals change or disappear, and school and much of life becomes "boring." Hobbies may be dropped, extracurricular activities abandoned, and former goal-oriented activities considered "uncool." When asked why she no longer is on the swim team, the young user may say, "I'm not into that anymore." There is evidence that this lack of drive is directly related to marijuana use.[21,22]

Others noting the same lack of motivation believe that the changes are due to selection of a new peer group. Association with these new "friends" who have little motivation is undoubtedly a factor. Children in this stage are seen to have a mixed group of friends. Older "straight" friends may still be a part of their life, but more and more their peers are from a new group usually considered less desirable by their parents. These new friends are often older, differently dressed, and less goal-oriented. The child finds acceptance with them, and, as his habit increases, he may achieve increasing prestige in their company. Often these new comrades are not seen by parents, because the child is less likely to bring them home, or when they do come, they stay briefly and avoid introduction. They may surface only as unidentified people who call at late and unusual hours.

Others believe the increasing lack of motivation relates to faltering school performance. Truancy (which may begin in this stage), hangover, headache, or being stoned in class will cause learning problems. Marijuana, with its effect on short-term memory and attention span, may contribute to school difficulties, and as school performance falls, life's goals may be readjusted. Many other explanations have also been given.[23] Whatever the causes, this is a changing child with decreasing drive and ambition.

Further problems are created for the youngster by the dual life he must lead. At home he is still trying to convince his parents and himself that he is okay by doing his chores, attending church, and participating in family activities. Away from home, he is apt to deny all of these activities as "uncool." A girl who leaves home neatly groomed may add makeup and dangling earrings and remove a bra to identify more closely with her new friends. Juggling two lifestyles produces strain, and for this young person, strain is most easily managed with further chemical use.

Temper tantrums and conning behavior may become increasingly common as a child tries to convince himself and others that he has the right to be left alone. He may come to feel paranoid and persecuted when asked to conform to family rules or when confronted about grades, friends, or drug use. He begins to closely fit the behavior pattern of the irritable and aggressive laboratory primates that were chronic tetrahydrocannabinol (THC) users (see Chapter 4 and Stage 4 in this chapter). This behavior further alienates him from his family and straight friends.

It may become increasingly difficult to stop the progression of drug use occurring in response to the problems such drug use has created. Strong parental reaction to such things as poor report cards may temporarily shock the youth into improved performance. If punishment or restriction is given without understanding the causative relationship of drug use to the offense, such improvement is not likely to be lasting.

The drug-using child will increasingly isolate himself from his family. He may treat home as a "pit stop" to which he comes for food and rest. The meals he would prefer are snacks not eaten with his family. The rest he seeks is in his room with loud musical accompaniment. When rested he may again plan to head out. If the changes seen in this stage are presumed to be nothing more than part of a growing up, the primary role of chemical euphoria in such change may be overlooked. Some would see these changes as signs of "normal" adolescent rebellion, search for independence, and ego identification. In the past, most such rebels would return to the family as adults. The concern now is that, with the widespread availability and acceptance of drugs, they may not return or ever achieve a reasonable and independent adult life. Instead, they may, and all too frequently do, become dependent on drugs and alcohol, a condition that does not improve with time.

As troubles mount, the teenager may decide, usually subconsciously, that "being high" is the main goal of life and enter stage 3. His third wrong decision has been made. This stage may also be entered by a less troubled youngster absolutely captivated by pleasure so easily gained.

STAGE 3: PREOCCUPATION WITH THE MOOD SWING (HARMFUL DEPENDENCY)

The 4.8% of high school seniors who drink daily and the 3.3% who smoke pot daily tend to plan their days around their trips to euphoria. Early in the day, they may make plans to smoke at the bus stop, on the bus, or in the school bathroom, or they may easily be tempted by friends to skip school altogether for a day of partying. Motivation to continue use at this level may stem from the need to elicit a sense of security, comfort or relief, often related to the child's initial reasons for regularly using the drug in stage 2. This psychological dependency is often reinforced by physiologic factors. Alcohol withdrawal, for example, may cause hangover, the pain of which can most easily be managed by taking more alcohol.

Cocaine/crack use increased markedly in the early 1980s and drugs such as LSD, phencyclidine (PCP), or psilocybin mushrooms are used, but alcohol and marijuana are still the most popular drugs for most of these young people.

The behavior changes of stage 2 become more obvious. Real academic problems exist for most, but those who are especially bright or adept at cheating may still pass. Stage 3 users tend to prefer the company of others in late stage 2 or 3. The appearance of many resembles the "hippie" look of the 1960s or is in emulation of the appearance of hard rock superstars.

By this stage it is costing money to be involved. Expenditures of $40 to $50 a week for alcohol and drugs are common and obtained from a variety of sources. Many of these young people have jobs, and parents should be wary of the child who spends more time at work than in study and school-related activity. Statistically, children who work are more likely to use drugs than those who do not. For adult alcoholics, job performance is the last thing to go. It is almost as if the alcoholic uses his employment to prove to his suffering self, his suffering family, and the world that he does not have a drinking problem. Adolescents at this stage may need to work and will often continue with fairly acceptable work performance long after their school work has dropped.

Where the job is babysitting, there is additional concern. At Straight, Inc., "20 Questions" is frequently played when visitors are in attendance to make these visitors more aware. One question often asked of the resident group is, "How many of you used to babysit?" Approximately half usually answer they did. The next question is, "How many of you got stoned while you sat?" (most did). Next is asked, "How many of you got the children you sat for high?" (many positive responses). "How?" "Blow smoke in their face."

Stealing is very common, and shoplifting is practiced by almost all at this stage. Others steal at home. Parents often are suspicious for a long time before they put two and two together. Many are guilty of breaking and entering neighborhood homes and stores. Most children in stage 3 sell drugs. School drug dealers are not typically underworld types making huge sums from innocent children. More often they are slightly older peers who sell at a modest profit to support their own habits. Unfortunately the younger children with whom they are in contact are most susceptible.

Sex and preoccupation with drugs go together. Euphoria is the goal. Intoxication may be used to break down sexual inhibitions in oneself and others. Not only may sex be attractive to the thrill seeker, but it may also be a way of procuring drugs. Girls do not need to buy drugs if they go with boys who have a supply. Intoxicated youths who have not reached a stage of firming up their sexual identity may experiment with homosexuality or be used for pleasure by older homosexuals. The scars and guilt resulting from such experiments may be most difficult to deal with in drug treatment.

Brushes with the law may be frequent for relatively minor offenses such as curfew violation, truancy, vandalism, and shoplifting. Also common but considerably more serious are such things as driving incidents, breaking and entering, or crimes of violence. For the physician, parent, teacher, and police officer, it is all too easy to focus on the child's negative behavior. It is easy to be angry at the brushes with the law and the defiance of family rules and to be frustrated at the potential gone astray. Most do focus on these aspects of the child, and many are ready to write him off as a loser. For parents this is not an easy thing to do, and they often intensify the same efforts at remediation that have previously failed. To succeed with the child, one must understand that there is more involved than the "rotten kid" who meets the eye. There is also a pained and unhappy teenager.

As the disease progresses, pain begins to outweigh pleasure. No child really wants to be at odds with his family, his church, his caring friends, his school, and the law. When not high, he is apt to be depressed and ashamed of himself and his actions. Self-image plummets and suicidal thoughts may become increasingly frequent.

In 1985 5,000 young Americans between the ages of 15 and 24 committed suicide. This is a number that has doubled in the last 20 years.[23a] Half of these young people saw their physician in the month before they died and still went on to their demise. They did not volunteer that they were going to kill themselves, that they had a drug problem, or that they were depressed. Instead they were apt to present with complaints such as abdominal pain, headache, or fatigue. The first questions asked of a teenager with abdominal pain should be how he is doing in school, how he is doing with his family, and what his goals are. His eyes should be checked for avoidance and sadness. Patterns of bowel movement are of lesser importance.

If drug use is unchecked, changes will continue to occur. The 18-year-old chemically dependent child may be seen as a delinquent (which he is) or as depressed (which he is), or he may be seen as a 13-year-old, which is the way he behaves if that is when dependency began for him. It is sometimes hard to believe that inside an 18-year-old body with a defiant attitude lives a frightened and depressed 13-year-old child. To reach him therapeutically, one must know who he is.

Many adolescents in stage 3, vaguely aware that their deteriorating life may in some way be related to their use of chemicals, will try to modify their use. They may want help with the complications of drug use, but they are not prepared to sacrifice the effects of the drug. Some are successful in abstaining for a period of time, but most have lost or never acquired the defense systems necessary for dealing with normal adolescent stress. By stage 3 they have usually alienated their family, their true friends, and their schools. They have usually stopped attending church and are often in trouble with the law. Without treatment or a new source of strength, there is little to defend them against their "need" to rely on drugs for feelings of comfort. Some may return to drugs with the intention of controlling their use more carefully. They may rationalize that perhaps a beer or two on Saturdays will cause them no problem. This line of reasoning has as much chance for success as that used by the two-pack-a-day cigarette smoker who decides he will limit his use to one cigarette after each meal. When a teenager has reached stage 3, he cannot go back to stage 1.

The teenager who does not recover from stage 3 use must go on to either death or stage 4. Continued downward progression to stage 4 is associated with a feeling that life is a "bad trip." The euphoria of drugs becomes rarer and harder to achieve.

STAGE 4: "DOING DRUGS TO FEEL OK"

The fun is gone. Larger doses of stronger drugs become necessary just to function. The temptation to try opiates increases. Suicide may be a frequent thought.

Kirk at age 17 was doing well in school and playing good basketball. He neither drank nor smoked. By age 21 he had been kicked out of his parents' home, had five counts pending with the police, and was unable to keep a job. Euphoria was gone. When he could afford it or remembered, he laid a few Quaaludes (methaqualone) on his nightstand just to get himself started in the morning (see arrow, Table 2–1).

Overdosing, which may occur in stage 1, becomes more regular, as do blackouts and amnesia. The chronic cough, which may begin earlier, is usually firmly entrenched, as are fatigue and problems related to malnutrition.

This child is not frequently seen by the pediatrician, because he has either entered his twenties or has left home, voluntarily or otherwise, and started to drift. He has fallen through a medical loophole. His only touch with physicians is apt to be in emergency rooms, where he is patched up and discharged, usually with little, if any, attention paid to his primary disease. He is not identified in school, because he has long since dropped out. The police, however, may know him, either as a drifter or a petty thief. What began as an experiment has ended in despair.

Most people are now aware of someone in their neighborhood who fits the description of a stage 4 user. This young adult, often in his mid to late twenties is at home and doing nothing. He just cannot seem to "get his life together," and to hear him tell the story, he has been the victim of a series of "bad breaks." Psychiatrists writing about this new "chronically" disturbed young adult acknowledge frequent drug use in such victims, but fail to see that such use may be the cause of the problems and not just coincidental.[24-26]

These lonely and impulsive young people strive for independence, satisfying relationships, a sense of identity, and realistic vocational choices, but fail in their efforts. They have been called victims of a social-breakdown syndrome.[27] They lack the tools necessary for dealing with stress and intimacy and end up anxious and depressed, often experiencing psychotic episodes. The rebelliousness of youth, control issues, and violence further compound their problems. They have been called "the new drifters" because of their tendency to drift from one living situation to another with intermittent stops at home, where they exist in a hostile-dependent relationship.[28] They have few skills and distorted reality testing, and they are prone to self-destructive behaviors. "Passive dependency" and "passive aggression" are terms that have been applied to these young people. Repeated failure becomes a way of life.[29]

The reasons given for the rise in number of such young adults are (1) the increasing numbers of young adults in our population and (2) a national policy of deinstitutionalization of psychiatric patients. There is some merit to both of these reasons. There were 91 million babies born between 1950 and 1965, which means that in 1987 almost one third of our population was between the ages of 21 and 37. The trend to deinstitutionalization does indeed put more disturbed people on the street, but the writers of articles related to the boom admit that neither of these factors accounts for the millions of such patients now being seen.[31,32] There are probably multiple causes of this new syndrome, but the similarity of many of these young people to the monkeys at the University of California, Davis, that were chronically exposed to THC (see Chapter 4) is hard to deny. That drugs may be the cause of such problems, and not just a related finding, is discussed in Chapter 3, where chemical dependency is set forth as a primary disease.

SUMMARY

Drug use is a progressive disease that progresses at a variable pace. It creates problems that too often are managed by further drug use, which induces further problems. Adolescents who are drug-free in April may reach stage 3 by October. Adults may drink socially (stage 1 and early stage 2) for 30 years before finally losing control and creating problems for themselves, their families, and their employers. Not all drug or alcohol users will move through these stages, but evidence indicates that the younger one is, the greater the possibility.

Many children sensing trouble make attempts at moderation or cessation of drug use. Some may be successful, but unless they have learned to deal with stress in an effective and mature fashion, their next crisis may lead them quickly back to the stage from which they fled.

Early diagnosis makes for easier remedy. Intervention in stage 3, which is more obviously needed than in stage 2, requires more therapy and is less likely to be fully successful. Understanding that each child may be placed in one of the stages, 0 to 4, and that chemical use is a progressive disease aids the pediatrician and parent interested in prevention and, where necessary, early remediation.

3

The Disease Called Chemical Dependency

An understanding of chemical dependency must precede any real understanding of a child with drug or alcohol problems. Efforts at intervention or treatment are not likely to be successful without such understanding. It was not until the mid 1950s that physicians began to consider alcoholism as a disease. Prior to that time, medical model treatment had been highly unsuccessful.

Earlier thinking about the cause and treatment of alcohol and drug addiction saw these conditions as symptoms of underlying psychopathology. The terms "addiction" and "alcoholism," though still widely used, are disappearing from medical literature and being replaced by the term "dependency." Earlier the study of addiction tended to focus attention on the physiologic effects of drugs, and confusion continues about whether particular drugs are physically addicting, psychologically addicting, produce physical tolerance, or are associated with withdrawal symptoms. Detoxification and drug withdrawal produce relatively predictable and short-lived problems that may be fairly easily managed and usually present no great problem. Dealing with the underlying dependency is the difficult part of treatment. Until this dependency has been dealt with, recidivism rates will be high. The chemical dependency model focuses on those behavioral and emotional changes that are present in a drug user and his family.

The terms alcoholism and drug addiction have been replaced in the newest *Diagnostic and Statistical Manual* (DSM III-R) of the American Psychiatric Association by the word "dependence" modified by the chemical involved.[33] By this classification, alcoholism is now termed "dependence on alcohol" and heroin addiction is called "heroin dependence."

The World Health Organization defines drug dependence as "a state, psychic or also sometimes physical, resulting from interaction between a living organism and a drug, and characterized by behavioral and other responses that always include a compulsive desire or need to use the drug on a continuous basis in order to experience its effects and/or avoid the discomfort of its absence."[34]

THE DEPENDENCY OF IMMATURITY

The concept of chemical dependency is useful in understanding the adult alcoholic and drug user.[19,35] The same principles apply to the youthful drug user, but an added problem for the adolescent is a preexisting natural dependency. In studying his particular susceptibility to drug use and the reaction of his family to changes in him, one must consider not just his dependency on chemicals but also this natural dependency, the dependency of immaturity.

The human infant is among the most dependent of all newborn creatures. Compared to the bird, who is shoved from the nest at a very young age, his survival requires more care for a much longer period of time. The ability to meet his own basic needs comes slowly and erratically. He will always be dependent on food, water, and shelter, but with time will come the ability to feed himself, then later to obtain his own food, and eventually to provide food for his offspring. Like the Harlow monkey, he is dependent on touching and warmth for adequate maturation. In some families children may be overprotected and given no opportunity or encouragement to strive for self-reliance. More appropriately, a child fortified with the security and warmth of his home and family should, with a slight nudge, venture forth into the world and meet age-appropriate challenges and independence. When these challenges are beyond his capability or when he escapes them through chemical use, he remains dependent.

"Drug rehabilitation" is most often an inaccurate phrase in describing treatment of the youthful user. It implies removal of drug and return to function. More accurately, successful therapy might be called drug "habilitation," because for the young user there may be little or no underlying base of independent coping mechanisms on which to build. His program will need to help him reach maturational independence, not just drug independence. There are many components to independence, and the rate at which they develop may vary greatly from child to child. One child may be early in developing the height and weight of physical maturity, but slow in learning how to budget time and money to best suit his goals. Another may establish a mature autonomy for himself within his family, but he may have difficulty dealing with girls. Progress in all the many areas leading to full maturation is likely to be uneven and erratic.

The World Health Organization declared 1979 "The Year of The Child" and in that year looked at the dependency status of children in many countries. To them, independence meant the capability of caring for oneself without parental support. In testing young people to see who might survive when left on their own, they found that, worldwide, the average age at which independence was reached was 16 years.[36] In this country it was 24. Said another way, the average 23-year-old American was still a dependent person.

Cultural differences might be given as explanation, citing such things as prolonged American educational time, but a related study seems to show that we have been truly losing ground. The same evaluation performed on Americans 16 years of age in 1954 showed that 60% were independent, as compared with only 40% in 1979.[36]

Prolonged adolescence and dependency surround us. Examples abound, such as young people in their mid twenties who are still at home trying to get their acts together. Many of these unfortunate young people are still dependent on their parents as well as upon alcohol and/or other drugs (see Chapter 2, stage 4). Taking on a new dependency does not replace the first. One just makes it more difficult to escape the other. These "new drifters," as they are called, have a psychological profile that is hauntingly familiar to the parents of many drug-affected adolescents.

Children change as they begin using drugs, and their parents "feel" the change. Neighbors may comment that the child is just going through a phase, but parents become uncomfortable. The child who may have such nice manners next door may be having mood swings at home that are very difficult to live with. Mothers who have loved and nurtured their child for 13 or 14 years are not happy with what is going on. The poor choice of friends, loss of ambition, falling grades, and worsening attitude at home concern them greatly. The old instincts of protecting and "mothering" may be called upon inappropriately to deal with a new kind of dependency as if it were simply a continuation of or relapse into the old normal dependency of immaturity. This sort of response, all too common, will act to promote rather than alleviate the symptoms of chemical use.

THE CHARACTERISTICS OF CHEMICAL DEPENDENCY

In the previous chapter, we looked at the clinical syndrome of chemical use and at the signs and symptoms characteristic of different stages of involvement. There are a number of characteristics that make drug abuse similar to other diseases. Understanding them makes possible effective management of the user. The characteristics of chemical dependency are that dependency is (1) a primary disease, (2) a progressive disease, (3) a family disease, (4) a chronic disease, (5) a contagious disease, and (6) a potentially fatal disease.

A Primary Disease

Many people still believe that alcoholism occurs mainly in people of low moral character who are not strong enough to indulge moderately or in people with underlying mental disorder. Still others believe that people become alcoholic because they are of lower socioeconomic class or have lost control of their lives due to a series of bad breaks. Some believe intelligence and education are adequate protection against alcoholism. In truth no amount of psychological maturity or strength of character guarantees protection against chemical dependency. This may be especially true when the chemicals produce such overwhelmingly euphoric experiences as those produced by heroin or cocaine. The immature and dependent adolescent may be at higher risk of becoming hooked, but he is not alone.

Those who see chemical use as merely symptomatic of underlying problems and cling to these older beliefs will fail to fully understand the plight of the user. Heavy nicotine dependence at age 40 is not a late symptom of curiosity in the early teens, but an independent phenomenon that is very difficult to handle. Alcoholism and drug abuse are diseases in much the same sense that tuberculosis is a disease. The tubercle bacillus and alcohol bring about a negative reaction in humans. The fact that some people may be more susceptible by reason of age, heredity, or other factors does not alter the fact that treatment aimed at the primary etiologic agent is the therapy most likely to be effective. Animal data suggest that anyone who drinks enough over a sufficiently long period of time will develop alcoholism. (This has not been established in humans.)[37]

An illustration of the concept of primary disease is given by Lynn Hankes, medical director of the Lakeland Regional Medical Center in Lakeland, Fla. Dr. Hankes makes periodic rounds on the medical-surgical floors of the general hospital and notes to his colleagues that approximately 25% of their patients have been improperly diagnosed. He tells them that the diagnoses of pancreatitis, rib fracture, hepatitis, and pneumonitis listed on their patients' charts are not diagnoses, but symptoms. The underlying disease in their patients is chemical dependency, and until they deal with that entity, their therapy will provide little more than symptomatic relief. Syphilis, once called the "great imposter disease" because it presented with so many different signs and symptoms, should now yield its title to alcoholism.

Does the adolescent in trouble "do drugs," or does the drug-using adolescent run into trouble (a "chicken or egg" question)? Both sides of this question are probably true, but for successful management, the second half must be considered first. Chapter 6 discusses the particular susceptibility of teenagers to drugs and personal factors that may increase the risks of drug use. On the other hand, Chapter 2 describes characteristic changes occurring in teenagers who progress beyond the stage of experimentation and points to the fact that drug use produces problem behavior.

In the earlier stages of drug use, the child's behavior may be the primary problem. Treatment aimed at altering such behavior can be very effective (Chapter 9). Implied in such behavior change is cessation of drug use. When the child is hooked (chemical dependency), the primary therapeutic focus must shift to separation of the child from chemicals. In early stage 2, a child with a poor report card may respond to strong parental intervention by bringing up his grades. If drug use continues with associated progressive dependency, the child will eventually reach a point where such parental action produces no response except rebellion or further retreat to apathy.

Illustrative is Shane's story of initiation to drug use in the summer after his freshman year. Subsequently he received poor grades for the first marking period in the fall. He was placed on restriction and did well the remainder of the year. Increased drug use the following summer was followed by poor school performance, which again was positively changed when restrictions were applied. A third summer of such behavior dropped Shane into late stage 2 or early stage 3 drug abuse, and efforts at restriction did not bring up his bad grades. Control of school performance may be the last thing to slip in stage 2, and when it does, this can be a sign of dependency.

The only effective treatment for drug problems must begin by removing the drugs. When alcohol dependency is treated as a Valium-deficiency disease, little benefit will accrue to patients. Underlying learning disabilities, personality disorders, or inadequate home situations may be dealt with effectively only after or in conjunction with making the child drug-free. Just as the adult alcoholic cannot be effectively treated until he gives up alcohol, the chemically dependent child needs to be divorced from his drugs. Chemical dependency is a primary disease.

A Progressive Disease

Characteristic behavior patterns of drug users have been described. Although some experts see these patterns as distinct and separate, at least three, Johnson,[19] Nizama,[16] and Newton,[18] view the patterns as belonging to one syndrome in which there are recognizable stages of progression.

The rate of progression through the stages of use described in

Chapter 2 may vary widely. Factors such as maturity, stress, boredom, and peer group all may play a part in the rate of progression. A dependent child who is smothered with everything he "wants" may be able to stop use, but he is likely to return when the going gets the least bit difficult.

There is some difference of opinion as to exactly when dependency occurs. The AMA defines addiction (dependency) as compulsion, loss of control, and continued use of the drug in spite of adverse consequences[15] (late stage 2 to stage 3). In contrast would be the nondependent drinker who, when arrested for driving while intoxicated, voluntarily modifies his behavior to prevent recurrence. By the time late stage 2 or stage 3 involvement is reached, consequences may be fairly obvious to all but the victim, even though some observers may not attribute the change to drug use. The less mature a user is, the less likely he is to have the insight necessary to relate negative consequences to his drug use. This makes it less likely that he will stop taking drugs to arrest progression. By late stage 2, he has often been able to "con" himself and others sufficiently to believe there is no relationship between habits and results.

Definitions of dependency vary. Chemical dependency may mean needing a chemical to deal with situations and/or feelings. Chemical dependency may be present when a beer is taken for relaxation or sedation for sleep. Amphetamines taken for weight loss may be a sign of dependency. More obviously, dependency is "needing" chemicals to feel good.

A Family Disease

A child with a drug or alcohol problem creates problems for his family. These problems are no less real in those situations where his drug abuse stems from family problems. A careful history may reveal family alcoholism or drug abuse as factors contributing to the child's problem, either genetically or environmentally. Children and their families are so closely interrelated that pathology in any member can cause problems for all the others. This close interrelationship may lead to a sick child making a family sick or to a sick family making a child sick. Other family factors that should also be considered are possible genetic predisposition to chemical dependency and parental practices and attitudes related to drinking. Drug abuse may be a family disease in more ways than one.

Adolescent Drug Use as a Cause of Family Problems

Outsiders tend to look at a family with a child in trouble and focus on family faults upon which they may blame the child's problem. They may rightly spot "lack of communication," "parental nagging," lack of family activity together, working parents, or divorce, but wrongly feel that correcting these problems will straighten out the dependent child. Few will see that the disarray in family life may be a result of the child's drug use rather than its cause. Their well-meaning efforts to help will fail the dependent child and his family if drug use is not accepted as the primary cause of current difficulties.

Drug use has become so acceptable in our "do-drug" society that many children from "good" families enter the stage of experimentation with no more basic family problems or psychopathology than those students of earlier days who swallowed goldfish or were involved in panty raids. This "harmless" experimentation and introduction to chemical euphoria may lead him to stage 2 drug use. When a child's behavior begins to change in stage 2, his family usually responds, and those responses most often add to his problems.

The Enabling Parent. One parent, most often but not always the mother, tends to become what has been called an "enabler" or a "rescuer." Generally daughters tend to con fathers better than mothers, while sons con mothers. Both parents are often enablers. One parent may enable one behavior (e.g., sex) while the other may enable another (e.g., alcohol). When the enabler is a mother, her natural maternal instinct may tell her something is wrong and it is her duty to respond. Her response, usually without knowledge of the cause of difficulty, is most often inappropriate. She tends to make excuses for her child's actions and to blame his troubles on others.

It is easy for a parent, especially a mother, to become an enabler. She has had a dozen or so years of being responsible for a child who came to her in absolute dependency. She has fed him, clothed him, cared for his wounds, and come to love him very much. She has enjoyed being needed and wanted by her child and will go to great lengths to protect him from trouble and insult. Reason is often colored by instinctive protective reaction. She has known the ambivalence of releasing her child to kindergarten. That joy of seeing her child moving on was tempered with the pain of loneliness at the loss of her dependent preschooler. Now with adolescence, she may again find it hard to release. When negative personality changes occur, she may instinctively know something is wrong but try to rationalize the changes and assure herself that she and her child are all right. Her denial may take the form of statements such as, "He's just going through a phase," or, "Don't all children try marijuana?" and reject any suggestion that he has a problem. She may especially cling to statements by neighbors who tell her he is a nice boy and well-mannered in their presence. The neighbors, of course, do not have to live with his late hours, falling grades, and mood swings.

In normal adolescence, parents should be releasing trust and privilege to their child as he earns them. Now they must deal with a child who has been given more privilege than he is capable of handling. The chief enabler, usually the mother, becomes the child's protector rather than accepting the fact the child may need tighter rein. If the school sees a problem with the child, she is apt to find fault with the school. Family honor is involved. The physician who is not aware of this denial mechanism and blunders into confrontation may lose this family to another physician who is less apt to confront them about their child's drug use.

Protecting one's child is normal and appropriate, but overprotection can cause problems. Enablers overprotect. They find it difficult to separate what their child needs from what their child wants. The price of overprotection is prolonging the dependency of immaturity and thereby aiding the progress of chemical dependency.

The enabler does more than just contribute to the child's problem. The enabler creates problems for herself. She builds defenses around feelings that may become increasingly painful to her. When her infant was small, she provided for his dependency and was rewarded with coos, smiles, and cuddling. Now her efforts may be rewarded with his sullen disrespect, withdrawal, and a general deterioration of the child's behavior. The more she tries, the worse things get. The worse things get, the more guilty and inadequate she feels and the more she tries to compensate.

Often, she will become sick herself as she builds defenses around her pain and the shame of having a child in trouble. She may be angry and afraid. She may believe herself to be a failure and suffer great guilt. No matter what she tries, things get worse. She is full of self pity. It is almost as if she is being punished for being too good a mother.

A common pattern is for the mother searching for answers to chide the father for his long hours at work and for not spending time with his child. She stresses the need for communication and family togetherness. Most families do need to work at spending more time together and doing things as families, but the enabler's efforts will fail because the problem now is not lack of communication. It is drugs. Counselors, psychologists, and well-meaning physicians may encourage these efforts of the enabler while adding to her guilt by suggesting that she, too, needs to communicate better with her child.

In addition to guilt, this enabling parent has anger that may be directed at schoolteachers and administrators for failing to make school interesting for their truant child or at the police for persecuting their child for "minor" traffic problems. With this anger parental denial of drug use or of the relationship of drug use to deteriorating behavior may become intensely pathologic.

The other parent (most often the father) may respond entirely differently and believe the child's problem is due to inadequate consistency and structure at home. He may come closer to understanding that the chemically dependent child is the cause, not the result, of family problems. He may be a generally successful person who believes in pulling oneself up by his own bootstraps. He, like the mother-enabler, knows something is not right, but his method of dealing with the problem, unless drug use is seen as a primary cause, also tends to make things worse.

He will cite rules that have been bent and curfews that have been violated without effective response as well as restrictions that have not been enforced. This parent, often well aware of the conning behavior of the child, is right in stressing structure and consistency, but he also will fail, because he does not understand that rule-breaking is only a symptom. He, too, will feel guilt over the way his child is turning out, but his overriding emotion is apt to be anger. This anger may be diffuse. Targets may be the enabler and the troubled child, who may respond to this anger and any tightening of controls by seeking additional chemical euphoria. Denial in this parent may be evidenced by the anger displayed if an outsider such as a school administrator, police officer, neighbor, or physician is not careful with his word choice in discussing the child and his problem. It is one thing for him as a parent to write the child off as a "bad seed," but others had best beware.

This parent usually cannot get the family to listen to him or follow his ideas, and he sees the child losing ground as the disease progresses. He may feel increasingly inadequate and powerless as the situation worsens. He may surround himself in outside activity at which he tends to excel. Inside, he is lonely, hurt, and confused. His inner feelings will cause him increasing turmoil as the disease progresses. Until the basic cause of the child's behavior is dealt with, there is little likelihood of change.

By the time the child has reached stage 3, things are worse. When mothers at this stage are asked how they are sleeping, their eyes tend to mist over as they say they have not slept well in over a year. Fathers who often sit grudgingly in a closed-off, arms-crossed position in a pediatric office will usually also admit to sleep problems. If both parents are on the same side of their assessment of the child and agree on a course of action, their sex life may be satisfactory. When they disagree, or as the child progresses downward, it is usually not. Feelings of inadequacy and frustration about a failing child are not hard to uncover.

If the child is adopted, there may be some relief in claiming a genetic basis for his behavior. If it is a stepchild, one parent may feel "off the hook" by blaming a previous marriage partner. For most parents, though, there is much pain. A profound grief reaction is in process with varying but increasing amounts of anger, denial, and guilt.

By stage 4, there is no family in any real sense. A few families continue to exist sharing a roof with a stage 4 drug user, but most have found other options. Divorce is common, as is departure of the child. Divorce may be encouraged by the conning child skilled at driving a wedge between his parents. Experience may have taught him that he is more likely to get his way when parental action is divided. Departure may occur by means of parental eviction, running away, or by suicide or other causes of violent death. Stage 4 is "hell."

Sibling Involvement. While all this conflict is going on, the siblings at home cannot help but be aware of the tension, anger, and futile efforts at behavior modification by their parents. The parents' energies may be spent almost totally on the disturbed child, leaving little for the siblings. Family dynamics may be seen as a mobile. When one component goes out of kilter, all will have to adjust. Parents who are not sleeping well or communicating well with each other will not have a lot of real warmth and openness to give their other children. Inappropriate attention-seeking behaviors may increase. Discipline is apt to be erratic, with punishment ranging from nonexistent to severe.

Siblings will not miss the fact that their drug-using sibling pays little attention to house rules and will be tempted to do the same. They may stay clear of him and his erratic mood swings when he is in a "mood," but when he is friendly, they may cling to him. Those periods of togetherness with the affected sibling may be times when drugs are offered. The temptation to use and thereby be accepted may be strong. Drug users offer drugs to siblings and others for a variety of reasons. One is a genuine belief that they have discovered something wonderful and want to share a "beautiful" experience. Another is the "fun" of seeing someone get high for the first time. Another is the hope of decreasing chances of exposure by having a sibling who, when involved himself, is less likely to tattle to parents.

Families as a Cause of Adolescent Drug Use

The child who uses drugs may be the marker of a previously diseased family. Family dysfunction, including child abuse and neglect, may lead a child to drugs. Families with a history of alcoholism are particularly suspect. Family members must respond to a parent with a drinking problem. Their responses often make them code-pendents in a dysfunctional organization that has been called "the family trap."[35] Each family member may become locked into a set of increasingly rigid survival defenses leading to compulsive patterns of behavior. The sicker the family, the tighter their compulsive roles of survival. Characteristics of codependency parallel those of chemical dependency: (1) denial and delusion, (2) "frozen" feelings, (3) compulsion, (4) low self-worth, and (5) physical symptoms.

The chemically dependent adult builds a shell of defenses around his inner feelings of shame, guilt, fear, hurt, and pain. His chief enabler, usually his spouse, has learned to repress feelings of hurt, anger, fear, guilt, and pain, and communication between the two may be limited to exchanges between their defense mechanisms.

The child born to such a marriage grows up in a home where feelings are controlled and performance is king. He will observe adult behavior and learn how to respond. He may get very close to the nondrinker and fear the drinker. Aware of pain in the marriage and in some way believing himself responsible for the situation may lead him to experience feelings of inadequacy and helplessness. Obvious success in the outside world may provide a defense for this child, who may learn to hide well his feelings of anger, hurt, and confusion. Later as a parent and marriage partner, this child may tend to be cold, never having learned how to express feelings. His children may have high rates of alcohol and drug abuse. A history of alcoholism in grandparents may be a helpful clue to physicians caring for children.

Social and economic problems may increase the risk of children becoming involved with drugs. One situation that is a cause for concern involves a parent who is not at home with the teenager after school or in the daytime if the child is away from school, legally or otherwise. With the increasing number of single-parent families, this pattern of inadequate supervision is becoming commonplace.

Treatment programs that address only the problems of the chemically dependent and do nothing for his family may return the child to an unhealthy environment, where his continued recovery is considerably less than certain.

Genetic Alcoholism

In addition to the effects of the family system on a chemically dependent person and the effects of a chemically dependent person on the family system, there may be a genetic predisposition for chemical dependency. Danish adoption studies looked at four groups of subjects, all of whom were sons of alcoholics.[38] One group consisted of sons of alcoholics who were raised by nonalcoholic adoptive parents. Second was a group of sons raised by their alcoholic biologic parents. Paired with each group was a control group of adopted children whose biologic parents were not identified as alcoholic.

Sons of alcoholics in the study were four times more likely to be alcoholics, and at earlier ages, than the sons of nonalcoholics, whether reared by nonalcoholic foster parents or their own biologic parents. High divorce rates were also noted among these children, but not increased use of other drugs. Studies suggest that female relatives of alcoholics tend to be depressed, while male relatives are prone to alcoholism.[39] Environmental factors appear more important in this depression than genetic factors, as judged by the fact that girls who were raised in homes of alcoholic parents were more often depressed than those who were adopted by nonalcoholics. Other adoption studies tend to confirm a biologic basis for alcoholism.[40]

A wide range of innate variation of responses to alcohol is seen in humans and in every other species studied. Few Orientals are alcoholic. Approximately 75% of Orientals have a cutaneous flush and unpleasant reaction to small amounts of alcohol.[41] The basis of this unpleasant reaction has not been established, but data indicate a high frequency of atypical liver alcohol dehydrogenase among Japanese.[42] This coenzyme may lead to increased acetaldehyde formation with subsequent flush and other ill effects, including nausea. These affected Japanese would be expected to be less at risk of becoming dependent on alcohol. Alcoholism among women is believed by some to be less common than in men, because, drink for drink, women have higher alcohol blood levels and experience more nausea and vomiting following "moderate" use.[43] Anecdotal evidence suggests that Jews may have more adverse physical reactions to alcohol than nonJews, which may contribute to the lower rates of alcoholism in Jews.[37]

To be an alcoholic, it is essential to be able to drink relatively large quantities of alcohol. In some, protection against alcoholism is provided by innate cutoff points, which appear to be under genetic control. Some people experience more euphoria from alcohol than others,[37] and because euphoria is a positive reinforcer, these people are more likely to become alcoholic. Alcoholics also experience dysphoric effects from their drinking, which may be self-treated with more alcohol. This may lead to binge drinking.

It seems likely that there is a genetic relationship to alcoholism. There is little, if any, evidence to date that dependence on other chemicals is so related, but it would not be surprising if some were found. Those who would ascribe to the theory that alcoholism is always genetic or biochemical may be guilty of the same overgeneralizations as those who blame all drug problems on the society in which we live. In terms of prevention and treatment, biochemical approaches are, at best, far in the future. For now, chemical dependency is a disease that makes families sick and that may cause dependency in other family members.

Parental Practices and Attitudes Related to Drinking

In addition to the genetic illness that may run in chemically dependent family members, there may be a relationship between "moderate" use in "healthy" families and problems with drug use and drinking in their adolescents. Surveys show that families who drink have more children involved with drugs or alcohol than those who do not.[44] Interestingly, parental tobacco smoking also seems to be related to an increased incidence of juvenile drug and alcohol problems.

Relationships between parental attitudes and children's drug use have been shown. In families where there was only mild disapproval of marijuana use, children were more likely to be involved than children from families where disapproval was stronger.[45] Strong parental control appears to be protective,[46] and it appears that large degrees of autonomy granted to adolescents may be related to increased drug use.[47]

In some cases parents directly introduce their children to drugs or alcohol by "teaching" drinking so the child may learn about "moderation" and "controlled" use in a family situation. Some quote the low rates of alcoholism among Jews who allow their children to taste sacramental wine. For 3,000 years alcohol in moderation was a tightly controlled Jewish ritual. Associated with this ritual were spiritual taboos against drunkenness. These traditions have been recently altered in those Jewish homes where children observe their parents reveling in the same spirits the night after the Sabbath. In spite of the possible genetic protection discussed earlier, this expanded social use of alcohol has been associated with the development of alcoholism and drug problems in increasing numbers of Jewish children. The practice of teaching social drinking by allowing the minor to indulge with his parents should be seriously questioned. Probably even more dangerous is the practice of some parents who give illegal drugs such as marijuana to children in the belief that the drugs are safe.

A Family Disease in More Ways Than One

Studies have identified three specific configurations of adolescent drug users. The first is the use of legal drugs or drugs considered acceptable and is primarily a social pattern. The second is tied to the normal, albeit difficult, process of growing up, which frequently involves experimentation with new behaviors. This process may involve strengthened extrafamilial ties, rebellion, and increased self-assertion. Both of these patterns of drug use may lead to dependency, as may the third, which involves children who use drugs regularly and compulsively and have high levels of personal dissatisfaction and depression as well as strong feelings of alienation from their parents.

Functional family structure appears to strengthen the resistance of a teenager to illicit drug use. The active, demanding, and involved parent who presents a model of strength and who monitors a child's interactions and familial and peer group activities tends to have a child who is less involved with drugs.[48] A close and affectionate father-son relationship is particularly helpful.[49]

Family therapists see drug abuse as having circular causation. Rather than viewing the drugs, the family, or the child as the primary cause of problems, they see all these factors as mutually reinforcing. From a treatment standpoint, it does not matter much which came first—the drugs, the dysfunctional adolescent, or the dysfunctional family. All must be attended to if recovery rates are to be good.[50]

A Chronic Disease

There has been recent controversy about whether a treated alcoholic can ever resume occasional drinking. The overwhelming majority of experts would still answer "no," as appealing as the thought of cure and return to "recreational" use might be. Relapse is all too common.

Alcoholics Anonymous (AA) members call themselves "recovering" alcoholics rather than "cured" alcoholics. All too many of them have tried alcohol after a period of sobriety only to learn the painful lesson that they were still dependent. Numerous young people who do marvelously well in treatment unfortunately learn the same hard lesson and quickly tumble back to stage 3 or whatever stage they were in before treatment. No one really knows whether the chemical dependency of children will be lifelong, but caution would suggest we assume that it is until we learn otherwise.

As with any chronic disease, chemical dependency is a disease with multiple implications. Just as the treatment of diabetes involves more than the injection of insulin, the treatment of drug abuse involves more than the giving up of drugs. The diabetic needs to pay special attention to diet, exercise, and intercurrent illness. The recovering child must be taught the need for an appropriate peer group, worthwhile recreational activity, and ways of managing stress. His life can be full and rich, but in being so it must not again include the experience of chemical euphoria.

A Contagious Disease

Chemical dependency is contagious, especially in peer groups. The child who attends "keg" parties is at high risk. The child who attends rock concerts where drug use is flaunted in the audience and encouraged on stage is at high risk. The more young people accept drinking and drugs as a part of adolescence, the more will additional children be pulled along. Parents wishing to protect their child should know his peer group and, where possible, protect the group as well. When each child in the group avoids drugs, all are stronger.

A Fatal Disease

Chemical dependency may be a fatal disease. With accidents, suicides, and homicides the leading causes of death in the 15- to 24-year-old age group and all three closely related to chemical use, this statement seems obvious. Include tobacco and lung cancer, and the seriousness of chemical dependency will be hard to deny.

SUMMARY

Chemical dependency describes the use of chemicals in such amounts and frequency that they create a progressive syndrome of trouble for the user and those around him. Seeing the condition as a disease seems essential to those who would provide therapy. Dealing with problems incidental to the drug use but allowing continued chemical intake will not solve the problems of dependency. The syndrome of adult chemical dependency is compounded and intensified in children, who are developmentally immature. Human children began life as very dependent creatures and are still dependent as they reach adolescence. This dependence makes them more susceptible to chemical dependency, which then arrests their progress towards the maturational independence we call adulthood.

4

The Drugs

Teenagers love to argue and compare. Many a child has sought to justify his marijuana use to his parents by saying, "You drink, and alcohol is more dangerous than pot." There are many things very wrong with this common teenage method of justification.

Drug comparisons are misleading. All psychoactive drugs are potentially more dangerous for the immature than they are for mature adults. Each drug has distinct physiologic side effects and toxicity. All have a strong potential to affect behavior and cause chemical dependency. The most dangerous drugs for adolescents are the ones they put into their bodies. By this definition alcohol and marijuana, the most widely used, are the most dangerous of the psychoactive drugs. If marijuana were to fall in popularity and be replaced by cocaine as the illicit drug most commonly used, then cocaine would become the most dangerous.

The AMA makes a similar statement in *Drug Abuse: A Guide for the Primary Care Physician:* "The degree of hazard associated with drug use can be assessed in terms of (1) the immediate psychic effects of the drug on the individual and (2) the consequences of continuous drug use for society as a whole."[15] Quoting another source, "In terms of incidence of use, complications from acute overdoses, long-term effects on the physical and mental state of an individual, and ultimate consequences for society, there is no close second to alcohol."[51]

When adolescents compare pot and alcohol, there are some real deceptions. First, it is the rare teenager who admits to pot smoking who does not also use alcohol, and his argument about which is worse is really moot. A second deception is when he compares his use with his father's drinking habits as an adolescent. A look at the current picture of alcohol use for high school seniors described in Chapter 1 is useful. Fewer of today's fathers drank as students, and, on the average, those who did drank less. A third concern is the very early age at which drinking now begins. It should be pointed out, though, that even the more moderate and delayed use of alcohol by the older generation was not without consequence. There are estimated to be over 10 million adults in this country who did not remain social drinkers and are now classified as problem drinkers or alcoholics. Unfortunately, widespread adult acceptance of alcohol has led many parents to make inappropriate statements such as "I'm glad my child only drinks and isn't into drugs."

Every drug has both short-term and long-term consequences. Teenagers tend to believe they will live forever, and for this reason long-range effects are given less emphasis than those more likely to present problems in adolescence. There is nothing wrong with pointing out that 30% of the adults who die in this country have had their lives shortened due to the use of alcohol, tobacco, and other drugs. It is probably more meaningful, however, when speaking with a high school group to ask if anyone who attended their school has died on the highway or committed suicide, and if so, were drugs or alcohol involved? It is also worthwhile to ask the group if they have seen children in their school who might be classified as "burnouts" or "space cadets" or who have gone through the behavior changes described in Chapter 2.

The effects of drugs depend on the chemistry of the drug, the amount used, and on many other circumstances—how, when, where, and why taken. Illicit drug effects are further complicated by unpredictable elements such as the concentration and purity of the drug and the nature and amounts of the contaminants that may go with it.

Drugs alone are dangerous. In combination, they are worse. Combinations frequently play a part in chemical dependency and accidental death. Teenagers use combinations of drugs for several reasons. In the early stages of involvement, new drugs may be added experimentally by the thrill-seeking and curious user who has discovered the euphoria of drug experience and the excitement of initiation into a new group of peers. If few repercussions have been experienced from drugs he had been taught not to use, he is often willing to experiment further. Later drugs may be combined to achieve desired effects or to cancel out the negative aftereffects of one class of drugs by adding another ("Valley of the Dolls" effect). Dead are John Belushi, who died "speed-balling" (simultaneous use of cocaine and heroin), and numerous other Hollywood personalities such as Alan Ladd, who forgot that sedative prescription drugs and alcohol do not mix. Less severe reactions are much more common. Alcohol is the most common cause of acute drug crises, both deliberate and accidental, in this country today, because of its interaction with a variety of substances such as tranquilizers, antihistamines, anesthetics, and sedatives.[52]

DEFINITIONS

A number of terms used to describe drug use have widely different meanings for different people. The words "addiction" and "abuse," particularly, have been so overused that they now are almost always used with adjectives to further define their meaning. Terms such as "physical addiction" and "psychological addiction" have taken on such legal, social, and moral connotations that they have lost much of their medical usefulness and have largely been abandoned. As Jaffe states, in the standard medical reference, *The Pharmacologic Basis of Therapeutics,*[53] "It is possible to describe all known patterns of drug use without employing the terms addict or addiction."[53] The key terms that are now increasingly used and accepted as pertinent to understanding the same addictions are "chemical dependency" and "physical dependency." For the sake of better understanding the vocabulary of drug pharmacology, the following definitions are used in this book.

"Addiction" is not defined in the AMA book *Drug Abuse,* which defines instead "abuse" and "dependence."[15] Jaffe says, "Addiction . . . means a behavioral pattern of drug use, characterized by overwhelming involvement with the use of a drug (compulsive use), the securing of its supply and a high tendency to relapse after withdrawal." By Jaffe's definition, "it is possible to be physically dependent on drugs without being addicted and, in some special circumstances, to be addicted without being physically dependent." By the World Health Organization's definition, addiction and drug dependency overlap.[34] The confusing word "addiction" is avoided in this book except on a few occasions to describe psychological dependency. When reading through these definitions, gray areas become obvious. The value of the stages presented in Chapter 2 should be apparent.

Abuse, according to Webster, is "improper or incorrect use." By this definition, there should be no difference in adolescent drug *use* and *abuse.* No child may legally or safely drink, smoke, or snort, and any amount of use is therefore abusive. In this book, abuse and use are considered synonymous when the user is a child. One popular definition of abuse says, "Drug abuse refers to the use, usually by self-administration, of any drug in a manner that deviates from the approved medical or social patterns within a given culture."[53] Using this definition, one might see adolescent alcohol use as not abusive in light of the fact that the majority (69.3%) of high school seniors drink every month.[2] The AMA definition, which seemingly allows even more loopholes, would not consider adolescent experimentation abuse: "When continued use of a mood-altering substance means more to an individual than the problems associated with such use, that individual can be described as abusing drugs" or "ingestion of a psychoactive substance that is capable of producing physical or psychological dependence, in an amount and at a frequency likely to result in overt intoxication or to lead to physical or psychological problems or anti-social behavior."[15] More consistent but less inclusive than the definition used here, are those definitions of the American Psychiatric Association (DSM III-R)[33] and the World Health Organization (ICD-9).[54] Both define drug abuse as all illicit use up to but not including the development of dependence. Dependence, in these definitions, implies the development of tolerance or withdrawal symptoms.

Acute abuse in the context of this book consists of use on a single occasion in such excessive fashion as to produce overdose symptoms. A common example would be the teenager who decides to experiment with alcohol, finds the early euphoria captivating, and continues to drink until emesis and passout. This scenario often occurs with a friend at home while the parents are out. When discovered, the child is cleansed and bedded and most often treated with new respect as befits one who has "successfully" negotiated a rite of passage. Rarely is this seen by parents as a cause of concern, nor by pediatricians, who may admit young people in near coma but send them home the next day glad that it was "only" alcohol.

Chronic abuse is repeated acute abuse or a pattern of use producing those symptoms and behavior changes described in the stages of chemical dependency (Chapter 2).

Compulsive use is described in the section in this chapter on cocaine.

Drug interactions may add to or detract from the actions of other drugs. Antagonistic effects may be sought by the user who combines cocaine and heroin ("speedballing") to facilitate his high or medically where naloxone hydrochloride (Narcan) is given to block the effects of opiates. Many "cold" remedies combine antihistamines (sedatives) and decongestants (stimulants) in efforts to reduce either side effect. Additive effects may be seen with alcohol and marijuana and are of particular interest to the pediatrician because of their effects on adolescent behavior and driving.

Chemical dependency as used here refers primarily to the need to use chemicals to deal with uncomfortable life situations and to dull or repress uncomfortable feelings. Chapter 3 deals with this subject at length.

Physical dependency is usually determined by the presence of symptoms when the drug is withdrawn. Such dependency may occur very rapidly. Some degree of physical dependency develops in patients who receive opiates while hospitalized for a few days, but the great majority do not go on to compulsive use. Physical dependency on alcohol may also appear fairly rapidly after a short period of continuous use, but need not lead to psychological dependency.

Psychological dependency is here used as synonymous with chemical dependency.

Tolerance is a loss of sensitivity to the effects of a drug, requiring larger and/or more frequent doses to produce the same effect. In the alcoholic, for example, tolerance is the ability to function at blood levels that would impair nonalcoholics. Each drug produces a variety of responses, and there may be a different rate at which tolerance develops to each of these. Toxic psychosis may develop when tolerance to a drug's euphoric effects leads to increased intake at a time when little tolerance has developed to the drug's other CNS effects. Tolerance may be part of and contribute to drug-seeking behavior. Three possible causes of tolerance have been suggested. First, tolerance may develop because of increasingly rapid metabolism as is seen with opiates. Another possibility is learned behavior. Third is an unknown path best called "brain adaptation," as is noted with marijuana.[55] In alcoholics tolerance may be due to a combination of all three possibilities. "Acute tolerance" is the phenomenon of getting used to drug effects rapidly. With acute tolerance the impairment of function noted in the phase of rising drug concentration following ingestion is greater than the impairment observed at the same blood level on the way down. For alcohol this means more staggering and word-slurring as blood alcohol is rising than at the same blood level in the descending phase.[56]

Withdrawal (abstinence) symptoms are those symptoms that occur after a drug is withdrawn, such as the seizures of barbiturate withdrawal or the delirium tremens (DTs) of alcohol withdrawal.[57] Milder withdrawal symptoms may be seen with marijuana, beginning about 4 hours after the last dose and disappearing by the third day.[58] These symptoms may include sleep disturbance, anorexia, restlessness, irritability, nausea, tremor, diarrhea, and cramps. They are similar to but less marked than those of withdrawal from opium, alcohol, and other sedatives. On abstinence, the symptoms of physical dependency tend to disappear faster than the user's return to normal tolerance.

GENERAL DRUG CHARACTERISTICS

The drugs discussed here are dealt with in the order and depth related to the rate at which they were used on a daily basis by graduating seniors in the class of 1987. Tobacco, the drug with the widest daily use, is mentioned here only in reference to marijuana. The drugs in order of daily use by seniors were (1) alcohol, (2) marijuana, (3) inhalants, (4) cocaine and other stimulants, (5) PCP, (6) sedatives and tranquilizers, (7) LSD and hallucinogens, (8) heroin, and (9) others.[2]

Marijuana

Use of this very crude drug derived from a plant used for centuries in hemp (rope) production has developed rapidly in a relatively short period of time. In the last 20 years, a huge commercial industry has arisen with considerable societal impact. Very sophisticated and effective horticultural advances have been made in this drug, which has exploded in potency, acceptance, and use in a society just recently learning of its hazards. For many young people, it has served as the "gateway" drug to new and devastating lifestyles inconsistent with the goals of reaching full potential and functioning as responsible adults.

Horticulture

Marijuana and two related drugs, hash (hashish) and hash oil, come from the cannabis plant, which has undergone remarkable change in recent years. The native North American plant, *Cannabis sativa,* with its well-recognized star-shaped leaf, is now being hybridized with a potent Asian variety, *Cannabis indica,* and a fast-growing variety from the Soviet Union, *Cannabis ruderalis,* which is said to be "the new super strain." Sinsemilla (Spanish for seedless) refers to strains that have been made more potent by a variety of cultivation techniques that include destruction of the male plants and removal of the seeds from the unfertilized female plants. The whole horticultural business is very complicated, incorporating much sophisticated and advanced technology. Chemical content of the psychoactive ingredients varies from leaf to leaf and from morning to afternoon in the same plant.

TABLE 4 – 1.   Marijuana Today

Contains
   421 chemicals
   18 chemical classes[62]
THC Concentration[60]
   1965 – 0.1%-0.2%
   1970 – 1%
   1983 – 2%-4% (average)
      5%-6% (high grade)
      13.56% (highest grade)
   1987 – 0.7% with samples as .25%*
Urine positive for cannabinoids: 7-10 days
* Source: Drug Enforcement Administration.

Chemical Makeup

To date, 421 different compounds from 18 different chemical classes have been isolated from marijuana (Table 4 – 1). When a joint is lit for smoking, this number rises to over 2,000. Many people equate marijuana with its main psychoactive drug, δ-9-tetrahydrocannabinol (THC), without understanding that THC is not the only biologically active drug present, nor the only psychoactive drug, nor in fact the only THC. There are 11 different THCs in marijuana, all important, but here the abbreviation THC refers only to the main psychoactive ingredient, δ-9-tetrahydrocannabinol.

Cannabinoid products seized in this country are regularly monitored for concentrations of component chemicals in the Analytical Laboratory of the NIDA Marijuana Research Project[59] at the University of Mississippi in Oxford. The strength of THC has increased markedly since the Beatles' John Lennon, a multiple drug user, called marijuana a "harmless giggle" in the mid 1960s. Strengths in those days (Table 4 – 1) of 0.1% to 0.2% THC[60] rose dramatically to a common 1% in 1970 and present usual concentrations of 2% to 5%. Newer techniques have produced concentrations over 13%, which are approximately 50 to 100 times stronger than the material of 20 years earlier.[61] Hash oil, derived from the oily resin found on cannabis leaves and added to tobacco or marijuana cigarettes, usually contains

THC in concentrations of 30% to 40%, with the highest recorded concentration in this country being 43.18%.[60] Hash or hashish, a product more commonly used in the Middle East and Asia, is also gaining popularity here. This compressed, resinous mixture may contain THC in the range of 10% to 20%, with the most potent sample to date analyzed at 22.89%.[60]

Storage in the Body

In addition to being a crude drug with many chemicals, marijuana differs in another important aspect from all of the other psychoactive drugs. All the others are water-soluble and excreted from the body relatively rapidly. By contrast THC is lipid-soluble and is retained in the body for a relatively long period of time.

For years young marijuana users insisted that marijuana was superior to alcohol because it made a person high more quickly and wore off more rapidly, leaving one safe to drive home after partying and able to wake up the next morning without a hangover. There is some truth to this, but also some important error. The truth is that marijuana does reach the brain very rapidly, acting within seconds after inhalation to produce a euphoric feeling that peaks at 20 to 30 minutes and disappears within 2 to 3 hours. This high is considerably more predictable than the high of alcohol, which relates to stomach-emptying times and other foods present in the stomach as well as the general metabolic state of the individual who drinks. Alcohol advocates might counter by noting that the alcoholic content of beverages is generally known, whereas the concentration and purity of THC varies in marijuana from leaf to leaf.

The main error in the teenage comparison of tobacco and alcohol metabolism lies in understanding the longevity of effect. The perception of a marijuana high may indeed disappear in 2 to 3 hours, but residual effects on driving are demonstrably present hours later.[62] Problems may be produced for the user who no longer feels affected by the drug. In terms of ability to follow a moving stimulus (tracking ability) and judgment, he may continue to perform more poorly than when not using his drug. Studies of critical tracking tasks have found deficits continuing for up to 10 hours.[63-65] At least as important as these intermediate-range effects of THC is the fact that marijuana stays in the body for considerably longer periods of time than was once imagined. Studies have shown that THC in active form may be retained for as long as 45 days after smoking, with a half-life averaging 72 hours.[61]

Because THC is lipid-soluble, it is stored in places where lipids are found, such as the brain, the lungs, the testes, the ovaries, and elsewhere throughout the body. In other words THC may accumulate. Whether accumulation is responsible for some marijuana users reaching a point where they seem to lose control of their habit is not known. The relationship is suspicious. The size of the person, his fat metabolism, his ratio of fat to lean body mass, and other factors affect the rate at which he excretes lipid-soluble material, and half-life may vary markedly from person to person.

The problem of being unable to eliminate THC may be a blessing when viewed in another way. This property makes it possible for a pediatrician to screen the urines of children who are not high, but who show evidence of drug use. Denial of use is so prevalent and usage rates so high that the urine screen can be a most valuable tool.

Marijuana Research

Obvious problems confront the marijuana researcher. Perhaps most serious is a prevailing attitude that the burden of proof should be placed on the shoulders of those who would speak out against the drug. This attitude is in sharp contrast to that applied to other drugs, which must be proven safe before they are considered acceptable.

Another problem in marijuana investigation is the diversity of chemicals and impurities, which may vary from joint to joint. Still another is the fact that marijuana is illegal. Because of its known harmful properties, great caution must be used when THC is given to a nonuser to evaluate its effects, especially if the subject is a child. Because of marijuana's psychoactive nature, double-blind study would be impossible unless the placebo used produced a similar euphoria. Research on the components of marijuana may be more meaningful, but investigators will still be faced with some of these problems. For these reasons, much of what we have learned about marijuana comes from retrospective studies and from accumulation of case reports and clinical experience. Despite these research limitations, there is more than ample reason to be concerned about the drug.

Pharmacology of Marijuana

The Central Nervous System. The drug's mind-altering properties and its ability to produce pleasure are the prime reasons for its use. Marijuana may also alter muscle activity, perception, hormone levels, and circulation through its actions on the brain. Behavior may be affected by its action on thoughts, emotions, and feelings.

The high of marijuana is a combination of sedation, tranquilization, and mild hallucination. The user may become preoccupied with himself or with an altered perception of sensory stimuli around him. His perception of time and space are changed, and his affect is flattened as a lag develops between thought and reaction. His thinking becomes less precise and his performance on some tasks will suffer. Short-term memory loss may occur, but remembrance of pleasure persists.[66]

The effects of chronic use on behavior discussed in Chapter 2 include lack of motivation and enthusiasm with reduced ability and interest in learning. More serious and permanent effects on the brain may be occurring along with these more easily observable behavioral alterations.

Heath and co-workers[67-69] studied the effects of marijuana in monkeys by implanting electrodes in a variety of deep brain sites. Electroencephalogram (EEG) recordings from those areas closest to the "pleasure" area of the hypothalamus showed changes in moderate smokers. These changes, which at first persisted for about 90 minutes, became more and more persistent as the trials continued into the third month. Smoking was discontinued at 6 months, and 8 months later the EEG abnormalities persisted. Monkeys that were sacrificed showed changes at synaptic junctions and in the endoplasmic reticulum of neurons, suggesting the changes (and brain damage) would be permanent. Heath's work has been criticized because of the high levels of monkey smoking that the investigator correlated with moderate human use. Critics seemed unimpressed by Heath's comments that monkeys absorb less smoke than humans from similar joints and by his presentation of evidence showing blood levels in the test primates similar to human levels.[67-69]

Heath's work has been complemented by studies at the University of California, Davis. Monkeys there were given doses of oral THC estimated to be equivalent to human doses received from a one-joint-per-day smoking habit. A pattern of tolerance developed in which higher THC doses were required to produce effects seen earlier with lower doses.[70] When stoned, the monkeys were "laid back," did not play or compete, and had perseveration of focus, much the same effects seen in humans. After 2 to 4 months of daily use, this pattern disappeared, despite the same dose of THC, and in its place irritability and aggressive behavior occurred. This negative behavior was most obvious in high-stress situations such as change of cage or entry of new cage mates. Other occupants of the cage avoided the irritable THC monkeys. In a sense, the THC users rose up in the pecking order among their nonusing cage mates, in whom stress was demonstrated by behavior change and by elevated cortisol levels. Higher doses of THC still at times produced the desired effects of relaxation and giddiness, but irritability and aggression remained and were persistent after the high was over.[71]

Monkeys who had been exposed to THC were evaluated by computed tomography (CT) scan in a study, admittedly small, but nevertheless remarkable. Four monkeys given the moderate dose of THC for a short time had scans indistinguishable from four control animals. The four long-term users from the primate labs, who were exhibiting aggressive and irritable behavior, had significantly enlarged lateral ventricles on coronal section.[72] In heads that had not changed in size, the cause of such ventricular enlargement must be interpreted as either cerebral atrophy or compression, neither desirable.

These findings prompt many questions. Would higher doses of THC cause the same findings to appear more quickly? What are the lifetime effects of chronic low-dose THC? Is there any safe lower level of marijuana use, especially given the long body retention of the drug?

The Lungs.   People often ask for a comparison of how many tobacco cigarettes compare with one marijuana cigarette. Statements have been made that one marijuana cigarette is equal in cancer-producing activity to 16 regular tobacco cigarettes, but there seems no easy way to measure this. It is important, though, to point out that there are major differences in the way in which the two are smoked that may make such an estimate correct. Tobacco smoke is filtered first by the length of the cigarette itself and then by any added filter. Marijuana cigarettes containing no filters are commonly smoked down to the very last bit with the help of a device called a roach clip, which is not used by smokers of tobacco cigarettes. This eliminates the protective effect of cigarette length. Another factor is that when marijuana smoke is inhaled, there is often a conscious effort to completely fill the lung and hold the smoke there as long as possible, knowing that increased absorption occurs in this way. Such prolonged inspirations increase exposure to all of the chemicals in marijuana, not only those producing the high. Marijuana smokers have learned how to further concentrate smoke, using clever little items developed by the drug paraphernalia industry. Among these are "bongs," which are devices much like the Turkish hookahs or water pipes of old. There is also a wide assortment of devices called "power hitters" used to force concentrated smoke into the lungs. Some of these resemble Ambu bags with masks similar to those used in hospitals for the delivery of oxygen, and others look much like futuristic "Star Wars"-type space guns, with a not-too-subtle appeal aimed at younger and younger children.

Like tobacco, marijuana contains chemicals with a variety of actions. For ease of comparison, tobacco constituents may be divided into those that are water-soluble, those that are gaseous, and those that are solid components or tars. The main water-soluble component of tobacco is nicotine, which is probably the main cause of its ability to cause habituation. Nicotine has a variety of physiologic effects, among which are cardiac stimulation, constriction of systemic blood vessels, CNS stimulation, and increased production of gastric acid. Marijuana, on the other hand, contains no nicotine, but instead has 61 lipid-soluble cannabinoids. None of these cannabinoids are found in tobacco smoke.[73]

Aside from these differences, many likenesses do exist in the two substances, all of which give us real reason to have concern for the smoker. Among the gaseous components, both tobacco and pot contain carbon monoxide. Regular tobacco smokers and marijuana smokers run carbon monoxide levels as high as 10%, compared with the average among nonsmokers of 1% to 2%. Other gaseous components of relatively equal content in both types of cigarettes are hydrocyanic acid, oxides of nitrogen, and assorted aldehydes, all of which cause lung damage and have been implicated in the production of chronic obstructive pulmonary disease (emphysema). The tars of both contain comparable quantities of polyaromatic hydrocarbons and polyphenols, which appear related to the development of lung cancer.

It has been estimated that it takes at least two decades of heavy smoking to see changes in the statistics of lung cancer and emphysema. There is every reason to suspect that by the year 1990 the devastation of marijuana on the lungs will become obvious as more and more young people have been induced to believe that pot smoking is harmless. The effects of smoking pot and tobacco should be additive. In terms of shorter-range effects, it has been of interest at Straight, Inc., to note how many young people continue to cough and bring up sputum for 6 to 12 months after they have stopped smoking pot and tobacco.

The Heart.   A clinically useful pearl was noted by Ingrid Lantner, M.D., an Ohio pediatrician who pointed out that she was aware of a relationship existing between anterior chest pain and marijuana smoking in adolescents. An awareness of this relationship may be helpful in evaluation of young people with anterior chest pain that has no obvious explanation. When cardiac abnormality or such things as pleurisy or costochondral tenderness have been ruled out, it may be helpful to ask how much marijuana has been smoked. Honest admissions of use are often more readily obtained in this situation, perhaps because of the fear that chest pain brings to people. In users, quitting may coincide with a rather prompt disappearance of chest pain. Of related interest is an attorney's wife who saw an article in my pediatric office. This article, which appeared in the *Reader's Digest,* referred to Dr. Lantner's observation and prompted the lady to ask if the relationship were true. When told that it might well prove true, she gave up her pot smoking with subsequent disappearance of her chest pain.[74]

Marijuana has an effect on heart rate and blood pressure (BP), the long-range significance of which is not known. Heart rate is increased and BP is usually decreased, but on occasion there has been slight hypertension. Exercise performance is negatively influenced, with a decreased capacity having been noted in some that is probably related to the observed elevation of the resting heart rate.

The Endocrine System, Male.   The question of testosterone and its relationship to marijuana smoking is most dramatically illustrated by a report of a 16-year-old boy who showed up at the Endocrine Clinic at Duke University Medical School.[75] Brought by his parents because of their concern about his short stature and delayed adolescence, at age 16½ he showed testicular enlargement, but no signs of maturation in those areas related to testosterone function. When evaluated he was found to have a very low testosterone level. It was not until his second visit that it was discovered that he had been smoking five marijuana joints per day since age 11. His testosterone levels rose after a period of abstinence, but he continued to show discordance between androgen effect and testicular enlargement when last reported at age 17½.

In rats and mice, cannabinoids have been shown to disrupt normal male reproductive physiology.[76] In vitro testosterone synthesis is decreased, and plasma levels of both testosterone and luteinizing hormone (LH) fall. These changes appear to be reversible. In humans, studies have varied with some investigators showing reduced levels of LH and/or testosterone and others not showing similar changes. Further research appears to be indicated.

Marijuana causes production of sperm with altered numbers, motility, and shape.[77] These changes, which have been noted in human and experimental animals, appear to be reversible with cessation of marijuana use. The effects on reproduction, both short-term and long-term, are not known, but a note of caution should be raised.

Other hormonal disturbances were noted in the early 1970s when there were reports of gynecomastia in males who were marijuana smokers.[78] In recent years such changes have not been reported with as much frequency, and the reports have been largely ignored or held up as a scare tactic used to dissuade youngsters from using pot. More recently, though, it has been learned that different varieties of marijuana contain different levels of estrogenic substances. Some estrogenic effect is contained in THC itself, but other substances found in marijuana, the dihydrostibenes and the noncannabinoid phenolic spiroindans, contain more. We now know that pot from different countries contains different levels of these feminizing substances.[79] The disappearance of gynecomastia as a frequent finding among users may be on the basis of a switch from one predominant source of pot to another.

Female.   Dramatic changes in the female menstrual cycle have been shown in the monkey and other nonhuman primates.[76,80] Anovulatory menstrual cycles have also been reported in marijuana-smoking women when compared with nonusers.[81] In experimental studies on nonpregnant female rats, THC does cause lowering of plasma LH and prolactin levels and a decrease in the preovulatory LH surge. These changes appear to be mediated by direct effect on the hypothalamic-pituitary-ovarian axis. All seem to be reversible with cessation of marijuana use.

Lactation.   I remember well the mother who, 7 or 8 years ago, asked whether marijuana passed in the breast milk. I told her I did not know. A month later the same mother notified me that marijuana did pass the breast barrier. She had ascertained this by noting that her infant had no trouble with colic on those evenings when she consumed one or two marijuana brownies. In my naivety at that time, I was more interested in the story than shocked by what I heard. It has since been shown by many others that THC does in fact pass in breast milk. Studies in animals have shown diminished lactation with marijuana use, probably related to impaired prolactin secretion.[80]

Immune System.   There is suggestive but not conclusive evidence that marijuana affects the immune system by altering the numbers and function of T- and B-lymphocytes and serum immunoglobulin levels.[82,83] Clinical reports of THC administration to patients on chemotherapy add to the evidence that marijuana in fact may have some deleterious effects on the immune response.[84]

The Fetus.   Infants of mothers who regularly used marijuana during their pregnancy may have increased irritability, tremulousness and exaggerated startle reflexes.[85] These may be a manifestation of the neonatal abstinence syndrome described for a variety of CNS-depressant drugs including alcohol.[86] Altered attention span has been demonstrated in the offspring of primates given THC during pregnancy.[55] The report of a fivefold increase in the fetal alcohol syndrome among mothers who used marijuana in addition to alcohol is also disturbing.[87]

Effects of Additives.   Marijuana naturally contains 421 chemicals, but it may on occasion contain many more. It may have additives such as PCP, LSD, hash oil, free-base cocaine, or other psychoactive drugs whose presence may or may not be known to the user. In addition disease has been reported from contamination with infectious organisms such as *Aspergillus*[88] and *Salmonella.*[89]

Potential Benefits of Marijuana.   Biologically active components of marijuana or derivatives of these compounds are being evaluated for a variety of potential therapeutic uses.[90] None of these applications is beyond the investigative stage, but it does not seem unreasonable to suspect that from such a large variety of chemicals, some beneficial effects may be discovered. Among the applications being studied are bronchodilator effects (asthma), antinausea effects (chemotherapy adjuvant), decreased intraocular pressure (glaucoma), anticonvulsive effects (epilepsy), muscle relaxant effects (spasticity), and decrease in tremors (multiple sclerosis.) The psychoactive properties of THC may make it unsuitable for any general use, but natural or synthetic analogues may be of value.[91]

The possibility that marijuana may have some medically useful components does not mean that it should be legalized any more than the knowledge that heroin is the most effective cough suppressant known means that we should legalize it. Some forms of cannabis or their derivatives may eventually find their way into the pharmacopoeia, as have such important and useful opiate drugs as morphine and meperidine hydrochloride (Demerol). If derivatives are approved by the FDA for certain uses, tight control of those that are psychoactive and habituating should be mandatory.

Statements made by the AMA Council on Scientific Affairs, by the American Academy of Pediatrics, and by the surgeon general of the United States strongly oppose the use of marijuana because of its negative effects on health, especially in the adolescent.[92-94] In making his strong statement, the surgeon general had considerably more data on which to base his recommendation than did his predecessor who condemned tobacco use 15 years earlier. The report of the Institute of Medicine, which led to their much less strongly worded conclusion that there was serious cause for concern about the health risks about marijuana, is packed with reports detailing the negative effects of the drug.[95]

Alcohol

As a social lubricant and euphoriant, ethyl alcohol is an important component of our society. Widely advertised and consumed in huge quantities producing important tax revenue, alcohol also has potential for great harm. Just a simple listing of all of the risks associated with ethanol ingestion is not possible in this section. The reader who wishes more complete information is referred to the excellent review article by Eckhardt and collaborators.[96] For one who regards alcohol as vaguely dangerous, a review of such literature is likely to change vagueness to serious concern.

Pharmacology

There is a common misconception that treats distilled spirits as hard liquor and implies that beer and wine are, by comparison, soft. Distilled spirits contain 40% to 50% alcohol, compared with only about 12% in wine and 4% in beer. When diluted and consumed in its most usual fashion, a highball contains a quantity of ethanol comparable to that found in a standard 12-oz can of beer or a 4-oz glass of wine.

Metabolism of alcohol varies with time of day, previous drinking history, nutritional factors, and genetic factors. It is excreted unchanged in breath, sweat, and urine, but primarily leaves the body after being metabolized in the liver.

Acute Effects

Alcohol produces a euphoria that might best be described as relaxation (sedation plus loss of inhibitions). For most this is preceded by a period of stimulation occurring while the blood alcohol level is rising. A positive feeling and increased social interaction may be noted. Subsequently sedation and hypnotic properties become prominent.

Because the absorption time of alcohol is affected by such things as gastric motility and pH, food in the stomach, and other individual differences, it is not unusual to see a desired level of euphoria exceeded without additional drinking as the stomach slowly empties its reservoir.

Overdose

The lack of judgment accompanying alcohol intoxication may lead to further drinking in the already overdosed. Concomitant use of marijuana, which has an antiemetic effect, may further add to the overdose problem by blocking protective nausea and vomiting. The frequent practice of taking tranquilizers or sedatives with alcohol can also produce dangerous overdosage, including severe respiratory depression.

The negative effects of alcohol on motor and cognitive functions become more severe with increasing levels of blood alcohol, and as the level reaches 250 to 400 mg/dl, more serious effects may be noted. Among these may be apathy, stupor, coma, depressed respiration, shock, subnormal temperature, and death. The chronic alcoholic may develop an alcohol tolerance that allows him to perform tasks surprisingly well with blood alcohol levels as high as 200. Tolerance of this sort does not seem to be accompanied by similar tolerance to the effects on such bodily functions as control of respiration and temperature.

Undesirable side effects such as aggressiveness vary with the individual, the drinking environment, and the amount of alcohol consumed. Intoxication may be associated with loss of coordination, sensorimotor process, cognition, and emotions. All of these may contribute to traffic accidents, violence, suicide, and crime. Most obvious are such motor impairments as staggering gait, unsteady balance, and slurred speech. Measurable body sway may be noted on testing with blood alcohol levels of 40 mg/dl, which are well under present legal limits of intoxication.[97] Processing of information is impaired as noted in testing of recovery from glare and eye-hand coordination tracking tasks. Problems are noted when it is necessary to process information from more than one source.

Hangover is common and may consist of fatigue, headache, nausea, and acute gastritis. This unpleasant aftermath may be worsened by constituents of the alcoholic beverage other than the alcohol itself. School and family function are likely to be suboptimal during this period.

Long-Term Problems

CNS Dysfunction.   Depending on the population surveyed, 50% to 70% of sober alcoholics entering treatment have CNS dysfunction.[98] Even social drinkers may show impairment of abstracting and adaptive abilities when off alcohol for 24 hours. Their degree of impairment is directly related to the amount of alcohol consumed per occasion.[99] Alcoholic neuropathy is common.[100]

Long-term alcoholics may develop the Wernicke-Korsakoff syndrome, also called the alcohol amnesic syndrome. The first phase of this problem described by Wernicke consists of confusion, ataxia, nystagmus, ophthalmoplegia, and peripheral neuropathy related to decreased levels of the vitamin thiamine. Correction of the thiamine deficiency results in improvement, but most are left with a chronic amnesic (Korsakoff's) psychoses.

Psychiatric Illness.   A statistical relationship exists between manic depressive illness and alcoholism. This may be due to depressed people drinking, drinking people becoming depressed, or both. There also exists a relationship with suicide. One investigator reported a 30-times-greater risk of suicide for alcoholics than for nonalcoholics,[101] while another said 6% to 12% of alcoholics commit suicide compared with 1% of the general population.[102]

GI Dysfunction.   From the point of entering the body onward, alcohol may cause problems. Alcohol's most prominent effects on the GI tract are those that involve the liver and include alcoholic hepatitis, "fatty" liver, and cirrhosis. In 1975 cirrhosis was responsible for 31,623 American deaths. Alcoholics have increased incidence of cancer of the mouth, pharynx, larynx, esophagus, colon, rectum, liver, and pancreas. Alcohol may cause gastric ulceration and chronic pancreatitis. Alcohol abuse has been suggested as the most common cause of vitamin and mineral deficiency in adult Americans. These nutritional deficiencies may be on the basis of alcoholic anorexia, nausea, and vomiting or secondary to altered digestive function.

Endocrine Changes.   Among the endocrine changes described in drinkers are testicular failure and atrophy,[103] impotence in men and women,[104] feminization of males, early onset of postmenopausal amenorrhea,[103] and increased incidence of breast cancer. Hormonal changes have been reported with alcohol use, including increased cortisol,[105] decreased oxytocin,[106] decreased antidiuretic hormone,[107] and decreased testosterone.[103]

Other Problems.   A listing of all of the physical problems that have been related to alcohol use is not possible in this book, but the list includes cardiac problems[108] and increased risk of pneumonia[109] and tuberculosis.[110]

Alcohol Withdrawal.   A specific and severe manifestation of alcohol withdrawal, DTs, are fortunately not an important consideration for adolescent treatment programs. This acute psychotic state is rare under age 30 or in drinkers who have not had at least 3 to 5 years of heavy alcohol consumption. The DTs usually follow binges and 2 to 4 days of abstinence. They consist of confusion, hallucinations, shakes, sweating, ataxia, and occasionally seizures and death. In 1975 there were 97,000 hospital discharges in this country for DTs and 316 related deaths.[111]

Driving, Drinking, and Drugs

Many of the effects of alcohol and marijuana are additive, and there is evidence that highway accidents may be increased by both drugs. Driving simulation was used to measure placebo, alcohol, marijuana, and the two drugs combined. Marijuana caused deterioration of perceptual motor performance, inability to maintain lane position, poorer emergency decision making, and prolonged mean reaction time in responding to peripheral lights.[63] Alcohol impaired the drivers' abilities to maintain their lane on curves and detect peripheral lights. Combined effects were slightly worse. Numerous other studies give cause for great concern,[62] as does the report that THC was found in 16% of blood samples obtained from nearly 2,000 drivers arrested for impaired driving in California.[112]

Fetal Alcohol Syndrome (FAS)

The suspicion that alcohol might have a serious impact on fetal development has existed since ancient times,[113] but only recently has a clinical syndrome been described. First described by Rouguette in 1957[114] and Lemoine and colleagues in 1968,[115] this syndrome identified a characteristic combination of birth defects in infants born to alcoholic mothers. These findings were largely ignored until 1979 when eight cases of infants with a variety of CNS problems were reported,[116] the most common of which were mental retardation, microcephaly, and irritability. The principal features of the FAS can be clustered into a triad: facial dysmorphology, prenatal and postnatal growth deficiency, and CNS involvement.

How much alcohol it takes to damage fetuses is not known. Evidence is accumulating that alcohol negatively affects growth and development of infants who do not have the full-blown FAS.[117,118] The bumper sticker that says "A Pregnant Woman Never Drinks Alone" says a lot.

A study quoted earlier in this chapter showing that women who used marijuana during pregnancy were five times more likely to deliver infants with features compatible with the FAS suggests that the effects of these two drugs on the fetus may be additive.[87]

The Stimulants: Cocaine and the Amphetamines

Cocaine

General.   The cocaine industry is big business in this country, with 40 tons the estimated amount imported yearly from South America and sales estimated at \$29 billion.[119] NIDA estimates that 15 million Americans have tried cocaine (also known as "coke," "snow," "gold dust," and "lady"), and Johnston and coworkers[2] in their survey found that 3% of all high school seniors in 1981 had tried cocaine in one form or another. In 1977, 19% of adults aged 18 to 25 years admitted experience with the drug, 4% within the preceding month.[120]

Cocaine produces such an overpowering euphoria that anyone may be swept into compulsive use. Strength of character and psychological maturity may not protect the experimenter from a rapid advance to dependency.

Compulsive use was well illustrated by experimental animals "who would press a lever more than four thousand times to get a single injection of cocaine. When given free access they immediately began self administering doses that might produce severe toxic effects and induce self mutilating behavior."[123] "All animals tested have worked (by pressing a bar) for cocaine more avidly than for any other stimulant . . . In an unlimited access situation monkeys will self-administer cocaine by bar pressing until they die of convulsions."[124]

The drug cocaine comes from the leaves of the Bolivian coca plant *(Erythroxylum coca)* or the Peruvian coca plant *(Erythroxylum novgranatense)* with 18 alkaloids and other chemicals. From these leaves, which contain 0.5% to 1% cocaine, a variety of psychoactive forms are derived. Adulterants, impurities, and varying cocaine concentrations distinguish the different preparations. Effects are dose-related, ranging from the very low-dose coca leaf up to IV cocaine.

Uptake of cocaine from most forms is fairly rapid, with a high being achieved within seconds after smoking of coca paste or IV use. The duration of the high may be no longer than 20 minutes and in some cases considerably shorter. The more rapid the development of euphoria, the shorter its duration. With freebase inhalation or IV administration there may be intense mental effects in seconds with a drop-off of effects in minutes. With sniffing, the high develops more slowly and lasts an average of 2 to 3 hours, with a number of users having effects for 6 to 8 hours. Cocaine is a very powerful reinforcer which frequently tempts the user to continue use. Such "runs" may last until either the product is gone, the apparatus for smoking is broken, or sleep ensues. Excretion is rapid, with half-life of 30 to 40 minutes and elimination of detectable forms in the urine in 50% of users in 24 to 48 hours.

Man may get high on cocaine using any one of its four drug forms. These are the coca leaf itself, coca paste, cocaine hydrochloride, and most recently "free-base" cocaine. The coca leaf is a relatively mild product, which has been used for centuries by workers high in the Andes. Chewing the leaf allows them to sustain their work efforts for hours with a sense of decreased hunger, decreased fatigue, and a general feeling of well being. Coca paste is the rather crude first-extraction product made during the manufacture of cocaine from leaves. Very high rates of absorption occur when it is smoked either in a tobacco or marijuana cigarette or when placed on foil and heated to yield fumes that are inhaled. The substance may contain anywhere from 40% to 80% cocaine.[127] Some of its effects may be related to alkaloids other than cocaine sulfate. Only recently used in this country, it has been very popular in Peru, where a psychotic syndrome was reported in 188 coca paste smokers between the ages of 16 and 25. The clinical picture was one of euphoria, hyper-talkativeness, irritability, stereotypic behavior, insomnia, weight loss, and toxic psychosis. Additionally, the sudden but brief high is similar to that of IV injection, but considerably cheaper.

Cocaine hydrochloride is the product that in various strengths and forms is known as "street cocaine." The product, extracted from coca paste by the addition of hydrochloric acid, yields a fine powder used for snorting or IV use. Concentrations may vary from near 0% cocaine to 85% to 90%. Estimates are that most street cocaine is "cut" anywhere from one to eight times. Cutting is done either with inert chemicals such as mannitol, glucose or, lactose or with substances that do have some CNS effects such as caffeine, lidocaine, or procaine. The great variability in the strength of street cocaine adds to the risk of overdose, which may occur when one unsuspectingly snorts a stronger form than he is prepared for. Extraction of free-base cocaine may be accomplished using any of a variety of readily available commercial kits. The high flammability of solvents made this a risky procedure but crack which is prepared without solvent extraction is cheaper, safer, and now more popular. Free-base cocaine need not be snorted or taken IV, but may be added to cigarettes or inhaled as vapor from heating.[127]

The effects of cocaine may be divided into three general categories: (1) anesthetic, (2) autonomic or epinephrine-like actions, and (3) euphoric. Cocaine is a marvelous anesthetic that has given way to its synthetic derivations because of its high potential for abuse. Autonomic effects include such signs as dilated pupils and increases in heart rate, BP, and respiratory rate. There may be increase in temperature and decrease in cutaneous sensibility as well as an increase in spinal and autonomic reflexes. Nasal septal perforation, which may occur with snorting is probably secondary to irritation, local anesthesia, and/or vasoconstriction. The dopamine-like euphoria that cocaine produces is an exhilarating high with an associated sense of power. Dopamine is the naturally occurring substance known to mediate the reward system for food in thirsty and hungry animals. There may be a feeling of calmness, even though the drug is a powerful stimulant. Thirst, hunger, and fatigue may all be diminished. During the relatively short euphoric phase, there may be hypervigilance, hyperactivity, anorexia, insomnia, and in some cases increased sexuality.

The euphoric high subsides into a "wired up" feeling of restless irritability that may be relieved if sedatives such as alcohol, methaqualone, or heroin are consumed with or between "hits" on the drug. This dysphoric phase may begin in seconds or may take 20 to 30 minutes to develop. Blood cocaine levels are usually still elevated.[129] Symptoms of anxiety, compulsion to smoke, sadness, apathy, aggressiveness, sexual indifference, anorexia, and insomnia are common. Continued use of the drug may lead to a third phase called the phase of hallucination.

Paranoia may occur, which can usually be relieved by taking more drugs, particularly the stronger forms such as coca paste and free base. This paranoia is more likely if cocaine is used in conjunction with a "calming" opiate. Symptoms may be visual, tactile, auditory, and olfactory delusions and hallucinations, delusional interpretations, psychomotor excitement, extreme suspiciousness, sexual indifference, and sometimes aggressiveness. This phase may last for hours or days.

Manic, paranoid, or depressive psychosis may develop after months to years of repetitive off-and-on use. Typical are hypervigilance, paranoid delusions, hallucinations, insomnia, and aggression. Disorientation and stereotypic behavior may occur. There may be death in this stage due to overdosing, suicide, accidents, or injury during fights.[128,130]

History. Cocaine seems destined to repeat its century-old history. This drug first came into popularity in the Western world with claims made in the 1880s by a number of medical experts about its great medicinal properties. Perhaps the most famous of these proponents, Sigmund Freud, wrote a number of articles extolling its virtue and usefulness for a variety of conditions. He described its value in warding off hunger, sleep, and fatigue and "stealing one's intellectual effort."[125] Coca Cola used cocaine with its stimulating and euphoric effects until the year 1903, and the Sears, Roebuck catalog of 1904 had advertisements for patent medicines containing cocaine. Then bad news began to surface. People became dependent, toxic, and died. Among the early victims was Halstead, the father of modern American surgery, who became dependent while investigating the use of cocaine as a regional anesthetic. He was cured from his cocaine dependency only by substituting morphine, on which he remained dependent until his death.[126] When the Harrison Narcotics Act was passed in 1914, cocaine was of more concern to the legislators than were the opiates. Those who are now calling cocaine the "drug of the eighties" might well review the history of the 1880s.[125]

Acute Overdose. Overdose may occur with severe consequences such as anxiety, hyperpyrexia, generalized seizures, respiratory arrest, cardiac arrhythmia, and death.[131] Because tolerance develops to the hyperpyrexic and cardiovascular effects, cocaine toxicity may be less likely to occur in the regular user. Cocaine-related deaths as reported by the Drug Abuse Warning Network (DAWN) doubled between the reporting periods in July to December, 1984 and January to June, 1987.

Detoxification. Withdrawal from cocaine may produce very similar symptoms, but of shorter duration than those due to withdrawal from amphetamines. Depressed mood, fatigue, disturbed sleep, or dreaming and suicidal ideas are common. With cocaine these symptoms are nearly gone in 24 hours, but the patient may have some continued guilt, embarrassment, and a few days of reactive depression, fatigue, and craving for drugs.

Tolerance. Tolerance develops to some of cocaine's effects, but not to others. This tolerance, which was disputed by experts for years, became obvious when IV and free-base cocaine appeared with their higher concentrations. In order to achieve a continued feeling of euphoria from cocaine, larger and larger doses may be necessary. In Peru much larger doses have been consumed than is customary in the United States.[133] Such an increase is apt to prompt the toxic symptoms of irritability, paranoia, and an eventual toxic psychosis to which tolerance does not develop. As mentioned earlier a protective tolerance may develop to such negative effects as hyperpyrexia, anorexia, and cardiovascular irritability.

Reverse tolerance or "kindling," though not conclusively demonstrated, is believed to occur in humans. In contrast to the phenomenon of tolerance, the experienced user with "kindling" may develop symptoms of toxicity with a relatively small dose. Kindling has been given as an explanation for rapid progression from euphoria to dysphoria to hallucinations to psychosis in some chronic users.[134] Such reverse tolerance might explain seizures and other serious incidents reported in some experienced long-term users.

The Amphetamines

A recent survey that showed rising use of amphetamines (also called "uppers," "speed," "black beauties," and "dexies") may partially reflect the appearance on the market of "look-alike" capsules.[2]

These widely sold replicas, usually containing caffeine, may be indistinguishable from amphetamines for the casual user. Another survey that suggests rising use found that only 5% of adults over 26 years of age had tried nonprescribed stimulants, compared with 21% of younger adults.[122]

Effects of amphetamines are in many ways like those of cocaine. In fact, experienced cocaine users were unable to distinguish between the subjective effects of IV cocaine and IV dextroamphetamine.[135] Amphetamine effects usually are slower in coming and last longer than those of cocaine. Both produce a euphoric feeling with associated disappearance of fatigue and feelings of enhanced physical strength and mental capacity. Loss of appetite may be the desired effect of those needing to make a lower weight class in sports such as wrestling. All of these effects have appeal for the young athlete who wants to give no competitive edge to opponents he suspects are users. With increasing dosage, toxic effects including psychoses may appear much like those seen with cocaine. The development of tolerance is similar to cocaine, as are symptoms of withdrawal.[53] Also similar is the tendency to use "speed" in runs and to try to balance the undesirable irritability with sedatives.

Sedatives and Tranquilizers

In general the effects of barbiturates and other sedatives are similar to those of alcohol. As with alcohol these effects may vary with dosage from user to user and from situation to situation.

Methaqualone (trade names Quaaludes and Sopor, also known as "ludes") is included as representative of the sedatives, because it is the most commonly used nonalcoholic, self-prescribed drug of sedation for adolescents. In 1980 less than 4 tons of methaqualone were made and distributed in this country. Estimates are that over 100 tons were smuggled into the United States that same year, of which 15 tons were seized by federal agents. By August of 1981, 30 tons had been confiscated. Youthful users have been lured by promises of a better high than with phenobarbital, one in which the hangover and the impotence of alcohol do not occur. Frequently counterfeits may contain substances such as Valium or PCP.

When first introduced in 1965, methaqualone was wrongly reported as nonaddictive and went on to gain popularity as a "love drug." Popularity waned as reports of severe withdrawal symptoms and serious overdose appeared, and methaqualone was reclassified as a Schedule II drug. Use among high school seniors rose until 1981 but by 1987 had to be returned to level off one third of those reported in 1978 when the high school survey was initiated.

In addition to its ability to produce chemical dependency, methaqualone may cause dangerous sedation and lack of judgment. Frequently used in combination with other drugs such as alcohol, methaqualone may lead to accidental death, accidental overdose, suicide, and homicide. In Broward County, Fla., Chief Medical Examiner Ronald Wright found methaqualone in 93% of 295 specimens obtained from drivers arrested for "driving under the influence" and whose roadside breath tests showed insufficient alcohol to account for their intoxication. Such laboratory assays are inadmissible courtroom evidence in most states.

As with the barbiturates ("yellow jackets," "red devils") and tranquilizers, tolerance develops to methaqualone that may hide the sleepy behavior that would be expected with regular use. Cross tolerance is common among members of the sedative-tranquilizer group. Withdrawal symptoms are similar with all and may be quite severe, including grand mal seizures and delirium. During the delirium, which usually occurs between the fourth and seventh day, agitation and hyperthermia can lead to exhaustion, cardiovascular collapse, and death.[53]

Inhalants

Approximately 11% of young adults between the ages of 18 and 25 in 1978 admitted some experience with inhalants.[122] Head shops did a good business selling products called "Rush" and "Lockerroom" to thrill-seeking teenagers. These products contain a liquid butyl nitrate that on exposure to air becomes amyl nitrate. Amyl nitrate, long used for relieving symptoms of cardiac angina, produces stimulation and a "rush" of blood to the head that some teenagers like.

Inhalants such as ether and nitrous oxide ("laughing gas") have a long history of use and abuse. Newer additions to the aromatic hydrocarbon field have been "glue" for sniffing, gasoline, lacquer thinner, and paint thinner. The latter chemicals all carry considerable risk, particularly of cardiac arrhythmia. Long-lasting brain damage has been shown in inhalers of aerosol paints.[53]

The Psychedelics

The primary psychedelic, LSD, gained popularity because of its advertised capacity to "expand consciousness." A state of altered perception is produced where sensory stimuli seem magnified and more vivid. There may be a sense of being able to ascribe meaning to routine facets of the environment and a sense of being closer to the cosmos.[136] On the negative side, "bad trips" or panic reactions may occur even in experienced users. Because it is easily and inexpensively produced, LSD is a frequent adulterant or additive to other street drugs.

Physical effects such as pupillary dilatation, hyperpyrexia, nausea, increased BP, tachycardia, and hyperreflexia are largely mediated by the sympathetic nervous system.[53] Dizziness, weakness, nausea, and paresthesia may precede the high. The half-life of LSD is 3 hours, with effects beginning to wear off in about 12 hours.

The great initial popularity of LSD has waned, and today there are few "acid heads." Tolerance develops rapidly, and with time the psychedelic "scene" tends to interest the user less and less.[44] Withdrawal symptoms do not tend to occur, but "flashbacks," a recurrence of the drug effects, may be a problem for some. Naturally occurring psychedelic compounds are contained in peyote cactus (mescaline) and some mushrooms (psilocin). These psychedelic plants are readily found in some parts of the country and have been fairly widely used by experimenters in stage 3 drug use. Their effects are much like those of LSD.

PCP

The psychedelic PCP ("angel dust," "killer weed," "crystal cyclone," "elephant tranquilizer," "embalming fluid," "rocket fuel," or "supergrass") has been placed in a class separate from other hallucinogens because of its ability to produce what has been called a dissociative anesthesia.[53] The altered state produced by this drug has elements of stimulation, depression, hallucination, and analgesia.

Most people who take PCP think they are getting something else. Inexpensive and easily manufactured, it is frequently smoked on a joint with marijuana or sold on the street as THC. First introduced in the 1960s as an aid to human anesthesia, its side effects soon became apparent, and its only legal use now is in veterinary medicine. At one time touted to be a psychedelic substance somewhere between marijuana and LSD in effect, most users were quick to discover its bad effects and not seek a second trial.

An early pleasant feeling can give way to a confused and agitated state. Incoordination similar to alcohol intoxication occurs, and thinking and decision making are affected. Some will become violent and aggressive, while others will be silent, withdrawn, and uncommunicative. Higher doses may cause muscle rigidity, tachycardia, convulsions, opisthotonos, coma and arrhythmias. Overdoses of PCP can kill, but deaths are more likely from accidents or suicide-related activity while high. Acute psychotic reactions have been reported with paranoia, suicidal ideas, delusions of grandeur, and hallucinations. Flashbacks may occur. Users may show long-term effects on memory, judgment, concentration, and perception. Clinical observation suggests tolerance does occur. Recurrent bouts of anxiety and depression have also been reported.

Despite all this, some continue to use PCP by choice. An estimated 10 million American teenagers and adults use the drug occasionally, and 1 million use it weekly.[137]

The Opiates

Heroin and other opiate use seemed to decline in use following international control efforts in the early 1970s. Street heroin was

"Mexican brown" with concentrations in the range of 3.5%. Newer heroin such as "China white" and "Persian porcelain" began to appear with considerably higher potency (15% to 20% not uncommon). This new heroin is so potent it may be smoked with tobacco or marijuana or its heated vapors inhaled. With the increasing availability of high-grade heroin, a new epidemic has begun. At first the users were primarily former users who gave up their methadone to return to "H." The national addict population is thought to be 450,000, primarily in the 26- to 39-year age group.[119] The 850 reported heroin deaths in 1980 were a 20% increase from 1979.

A report from Southern California showed a dramatic increase in young heroin addicts in late 1981. The executive director of the Los Angeles-based Community Health Projects, which treats more than 1,000 clients daily, reported more young addicts in 3 months than in the previous 7 years combined. "To be an addict at 16, it means they would have had to start smoking and drinking at 8, moved into marijuana, then something like PCP, and then try heroin."[138] In 1977 an estimated 2.3% of young adults (between the ages of 18 and 25 years) admitted to heroin use at some time in their lives.[120]

Opiates are potent pain relievers, hence the medical use of morphine and meperidine hydrochloride (Demerol). Such medical use may induce dependency, but awareness of such danger has decreased its occurrence. The "rush" of IV heroin produces a lower abdominal sensation similar to orgasm and is very addicting. In 1971, 42% of enlisted servicemen in Vietnam reported using opium at least once, and one half of these said that at some time during the year they were physically dependent.[139] Some who believe that an individual's pattern of drug use is most frequently situational point to a follow-up of these seemingly dependent servicemen, only 14% of whom were unable to cease use upon returning to civilian life.

Death is usually due to fatal overdosage and respiratory paralysis related to inexperience of the user, higher purity of the drug than expected, or a dangerous combination with other sedative drugs such as alcohol. Anaphylactic-like reactions have been noted that are believed to be related to injection of impurities. Contaminated needles may cause hepatitis and a variety of other infections such as septicemia, acquired immunodeficiency syndrome (AIDS), and endocarditis. Withdrawal symptoms, which peak at 2 to 3 days, may be severe.

Other Drugs

Teenagers love to experiment and have reported smoking or ingesting a wide variety of substances including nutmeg and morning glory seeds, which may have some CNS effects.

The relationship of caffeine to other psychoactive drugs is unclear, but it does indeed have properties of stimulation, tolerance, toxicity, and withdrawal symptoms, because of which some would include it on the "bad" drug list. Its social acceptability and relatively low cost and risk justify its use to many.

SUMMARY

It is not possible in this book to do an in-depth review of drug pharmacology. Most emphasis has been given to the drugs most commonly used by teenagers. All psychoactive drugs may cause dependency and subsequent destruction of personality. For more detail on alcohol, see Eckardt and colleagues[96]; on marijuana, see Nahas and Frick[140,141] and Russell[142]; and on drug pharmacology in general, see Jaffe.[53] An excellent series of monographs on marijuana and cocaine may be obtained from the American Council for Drug Education (ACDE).[143]

5

"Do-Drug" Messages: Happiness, Drugs, and Dollars

HEDONISM AND HAPPINESS

We live in a society where pleasure and happiness are considered the main goals of life by many. Pleasure-seeking behavior and avoidance of pain are natural human instincts that seem to have gotten out of control. Phrases like "do it now," "whatever turns you on," or "if it feels good, do it," are widely subscribed to even when acceptance of such immediate gratification may be detrimental to the long-range goals of self or others.

This hedonism, so pervasive in adult society, has reached down to involve parenting and the desire of parents to see their children's desires gratified. When asking parents what they want their children to be when they grow up, be prepared for an answer that coincides with this desire. At prenatal visits, at PTA meetings, or in casual conversation, one response to this question has become predominant. The all-too-common answer is, "I don't care what Charley becomes as long as he's happy."

Happiness is great, but not when it becomes the number one goal in life. When it does, deferment of gratification, self-sacrifice, sharing, and caring about others may be pushed aside. Better goals are to have a child grow up feeling good about himself, living up to his potential, having a spiritual awareness, and caring about other people. These goals are often interrelated and may lead to happiness.

The joy of accomplishment and helping others can be great. Putting happiness first may prevent the attainment of such joy.

Happiness has in many ways been equated with intoxication. "Happy Hours" are times for chemical euphoria with the added benefit of reduced prices. It is little wonder that children led to believe happiness is paramount and bombarded with drug messages take the bait.

Historically almost every culture has identified for itself an acceptable psychoactive substance. For Americans this substance has been alcohol. For some American Indians, it was mescaline (peyote). For Arabs it has been hashish. The phenomenon of multidrug use that now exists is new. In a society that talks of legalizing marijuana and where there is indiscriminate use of tranquilizers and even cocaine, the messages given to children have become blurred. Not only are there more types of "popular" drugs available, but there are additional "acceptable" reasons for drug use. In the past socially accepted drug use has been limited to medicinal, social, and spiritual or ritual purposes. To these traditionally accepted uses, our society has added use for the purpose of dealing with stress.

The way a society views intoxication bears strong relationship to its patterns of use. In societies that accept alcohol use but see intoxication as shameful, there are fewer problems. In our society intoxication is often viewed as humorous. Young drinkers have come to accept staggering, word slurring, and even vomiting as part of the cost of having fun.

The message of "happiness at all costs" has become firmly entrenched in child-rearing practices from nursery onward. Pediatricians and parents have subscribed increasingly to the belief that it is a parental responsibility to shield children from all trauma. Children are not to face death, discomfort, boredom, loneliness, frustration, or anxiety. Parents, in trying to shield children from these situations, have only postponed reality. These "traumas" are real, and the role of parenting should be helping a child learn to deal with them. Careful, loving, and age-appropriate teaching of coping skills allows the child to learn from his experiences.

When a child's unhappiness has boredom as its root, early messages given to the infant may be lasting ones. When a child is 8 months old and cries in a pediatric office, it is appropriate for the physician to ask the mother why the child is crying. If she says hunger is the cause, then the obvious solution is to feed him. If she says he is dirty, changing his diaper makes good sense. If she says he is bored or it is his fussy period, further inquiry should be made as to her usual response to such crying. Saying that she offers breast or bottle or cracker at these times should be considered wrong answers. Saying she moves him, picks him up, or winds up his swing may also be indicators of overprotection. The wise pediatrician may point out that the attention span of infants is very short. It is not unusual for them to lose interest in things after relatively short periods of time. If their fussing is observed and timed, many of these infants will shortly focus on something else and content themselves for another short period. The child who does not learn to deal with such boredom may be demanding stories for boredom at 2, Atari cartridge refills for boredom at 10, and keg parties for boredom at 16. Happiness to some means constant mollification and/or external diversion. Parents who see it as their duty to provide such happiness may be heading for trouble.

Crying, one sign of unhappiness, must be avoided at all costs. This is a dangerous belief shared by many parents. Crying mobilizes people to action; no matter what the cause, adults in the area of a crying child will respond with efforts to make him stop. When a pet dies, his youthful master is told not to cry. Where reassurance will not work, perhaps a bottle, candy, or medication will. More appropriate responses are often available. If a child is in pain, a caring parent might better hug the child, pick him up, and make an offer of help. Crying is a symptom of distress, and not a disease. The wise parent will learn to read the message and respond. Shutting off the symptom is not the correct response.

Many have suggested that a major emphasis of drug prevention efforts should be the provision of the "alternative highs." If young people could be made to appreciate sports and music, for instance, as capable of producing real feelings of joy, they would be less likely to indulge in euphoria-producing chemicals. This may be only partially true. Part of the problem with this solution is that again the emphasis is on merit being given only to those things in life that provide gratification in a fairly short-term sense. Another difficulty in this solution is that many young people who have accepted the fact that music or camping can produce euphoria have chosen to "enhance" the natural euphoria with chemicals.

THE PLOP-PLOP, FIZZ-FIZZ SOCIETY

Our children are taught to open their mouths and find relief. Widely promoted are drugs for "minor aches and pains," "tension headache," "night cough," "tired blood," and a variety of other ailments and symptoms. For those needing even more help, "extra-strength" preparations are available. Our children grow up with vitamin pills, aspirin, and cough medicines. Family medicine cabinets often look like branch pharmacies. The message given to the child is clear: the answer to whatever ails you can usually be found in capsule or syrup form.

Often overlooked is the fact that almost all of these remedies have negative side effects. Such effects are generally downplayed. Relief of discomfort is often given precedence over making a diagnosis or allowing a disease to follow its natural course. Despite the fact that many of these home remedies do not work, parents feel better thinking they are doing their share to stamp out discomfort. The economic costs of such practice are great, but may be dwarfed by the costs related to teaching that drugs can relieve all ills.

Alcohol is widely promoted as a key part of all sorts of social and athletic activities. Fun is drinking. It was once a common belief in this country that weekends were for family, church, and relaxation. Now the message is clearly that "weekends were made for Michelob." Sports stars look forward to retirement so they can join their mates in the debate over various lite beers. Mountains are climbed not just for exercise, view, and companionship, but with the hope that your favorite beer will be chilled when you reach the top. The message one gets when watching such commercials is that the beer at the end of the activity is more important than the activity itself. The wine and beer industry speaks out against teenage drinking, but sponsors ads that seem most aimed at youthful audiences. From a commercial standpoint, the money is well spent.

More insidious, perhaps, are the television ads that are not billed as such. "Dallas" almost always has a family cocktail hour, Quincy wraps up in his favorite bar, and the medical heroes of "M*A*S*H*" frequently adjorn to their tents for liquid relaxation. Family togetherness and relaxation are closely tied to liquid refreshment. Cigarettes are not openly advertised on television, but tennis tournaments are named for favorite brands. Macho men ride horses and smoke. Ads promoting alcohol and tobacco surround the highway. The exposure is tremendous, and kids are getting the message—drink and smoke. This is in spite of the fact that approximately 30% of the people who die in this country have had their lives shortened as a fairly direct result of alcohol or tobacco consumption.

Drug Paraphernalia

In 1972 a man named Burt Rubin noted that marijuana smokers could not get a full load onto a sheet of standard tobacco rolling paper and were using two instead. He invested $6,000 in making and distributing a product called "EZ Wider" papers to answer this need and by 1978 had a $9 million business with an annual advertising budget of $500,000. What began as a product for adults sold only in inner city stores became such a success that paper sales spread to boutiques and record stores, then supermarkets, convenience stores, and vending machines.

Noting the instant market in paper sales, other drug-related items were pushed on the market. Bongs, originally vertical bamboo devices, were joined by a variety of other contraptions for concentrating marijuana smoke. For the younger audiences, there were "candy quaaludes," "practice grass," and smoking devices resembling "Star Wars" guns. To promote their products, the industry supported *High Times* magazine, which from a difficult start in 1974 reached a readership of 4 million in 1980.

The drug paraphernalia industry, which did not exist in 1970, had by 1979 become a multimillion-dollar giant. (Since then, primarily due to the efforts of angry parents, this industry that openly promoted drug use has been made to retreat.) Shopping centers around the country saw the appearance of "head shops" stocked with a variety of devices with unusual names like "roach clips," "power hitters," and "isomerizers," all used to concentrate marijuana smoke. T-shirt sales boomed with messages such as "Drugs, Sex, and Rock and Roll," and the leaf shape of the new euphoric plant was seen everywhere. Bumper stickers proclaimed "Arrive Stoned" and "A Friend with Weed is a Friend Indeed."

A major target was youth. Frisbees with pot pipes in their centers appealed to young people. Comic books told how to snort cocaine. *McGrassey's Reader* explained the hows and wherefores of pot smoking in grade school language. Youngsters found it exciting to hang around head shops and be treated with respect by the cool characters who ran them. These same quasilegal operators denied community allegations that they were in any way responsible for the epidemic of marijuana use among young people. As head shops were closed down by legislatures and courts across the country, marijuana usage rates by adolescents began to turn around.

Illegal Drugs

Endorsements for illegal drugs like those for pharmaceuticals, tobacco, and alcohol increasingly appear in the media. These "advertisements" took the form of making use appear acceptable, as in the movie "Nine to Five." Drug use was seen as funny in the "humor" of stars such as Johnny Carson. The television show "Fridays'" weekly "ganja" smoking episode became standard. Two marijuana-promoting comics, Cheech and Chong, rose to fame with movies with such obvious titles as "Up in Smoke" and "Still Smokin'." Many played up the fun of drug use. "Opium," an exotic and widely advertised perfume, has had great commercial success with an ad campaign linking glamour, euphoria, and drugs. This perfume was not promoted by a quasilegal paraphernalia company, but by an "ethical" pharmaceutical company, the same company that produces "Life Savers." Concern expressed by William Pollen, M.D., director of NIDA, about the product's prodrug message was rebutted by the chairman of Squibb, Inc. as government meddling in private enterprise. Success with "Opium" perfume spurred imitations with names like "Stash," "Grass" and "Sinsemilla."

The rock music industry, where drug use and drug songs have proliferated, has been strongly criticized for its role in the epidemic of drug use. The relationship of drugs to the death of stars such as Jimi Hendrix, Jim Morrison, and Janis Joplin have been largely ignored. Recovering heroin-cocaine addict John Phillips of "The Mammas and the Papas" and his cocaine-recovering daughter MacKenzie Phillips of television's "One Day at a Time" tell of the close relationship of drugs and the rock music industry. Los Angeles drug dealers speak of their "regular rounds to the homes of executives, performers, and technicians in the film, television, and rock music industries, some of whom are spending as much as $1 million a year on cocaine."[144] John Belushi, a hero to millions of our young, was not alone.

Rock music grew up in a time of youthful rebellion. Interwoven with the music were messages of sex, drugs, and protest. More recently homosexuality and satanism have been added to these themes.

Rock music has become the music of the young. Some is very good. Many teenagers understandably enjoy the beat and the use of fascinating electronic effects. Much of the music, though, is definitely counterculture. Strong messages to "let it all hang out," "do drugs," and "have sex" abound. Pleasure is king. Popular rock star Eric Clapton sings, "Cocaine, cocaine, she's all right, she's OK." Adults who largely ignore these media messages are seen by children as passively accepting them. Outrage might be more appropriate.

DOLLARS

As important to an understanding of the drug explosion as awareness of hedonism is an understanding of the economy of drugs. Drugs, legal and otherwise, are big business, and efforts to moderate their use that do not address this issue are likely to fail.

The American tobacco and alcohol industries are big business, with gross annual tobacco sales alone of $27 billion.[145] As impressive as those figures are, they are dwarfed by the profits from illegal drugs. It was estimated that "in 1980 the retail, street-level transaction value of the drug trade in the United States was about $79 billion," which was up 22% from 1979, with escalation continuing.[119] When compared with sales of the largest U.S. business corporations in 1980, only Exxon at $103 billion was greater. Number five was Standard Oil of California, with sales of $40 billion. The profit motive for traffickers has been powerful and compelling. "Narcodollars" have strong effect on the economics and politics of a number of countries in South America, Southern Asia, and the Caribbean.[146]

Cocaine use is big business for the user also. In the stage of social recreational use, it costs $200 per month. Intensified users report spending $500 to $1,000 per day. Compulsive users may spend $2,000 to $12,000 per week.[127]

Most illegal drugs come from outside the country. Drug traffic is estimated to be the major industry in the state of Florida. The domestic crops, although dwarfed by imports, are not small. The largest cash crop in the state of California is estimated to be marijuana, with a gross revenue of over $1 billion annually.[119]

SUMMARY

Children are growing up in a society where drug use and intoxication appear to be socially acceptable. Pleasure and happiness are seen as the major goals of life. The profits for delivering chemical euphoria are huge enough to guarantee that the message "if it feels good, do it" will be actively promoted. The main target for increasing sales will be the market that has not yet decided how they will personally deal with drugs and alcohol—our children. Living in our society might well be called stage 0 of the drug use disease. No child is uninvolved.

6

Peer Pressure and the Susceptible Child

"The single main determinant of whether a young person uses marijuana is whether or not his best friend uses it."[147] Peer pressure is a strong force indeed. It is felt by all ages, but by the adolescent most of all. In testing new behaviors and seeking to establish his identity, he has a particularly strong desire to relate to and be accepted by people his own age. Peer pressure is generally seen as a negative force, but it need not be. The innovative approaches to drug prevention discussed later in this chapter and the use of group process in drug therapy are strong examples of effective use of positive peer pressure. To avoid peer pressure, as some would suggest, would require placing children in glass bubbles.

Peer pressure affects us all. Codes of dress and style may vary widely, but within each group there are norms and standards ignored only by the eccentric, the clod, or the trend setter. Neckties, for example, serve little useful purpose other than meeting certain group standards for business and social functions. The child who is looking for his own identity most often finds it in establishing his position within a peer group.

Young people do not talk about peer pressure in the same way adults do. They talk about looking for acceptance and wanting to fit in and belong. Adolescent drug users are often asked why they began drug use. Their answers are most often vague and should not be considered highly reliable. Peer influence objectively and observably influences drug use, but the drug-using teenager will not necessarily perceive this as a causal factor.

PEERS

If smoking and drinking are considered acceptable and are indulged in by a child's friends, he is in jeopardy. Where keg parties for 16-year-olds have become fashionable, it is much harder for a child to say "no." Young people need the friendship and acceptance of other teenagers. The desire to be popular is very strong, and if the popular crowd drinks, the child looking for acceptance will be strongly tempted. In order to counteract this pressure, efforts should be aimed at making drinking and other drug use unfashionable.

While peer pressure may be the main factor leading children to experiment with drugs, immaturity and other intrapersonal factors are the main causes of their high rate of chemical dependency.[148] Normal adolescent behavior and developmental immaturity make teenagers more at risk than adults. Those who have inappropriate attitudes and lack coping skills are even more susceptible. Modified and/or reinforced parenting skills and efforts may go a long way toward helping these marked children. Efforts aimed at diminishing or eliminating harmful attitudes and building appropriate skills can make children stronger.

Anticipatory guidance may offer great hope when aimed at prevention of those risk factors discussed later in this chapter under "The Susceptible Child." By age 12 these factors, by their prevalence, have almost become the norm. It has been suggested by the sociologist who compiled the data from which the deficiencies were outlined that we had best accept such "normality" and help children learn to deal with it.[149] Pediatricians and others familiar with behavior modification and prevention of disease might more properly elect to use the information to offer guidance to parents. Improving the child's coping skills and attitudes is a reasonable and worthwhile goal.

ADOLESCENCE

Many seem to have forgotten that adolescents are different from adults. A society where 12- and 13-year-old girls are paid huge sums of money to look suggestively older and more experienced in the ways of the world needs a refresher course in child development. There is more than the normal adolescent's search for identity and independence that make him particularly susceptible to drugs and alcohol.

What makes children most susceptible to drugs is the fact that they are children. When a child falls into chemical dependency, his progress to mature independence will be interrupted, and he may remain a child forever. Acting like a teenager at age 13 is appropriate. At age 27, it is not.

Normal teenage attitudes such as their love of danger, the "group," and the "here and now" also increase the risk of drug use. Observe a teenager on a dirt motorbike or at a roller coaster park, and you will gain some increased appreciation of the thrill they get from challenging fear. Observe the hairstyles, dress fads, and musical tastes that identify each generation of adolescents, and see young people looking for an identity of their own, separate from their parents and from the teenagers who preceded them. Teenagers do not see long distances into the future. Scare tactics that talk about long-range consequences such as the relationship of lung cancer to cigarettes are given low priority on their rating scale. What counts most is now.

Comparing, competing, testing, experimenting, looking for thrills, and tuning out parental advice and instructions have always been a part of adolescence. Warnings, which are often the result of past parental experience, may be disregarded by young people looking for their own answers. A certain amount of rebellion is normal. When maturity is reached, most adolescents come to realize that their parents were not so dumb after all or are surprised that their parents have learned so much over the course of a few adolescent years.

Some who look at the behavior changes described in stage 2 drug use, "Seeking the Mood Swing" comment, "Aren't those the changes we all went through as part of growing up?" I do not believe so. Most of us did not change friends, become truant, or have such drastic changes in school performance. Some, of course, did and eventually returned to the mainstream. Others continued to drift. Early drug use on the part of older children and early adolescents has changed things. Now as children become alienated, by choice or otherwise, from their families and friends, they frequently involve themselves with an all-too-easily available chemical euphoria. When this occurs, return to acceptable behavior becomes less likely. Their experimenting and rebellion become not a vehicle for achieving maturity, but a trap leading to the continuation of immaturity known as chemical dependency.

The tasks of adolescence are developing individuality and autonomy, separating from parents while establishing a sense of belonging, forming commitments, establishing an adult value system, and growing to emotional, physical, and sexual maturity. Drug use may interfere with all of these.

Freud, Erikson, Piaget, and all the great developmental psychologists stress the importance of adolescence. Great changes are said to occur in the teenage years as transition is made from childhood to adulthood. Piaget says that problem-solving skills change during this period, progressing from what he calls "concrete" to "formal" (abstract) operations.[150] This means that the preteenager tends to view the world egocentrically and sees things only as they relate to him. Abstract operations such as algebra or geometry contain much that is beyond his comprehension. When the teenager reaches the point where he is able to manipulate abstract ideas, a whole new range of sophisticated adult thought becomes possible, such as deductive reasoning, scientific experimentation, assimilation of new ideas, philosophy, and political theory. Children who have not reached this point may have difficulty with ethical or moral concepts that do not directly relate to them. They may memorize the Golden Rule, but have no personal understanding of the ethics involved beyond what is in it for them. Although well schooled in the story of Christianity, they may have no real understanding of the concept of God or of more abstract beliefs such as the "Holy Spirit." When faced with moral or ethical choices, the adolescent at this stage is still a baby. Growing up with development that is arrested at this stage produces an "adult" who is amoral and without an ethical code except as it relates to personal desire. Unfortunately, there are all too many examples of such arrested maturation, many of which are due to early chemical dependency. The "new drifter" discussed in Chapter 3 fits this description well.

Adolescence is built on the foundation of earlier experience.

Late childhood is a stage of industry and striving for mastery.[151] Previously used rules of the game are summoned to combat feelings of inferiority and enhance self-esteem. Drugs get in the way. In this stage, which is normally goal- and achievement-oriented, drugs may lead to failure to reach goals, with consequent loss of self-esteem.

Sexual drive is a major adolescent force. There may be "varying degrees of sexual exploration and experimentation with temporary romantic attachments in which the beloved is idealized or perceived as an extension of self. Self-gratification is more a goal than is sharing. In late adolescence, sexuality and emotional attachment may become fused in a relationship of mutual concern, sharing and intimacy," which is a prelude to mature and lasting adult attachment. Such process, aborted by drug or alcohol use, leads to a formless groping expressed either as promiscuity or shifting bisexuality.[152]

Freud talks about adolescence being the time when one's psychosexual identity is confirmed. When the thrill seeking and experimentation of normal adolescence are enhanced by a chemical release of inhibition, inappropriate sexual or homosexual activity may be initiated. The progressive increase in thrill seeking, characteristic of the child involved with drugs, makes such possibilities increasingly likely. Dealing with the shame and confusion that may result from such experience may make later heterosexual identification difficult if not impossible. In treatment for chemical dependency, the guilt associated with homosexual experience may be so great as to jeopardize recovery from either problem.

An understanding of the developmental immaturity of children coupled with the known dangers and widespread availability of drugs has great implications for a society wishing to protect its future. Ample safeguards must be provided for children to allow them to reach full maturity without being diverted from their potential by pressures, which without help, they may have too little power to resist.

THE SUSCEPTIBLE CHILD

Researchers in Boulder, Colo., identified a group of children particularly susceptible to problem behaviors. They studied 218 middle-school children who had not begun to drink alcohol. Using a variety of psychological and social testing instruments, they were able to demonstrate a characteristic profile identifying those children who would likely begin drinking in the next 3 years.[153] Subsequent studies by the same group have looked at a correlation between personality, perceived social environment, and behavior and alcohol and marijuana use.[1,154] In these subsequent studies with much larger samples, it has been shown that a definite correlation exists between all these factors. Unfortunately the studies do not indicate whether drugs may have caused the problem behavior, problems led to drug use, or whether the two occur in the same young people, but with neither causative of the other. The earlier smaller study has been criticized, because it was done in 1969 (before the current adolescent marijuana epidemic) and because it is often difficult if not impossible to control the multitude of factors affecting adolescent behavior. Despite their limitations, the studies do have value for those wishing to aim prevention efforts at high-risk children.

Jessor statistically identified those youngsters who would by the 12th grade be most likely to have difficulty with drugs, alcohol, sexual promiscuity, and delinquency. All four of these problem behaviors occurred in the same group of children. The profile of the child most likely to be sexually promiscuous was no different than the profile of the potential alcoholic.[153,154]

These profiles of children at risk provide insight for parenting and for prevention of drug and alcohol abuse. Stephen Glenn has done an excellent job of translating the data on the preexisting status of the drug user into a workable scheme for prevention.[155] The children at risk all had (1) low self-esteem and (2) a feeling of not belonging. They lacked (3) intrapersonal skills, (4) interpersonal or communication skills, (5) situational skills, and (6) judgmental skills.

Low Self-Esteem

Low self-esteem is a by-product of progressive drug use in the developing child. Drug use produces low self-esteem, and low self-esteem promotes drug use. Preexisting poor self-image was identified in almost all the adolescents who went on to dangerous drug use patterns. These children were the most apt to experiment, and once they discovered the good feelings of chemical euphoria, they were the most likely to become victims of progressive use. This cycle of poor self-image leading to drug use/leading to lower self-image / leading to more drug use may be interrupted in two ways. One is by keeping the child away from drugs, and the other is by strengthening his self-image. Self-image, like happiness, is a consequence, not an end, of certain kinds of behaviors.

Self-image is not static. It varies in all of us from day to day and at the "down" points, we are all more susceptible to inappropriate behavior. Routine adolescent happenings make teenagers especially prone to problems with self-esteem. Such normal events as acne, changing voice, being turned down for dates, and the competitive nature of approaching career choices may readily lead to a questioning of one's self-worth and value. It is the rare teenager who does not have more than occasional self-image problems.

Being a teenager is tough enough if all is going fairly well. The job is made considerably more difficult if there is added divorce, death, or a move to a new area or school. Some believe that adolescents' drug use may be related to fears of nuclear war and more global concerns about the future. Learning disability, delayed puberty, or chronic disease may add additional burden. Families that spend little time together, relate poorly, and show little love do little to enhance a child's self-image. More disastrous are those in which there is an alcoholic parent, a child abuser, or incest.

A child with low self-image may have little interest in school. There is little sense in studying to be a nurse, teacher, or physician if one feels incapable of reaching such goals. Man by nature seeks pleasure, and if the pleasure of long-range success is nowhere in sight, the euphoria of drugs is especially attractive.

Four major factors are the antecedents of the personal judgment of worthiness, which we call self-esteem.[156] First and foremost is the respect, acceptance, and concerned treatment that an individual receives from the "significant others" in his life. In his early years, a child's "significant others" are his family. At about the sixth grade, his need for acceptance shifts, and subsequently his peers may become the most "significant others" in his life.

Acceptance is warmth, responsiveness, interest, and liking for the individual as he is. The bumper sticker "Hugs, not Drugs" speaks to the relationship. Children in trouble with alcohol who were asked for insight on their families commented as follows: (1) Their mothers lacked control, (2) their fathers lacked time, and (3) there was little affection. Much of what becomes of children is a product of what the parents do and how a child perceives it.[157]

Parents who reject and severely punish their children do little for self-esteem. Basic anxiety is produced by domination, indifference, lack of respect, disparagement, lack of admiration and warmth, isolation, and discrimination.[158]

The second antecedent of self-esteem is a history of successes. Success, interpreted differently by each individual, may be measured against approval of accomplishments by a child's family and friends or by their relevance to his own personal goals. Good behavior and accomplishment that are rewarded are apt to make a child feel good about himself and lead to continued successful performance.

Values and aspirations are the third antecedent of self-esteem. The child in high school who is unable to express any plans for the future is at greater risk than the child who has a career goal. Parents who leave the guidance counseling of their children to others miss an important opportunity to assist their child in his drive for self-esteem. His successes may have little meaning for him if they relate to no long-range goal.

The fourth antecedent is the manner in which the child is able to deal with his errors, defeats, and frustrations. We all must learn to lose and face occasional rejection. The child whose parents have overindulged him is apt to have troubles. The self-centered child will be poorly prepared for dealing with failure.[159] The parent who feels duty-bound to protect the child from boredom, loneliness, and a variety of normal frustrations would do better to allow the child to experience these realities. Wise parents will support their children as they cope with insecurity, but minimize situations where insecurity is excessive. Parents should avoid the temptation to totally insulate children from the realities they must eventually face.

A Feeling of Loneliness

Loneliness was also typical of the children who were most susceptible to drug problems. As a group, drug-abusing children do not hate the world around them (although some do) as much as they do not feel a part of it. Many like and respect their families, but just do not feel they belong or are needed. There is a basic human need to belong.

The child psychiatrist who authored a series of pamphlets that sits in racks in pediatricians' offices across the country speaks strongly to this issue. For years he advised pediatricians to insist that children do family chores.[160] At first thought, the assignment of chores may seem impractical and unnecessary, especially with the advent of such things as electric dishwashers and garbage disposals. Families that "need" children to assist are largely a thing of our agrarian past. The relationship of chores to survival of families, however, is still very real. One must contribute to become a part of any organization. For a child to feel himself a full family member, he must participate in the work of the family. Children who have no responsibility to their schools, churches, and country are not likely to have school spirit, church spirit, or patriotism.

The rise of cults in this country may be related to the desire we all have to be needed and listened to. The Moonies, Scientologists, and Hare Krishnas seem to know this. Converts are put to work and made to believe that their work is meaningful and important. It would be much better if families learned this important principle first.

Inadequate Intrapersonal Skills

The intrapersonal skills of the high-risk children were inadequate. These adolescents were unable to separate what they "needed" from what they "wanted." They were unable to defer gratification for greater gain later. These skills are not easily practiced by adolescents who have not learned them earlier. The infant who is given a juice bottle whenever he screams for one is not being well prepared to cope with life. The oral gratification received from this sugary substance may be a strong contributor to later dental caries and obesity, hardly a fair trade for momentary relief of boredom. What he "wants" is attention. What he "needs" is a meal schedule. Even more importantly, he may need to learn to deal with boredom or getting himself to sleep.

Inadequate Interpersonal Skills

Communication, or interpersonal skill, is also lacking in high-risk children. Teenagers communicate poorly, but this should come as no great surprise. Good communication requires time, periods of closing one's mouth to listen, and learning to use language effectively.

Too little time spent conversing with children is a major factor. The average American father spends 14½ minutes per week in conversation with his adolescent child. Much of this time may be spent making statements such as, "How come you didn't take out the garbage?" "Get your feet off the sofa!" and "Please explain the 'D' in algebra." This 14½ minutes per week compares very poorly with the time teenagers spend in front of the television or listening to rock music. A recent Atlanta survey revealed that the average teenager in that city listens to 3 to 4 hours of rock music each day. The average American child watches over 18,000 hours of television before he leaves home.

Communication skills take more than just time. They also require periods of active listening. When a child of 2 years talks constantly, it is exciting. At age 4, it is sort of cute, at 7 it is a bother, and at 17 it is a disaster. This pattern of constant chatter may be modified. Parents too often allow their children to interrupt repeatedly. Pediatricians who observe such behavior in the office should ask mothers how they feel when their child acts to cut off all adult conversation. Most will admit that they do not like it. When asked if they have done anything to change the pattern, many will respond as if they did not know it was permissible or possible to make such change.

Parents who seem reluctant to shape their child's behavior should be questioned further. Some may fear that in doing so they will inhibit their child. They should be told that some behaviors need to be inhibited, not only for the family's sake, but, perhaps more importantly, for the child's sake as well. Other parents may be unwilling to modify their child's behavior, fearing that if they do so, the child will not love them. This sort of reverse dependency, where the parent needs the child's love, should be addressed. When the mother of a teenager says that she and her daughter are best friends, the physician may wonder who is filling the role of parent. Parents need to make decisions for their immature children that they believe are in the child's best interests. Whether the child approves or disapproves of such measures should not alter the parents' honest judgment. The physician may even comment that parents are allowed to make mistakes, that none are perfect, and that they must do what they believe is right for their child. In truth those parents who exert firm, consistent, and loving discipline will in the end be the most loved.

The physician who volunteers to help families reduce constant interruptions from their child may be rewarded by a quieter and more relaxed atmosphere at the child's next visit. The child and family will be rewarded by a better ability to communicate with each other.

Parents are not infrequently bored by children who tell long and rambling stories that seem to have either no point or a point too long in coming. These parents do not fool children by pretending interest. Another component of communication is teaching proper use and organization of language. Constructive suggestions may help children learn to express themselves in more concise and effective speech.

Four cautions in teaching children to speak and communicate are as follows:

1. Do not expect more than age or experience make possible.
2. It is better to instruct with praise than with criticism.
3. Teaching takes a lot of time and patience.
4. A good communicator is first and foremost a good listener. When the child does become a good communicator, the rewards can be tremendous for all concerned.

Assertiveness training is a part of most drug treatment programs. This important element of successful communication is often missing in the child who becomes entrapped with drugs. Being able to say "no" is only part of this skill that allows a child to express his wishes while drawing a line between being overly aggressive and overly submissive to the will of others.

Deficient Situational Skills

The "con artist" of stage 2 drug use believes in "magic." After an automobile accident, he is likely to really believe that the cause of the crash was wet roads or some old lady who did not know how to signal properly. Pointing out to him the fact that he was stoned and driving 72 mph often does little to change his belief as to the cause of the accident. He may believe the reason he failed an examination was that the questions were poorly worded, the material was not covered in class, or that he recently had mononucleosis. Trying to convince him that his grade may have some relation to his lack of study time is often futile. Too often we hear "adolescent" adults who blame their unemployment on "bad luck" and refuse to acknowledge that poor job preparation, absenteeism, or poor attitude might be the real culprits.

These people have never learned to analyze situations and see that their behavior has consequences. An infant who purposely dumps his milk and is promptly removed from his meal learns a lesson that will be helpful to him later. A child who is rewarded for a task well done is learning a valuable lesson. A teenager who has never been taught the negative and positive consequences of his actions is ill prepared to refuse a beer that might lead to a brush with his parents or the law. Responsible parenting prepares children for adolescence and teaches the child that he can affect what happens to him.

Poor Judgmental Skills

The ability to make judgments on an ethical basis prepares children to say "no" to drugs. As noted earlier, Piaget says that this is not a well-developed skill in early adolescence. Protecting the adolescent until this skill is acquired may enable him to make appropriate and informed decisions when he is more capable. In times of stress, we all tend to fall back to the level of decision making at which we are most comfortable or that has become habitual. The adolescent exposed to social stresses may put aside the newly acquired formal operational methods of Piaget and fall back to the concrete level of reasoning with which he is more familiar. Parents who are aware of this tendency will provide some protection from situations that may produce dangerous stress.

All of these skills are relative. No one communicates perfectly or is completely prepared morally to withstand all temptation. Many factors influence the rate at which these different skills are attained. In the right environment, however, a child should continue to gain judgmental skills commensurate with his age. An understanding of this point is basic to acceptance of a "double standard": children are often not capable of surviving situations that adults are able to deal with.

This profile of the susceptible child, the work of sociologists, counselors, and psychiatrists, differs very little from information obtained by talking with young people. All of the risk factors just described were mentioned by adolescents asked what they thought youth needed most.[161] Seven needs were identified by teenagers as particularly important to them. These were (1) increased respect from adults, (2) more time and involvement with adults, (3) more constructive opportunities to experiment with life, (4) more help in developing social competence, (5) better qualified adult youth leaders, (6) more opportunities for moral development, and (7) help in finding the meaning of life.

POSITIVE PEER PRESSURE

Too often the pleasure-seeking behavior typical of stage 3 drug use is viewed as characteristic of all teenagers. It is hard to ignore such behavior, but there is more to the well-rounded teenager than thrill seeking. If all adolescents are labeled self-seeking hedonists, the idealism and enthusiasm so typical of many may be overlooked. Teenagers such as those who identified the needs outlined in the previous paragraph have much to offer and appear willing to do so.

Drug prevention efforts aimed at providing alternative highs have merit, but those aimed at putting adolescent idealism and energy to work should do more. Positive peer pressure approaches do not ask children whether they need help, but instead ask if they are willing to help.

Drug prevention efforts utilizing positive peer pressure and young people's desire to help may be divided into four general groups: (1) peer influence programs, (2) peer participation programs, (3) "kids teaching kids," and (4) peer counseling.[162] The first two may offer great hope. Proof of their value, however, is still lacking, as there are few, if any, mature and effective programs 5 years old.

Peer influence programs provide options. Courage is required by those teenagers who are the early organizers of these peer activities, which are outside the mainstream of popular adolescent activity. Parental support and encouragement is important and must precede adolescent action. The goal is to reach young people who either do not want to be involved with drugs, have not yet made a decision, or who are minimally involved. Without reinforcement many of these young people will be unable to withstand social pressures pushing them to experimentation and "recreational" use.

Successful parties have been arranged for teenagers where the price of admission was observance of no-drinking-or-drugging rules. In Palo Alto, Calif., a small group of teenagers began meeting weekly and worked to plan a drug-free party. They hoped 30 would attend and had a crowd of 250. In Grand Junction, Colo., 500 came. Those who did attend had fun, and many agreed to sponsor drug-free parties at their own homes. No young person was excluded on the basis of his reputation as long as he agreed to arrive sober and stay that way. The large numbers who showed up may have pushed attendance beyond the ideal number for teenage parties, but illustrate clearly that interest exists. Whether this sort of interest is curiosity or a desire for options must await the test of time.

Some peer participation programs are working; others are not. Channel One, a coordinated effort of government and the private sector, involves adolescents and community leaders.[163] Young people analyze community needs and decide what they want to do for their community. Adults assist. Prudential and the Metropolitan Life Insurance Companies have offered strong support to Channel One projects. Other major corporations are becoming involved in an expanding program of putting young people to work constructively in the community.

In Kansas City, Mo., student leaders with training in alcohol and drug abuse approach new students and tell them it is not necessary to do drugs at their high school. They reach out to these susceptible young people and inform them of alternative parties and activities.

In Minneapolis young people between the ages of 12 and 18 are used as health educators to teach younger children the facts about drug effects. The adolescent teachers receive job training from qualified leaders. In reality, the student teachers benefit more from the program than those they teach, but this in no way makes the program less valuable.

A fourth approach is peer counseling, which is based on the belief that many adolescents trust their peers more than adults and would benefit from trained listeners.

In Illinois, several hundred campus leaders selected as peer counselors attend the Illinois Teenage Institutes, where they spend 6 summer days training with teachers and administrators.[162] They are taught to support and listen. Operation Snowball, sponsored by the Illinois Alcoholism and Dependence Association, was designed to build on the enthusiasm generated by the summer institutes and carry prevention programs back to local schools. Groups similar to Operation Snowball exist in New York City, Minneapolis-St. Paul, and elsewhere.

Hastily thrown together and poorly supervised peer counseling programs can be dangerous. Counseling requires maturity and knowledge of when and how to refer emergencies such as possible suicides. An inclination on the part of peer counselors to provide therapy in contrast to listening and supporting must be discouraged. Advocating moderation or responsible use are also not in keeping with drug-prevention efforts. In the course of peer counseling, major benefits may accrue to the counselors themselves. Many are enthusiastic about peer counseling. Others view peer counseling as a way to stay in touch with drug use and drug problems, but contributing nothing directly to cure or rehabilitation. Caution in selection, training, and supervision of peer counselors should be urged.

SUMMARY

Adolescents have traits of adventurousness and willingness to test danger that make them particularly susceptible to drug use. This susceptibility is increased when they are younger and have low self-image. If they communicate poorly, are unable to separate needs from wants, and see no relationship between their actions and their consequences, the risk is increased. Peer pressure, a powerful force in the adolescent drive for establishing identity, may be a positive as well as a negative influence. To be successful in drug abuse prevention, one must address these issues. The best approaches will work on building and employing adolescent strengths and providing adult support and encouragement. *Until mature adulthood is attained, children need protection.*

7

The Parent Revolution

By the mid 1970s, parents knew something was wrong. They could not ignore what they were seeing at home. Many medical experts saw nothing wrong with marijuana. Pediatricians spoke of "responsible" and "moderate" drinking by adolescents. Others told them to accept experimentation with drugs as an inevitable and even acceptable part of growing up in our stress-filled society. Neighbors told them not to worry, that their children were just going through a phase. A small handful of parents refused to accept the advice of these "experts." Their instincts told them their children were in trouble, and they realized that if no one else would save their children, they must. Concerned parents found concerned parents, and a national parents' movement, The National Federation of Parents for Drug-Free Youth (NFP), was launched. From these roots grew a strong organization. The goal was drug-free adolescents.

The Coming Parent Revolution is a popular book that presents an action plan for strengthening the family.[164] Taken to task are social engineers and child-rearing "experts" who believe that parenting is too difficult to be entrusted to "amateur" mothers and fathers. Other angry parents calling themselves the "voice of the victim" joined together as the Mothers Against Drunk Driving (MADD). Their motives for action were somewhat different from those of the parents who organized the NFP, but their goals of alcohol control made them allies. As an organization MADD has been a major force in making elected officials take action aimed at curbing highway mayhem.

Pediatricians are familiar with parent movements. The La Leche League persisted in the face of medical nonsupport and derision to insist that breast milk was the best for babies. Because they were persistent (and right), medical opinion changed from lip service to active support. Much of the change was due to the economic pressure of mothers who sought out pediatricians who would listen. The International Childbirth League had similar success with even more forceful methods aimed at putting fathers with mothers in labor and delivery rooms. Those obstetricians who continued to deny such "privilege" to fathers, claiming they would faint and get in the way, saw their practices shrivel. Physicians who listened learned that parents have much to teach.

Advocacy for children's rights is a great idea that may have gone too far, possibly because of the vague definition of the relationship of children's rights and responsibilities to their parents' rights and responsibilities. One problem is that children often define rights more globally than their parents do. Some wish to include the "right" to set their own code of behavior even when such behavior interferes with the rights of others or with their own right to reach independent maturity. Parents found themselves increasingly unable to control these children. The right of parents to protect their children and set limits consistent with demonstrated behavior were often forgotten as children's rights became children's license to do as they wished. An organization called "Tough Love" became national as angry and frustrated parents fought for family survival in the presence of children seemingly gone berserk with "rights." A feeling of helpless uneasiness prevailed as parents became vaguely aware that their children might be dabbling in alcohol, drugs, sex, and delinquency. Many parents found themselves without the know-how to respond and found solace only in the hope that adolescence would not last forever.

Parents are often possessed by an ambivalence that says, "I guess my children will try marijuana, drink some, and experiment with sex." Few think that parents have the right or the wherewithal to protect their children from these potentially very dangerous experiments. Those who do are frequently discouraged by the overwhelming pressures of a society that seems to have forgotten that adolescents are not mature people. "Double standard" is seen as a dirty word. In the midst of newly evolving patterns of family life and child-rearing practices often far different from those of the past, a number of parents took action. It was their belief that they could do no worse than the "experts." They began to do what they could to save their children from what they saw as a sure path to disaster.

A concerned Atlanta mother became a founder of a growing national movement.[165] Necessity forced her and her husband, both university professors, into the drug education business. Neither became involved because they were seeking a cause. At a party given by their 13-year-old daughter, they had their eyes rudely opened to the phenomenon of adolescent partying involving drugs and alcohol. The obvious acceptance and prevalence of marijuana and alcohol use by a nice group of children from good families stunned these parents and spurred them to action.

The morning after this social function, Dr. Manatt and her husband told their daughter of their concern and asked for the party invitation list. They stressed their love for her and their amazement at what they had witnessed. From the invitation list, they put together a list of parents whom they contacted and invited to a meeting. They encountered considerable resistance from some. Despite the anger and denial they experienced, they persisted until they brought together a group to whom they told their story.

No accusations were made, but a description of suspicious incidents that had occurred at the party and in the neighborhood in the preceding months was given. Other parents were led to believe that perhaps their children might also be involved. Some, as might be expected, believed that the Manatts were overreacting. Others of the assembled parents agreed that there was a problem and set out to do what they could.

At first they had few allies. The prevailing consensus in 1976 among counselors, physicians, and the media was that marijuana was a relatively benign substance, and parents should not "hassle" their youngsters for using it. This group of parents believed otherwise. Their instincts told them that their pot-smoking youngsters were deteriorating in appearance, personality, intellectual function, and physical health.

Their first mission was to educate themselves, and they had to read a lot of outdated and inaccurate material before they began to find experts who agreed that marijuana might be harmful. They identified Gabrial Nahas, Professor of Anesthesiology at Columbia

University, and Robert Heath, Professor of Psychiatry and Neurology at Tulane University, who willingly talked to them and shared their fears about the risks of marijuana. These experts assisted them in further search that confirmed their belief that their children were playing with poison.

Armed with this information, each set of parents spelled out a strict antidrug position for their family. They went on to establish common behavioral codes for their group of families, involving age-appropriate privileges, limits, and responsibilities for their children. The families met regularly and shared information and support. As a result of much time, work, and patience, they began to see change in their children.

Observers were impressed with what they saw. Robert DuPont, then director of NIDA, was so impressed when he visited Atlanta that he asked Dr. Manatt to write the story of their group's success. *Parents, Peers and Pot,* the result of that request, has over 1 million copies in print and has been used as a reference for parents' groups across the country.

Dr. DuPont then put Dr. Manatt in contact with Thomas "Buddy" Gleaton, another Atlanta professor. Dr. Gleaton, also a concerned parent, had been sponsoring a professional drug conference since 1975. He was excited about what he heard regarding family involvement, and in 1978 his Southeastern Drug Conference was titled "The Family vs. The Drug Culture." With Dr. Manatt he formed the PRIDE[167] (Parent's Resource Institute of Drug Education) office later that year, and the movement was firmly under way.

Parents' groups began springing up across the country. Their immediate concerns varied and they had no set structure, but all shared several beliefs. They all believed that children should not use drugs or alcohol, and all believed that parents had a right and responsibility to protect their children.

These parents were smart enough to know that efforts to choose their children's friends for them would most likely fail. They also realized that efforts aimed at having their children give up friends, no matter how undesirable, were likely to be met with resistance. Rather than do nothing, the Atlanta parents and those who joined them concentrated on strengthening the peer group their child had chosen. They would not pick their child's friends for him, but they would have some say about what went on in the peer group.

Most groups began by adopting a set of rules. Some groups were very restrictive, and others were quite loose with their guidelines (see Appendix A). All seemed to share the belief that they needed to know where their children were at all times. This might mean mothers would call ahead when their child was going to Charley's house to see if it was all right. Early on they might find that no parent was home at Charley's or that Charley's parent had been told that Charley was coming to their house.

Before allowing their children to attend parties, these concerned parents made a phone call to find out such things as what precautions were being taken about drink and drug use and whether there was anything they could do to assist with the party. Where anger was encountered or where parents felt uncomfortable about what they heard, attendance by their child was prohibited.

Along with this restrictive approach, the parents planned activities for their families to bring them closer together. The parents wanted to be positive forces in their children's lives and not come across as opposed to everything. When activities were denied, parents often substituted acceptable alternate activity. They did not assume responsibility for keeping their children constantly entertained or boredom-free. They helped their children find fun-filled, drug-free activities in the company of their friends. The youth resisted at first, and two steps forward were often followed by one step back. But the new peer groups found identity and strength within themselves. The parents were smart. They used a child's newly controlled peer group, chosen by the child, to provide mutually reinforcing positive peer pressure. Many of the kids were secretly relieved. Parental interest had given them support with which to resist situations that made them uneasy. Earlier parental efforts that had removed children from their peer groups had largely failed. Children need children to complete the tasks of adolescence. As success grew at home, many groups went on to community action.

An early target was the paraphernalia industry. Head shops or "little learning centers for drug abusers"[147] were an overnight success in the 1970s. When the head shops hit the malls of this country, parents began to notice the fascination they had for young people. Testifying before the U.S. Senate Select Committee on Narcotics in 1980, Mitchell Rosenthal, M.D., director of Phoenix House in New York City, expressed his concern: "There is no question in my mind that the great increase in adolescent drug abuse can be blamed on the proliferation of head shops . . . and so can the nature of that abuse and the sophistication kids have about how and what to smoke or sniff or swallow."[147]

In New Jersey, a PTA mother traveled the state with a "Bong Show," shocking citizens with her bag of goodies purchased in their town. Another mother in Wisconsin and more in Georgia and elsewhere went to war. Antiparaphernalia laws began to pass in 1977. The Federal Drug Enforcement Agency drafted a model paraphernalia bill. Courts overturned some of the earlier statutes, but it was not long before the head shops began to disappear. Flushed with victory, the parents moved on to other laws and other projects. School approaches to drug education and drug use were changed.

Parents' groups reached out to involve community organizations such as the PTA, the Junior League, and the Medical Auxiliary. In them they found mothers who were interested, concerned, energetic, and talented in community action. They sought out men's organizations such as the Lions and Rotary, who added their talents. The governor of Texas was recruited, and he named industrialist H. Ross Perrot to lead a task force in his state. A highly effective "Texas War on Drugs" went underway. Other states followed suit.

Each parent group had slightly different talents and directions. Some went to the schools and churches. Others went to police and legislatures. Others pursued the media. They all sought to keep themselves informed on drug abuse and worked on parenting skills and techniques for their own families.

At the 1980 PRIDE conference, hundreds of parents from across the country met to form the NFP.[166] This organization began serving as a focal point for a rapidly growing network of parents' groups committed to saving their children and communities from the ravishes of drug use.

Parents whose children had drug experience were joined by

parents who wanted to protect their children before that involvement began. Little League coaches, grandparents, and concerned professionals joined in support and encouragement and participated in meetings sponsored by the organization. Leaders of industry, professional sport leagues, the AMA, and others contributed money and support, and the organization grew in numbers and strength. As an organization NFP has become a strong federation of concerned adults who know the dangers of drugs and fear for society and its children.

Then the strongest ally of all was added. Early efforts had focused on young people who were involved with drugs. Less attention was paid to those children who were not involved and those who did not want to be involved but seemed to have no choice. A highlight of the 1981 PRIDE conference was the appearance of 16 articulate and action-oriented young people from two high schools in Palo Alto, Calif. These youngsters inspired the audience with their story of forming a student group aimed at helping other students find alternative drug-free activities in their school. They told of well-attended drug-free parties and of upperclassmen approaching new susceptible students and informing them that drug use was neither "cool" nor necessary at their school. Their enthusiasm was infectious, and few were surprised when they reported on the growth of their organization. By the 1982 PRIDE meeting, there were hundreds of students representing groups from many states who were working to help themselves and their peers reverse the trend of youthful alcohol and drug use. With the ingenuity and enthusiasm of youth, they reported on a variety of programs that were already producing clear results.

SUMMARY

Not until concerned families took action aimed at what they considered a horrible epidemic was there a change seen in the epidemic of adolescent drug abuse. Rather than the professional community, it was parents working with their own children who brought about decreased marijuana use, stepped-up legal efforts, and renewed involvement of the schools. Concerned parents' groups have joined efforts as a national organization whose purpose is to provide children with an adequate opportunity to grow up completely drug-free. Their efforts appear to be bearing fruit. Useful information and helpful pamphlets on drugs and the antidrug movement may be obtained from the NFP[166] or PRIDE.[167]

8

Diagnosis

DIAGNOSTIC DIFFICULTIES

Adolescent drug or alcohol abuse is probably the most commonly missed major pediatric diagnosis. For every child in treatment, there are many, many more whose disease continues to progress because it is never diagnosed, only partially diagnosed, or diagnosed too late. There are a number of reasons for failure to make an accurate diagnosis, all of which should become increasingly unacceptable as our body of knowledge and experience increases. The most common diagnostic difficulties are (1) low index of suspicion, (2) outdated conception of drug abuse, (3) missing the early stages, (4) failure to realize the primary nature of chemical dependency, (5) concept of "soft" or "recreational" drugs, (6) ambivalence about adolescent experimentation, (7) relating drug use to the physician's recollection of his own adolescent experience, and (8) overdependence on physical, laboratory, and other hard data.

Low Index of Suspicion

Failure to seriously consider drug abuse as a possibility in middle-class suburban patients is perhaps the most common cause of missed diagnosis. Studies have shown that the high index of suspicion most physicians have prior to making most medical diagnoses does not generally exist in cases of chemical abuse or dependency. Most physicians seem reluctant to diagnose chemical abuse or dependency until clear signs of intoxication or withdrawal are present.[168] In 1980 I spoke with 25 teenagers in treatment about visits to their doctors in the 6 months prior to their admission to a drug program. Eleven told me their physician had asked about drug use. Six of these lied to their doctor and denied drug use. Five admitted they had tried drugs but stated they had no problems, and the issue was not pursued.

I missed the diagnosis for years. The main reason was that I did not seriously think that children in my practice could have such "low-class" problems. Like venereal disease and child abuse, chemical dependency is a disease that shows no respect for socioeconomic situation. In truth there is much to suggest that affluence, free time, and drug abuse are related. The physician aware of the prevalence of drug and alcohol use should consider the possibility of such use in all adolescents, especially those with negative behavior change or suggestive physical symptoms.

Outdated Conception of Drug Abuse

Adolescent drug abuse of the eighties is not like drug abuse of the fifties. The two main drugs of abuse at this time are alcohol and marijuana. Looking for needle tracks in the arm or cocaine erosion of the nasal septum are worthwhile examinations, but the overwhelming majority of teenagers in trouble will show neither. The new-style adolescent victim is most often trapped by what he has been led to believe are socially acceptable and harmless drugs. Experimentation with cocaine may, of course, occur, but continued use is most often beyond his economic means. The cocaine available to the novice teenager in middle-class America has usually been "cut" many times and is not the same as the jet-set product of superior grade. Heroin use most often signifies stage 4 use or a close approach to it.

Missing Early Stages

The early stages of chemical dependency are often subtle and usually missed, because they are assumed to be an expected and important part of growing up. Erikson[151] has stressed the importance of experimentation in the normal maturation process that occurs during adolescence. A change in friends, hairstyle, or disinterest in school may be seen as part of a normal separation from parents and a search for peer group identity. Certainly such behavior is nothing new and has been associated with adolescence for quite some time. Mood and attitude swings may be blamed on hormonal imbalance and accepted as temporary. Rule testing is normal, and arguing is expected. Separating these changes, all of which may be normal, from those of early drug involvement is often difficult. Unfortunately what begins as a normal adolescent quest for identity may lead to entrapment in a net of chemicals that are highly promoted and have become increasingly available.

There are some clues that are helpful to parents and physicians trying to separate normal from pathologic adolescent behavior. Parents, especially mothers, have strong instincts about their children. They tend to have a feel for when their child is lying, avoiding them, or in trouble. When they feel uncomfortable about their children, it is often with good reason. The reason may not necessarily involve drugs, but should arouse suspicion and concern. Many parents, often on the advice of physicians or counselors, accept pathologic change as a "phase" and fail to respond to their instincts for fear of overreaction.

Overreaction does indeed occur and can drive a wedge of rebellion into communication with adolescents. Appropriate strong concern and reasonably firm control as outlined in Chapter 7 should not drive such a wedge. This is especially true if the relationship is built on a previous base of parental care and concern that has granted trust and permission based on demonstrated performance. Trust should be given based on the situation involved and the maturity of the child. Not responding to stage 2 drug behavior is risky and will make progression to stage 3 more likely.

Failure to Realize the Primary Nature of Chemical Dependency

Understanding the primary nature of chemical dependency is essential to making an accurate diagnosis. Almost all of the young people in treatment at Straight, Inc., previously received counseling that in retrospect proved to be off target. The most common occurrence was counseling that advised parents that they needed to make change and communicate better with their adolescent. These parents were told that adolescence is tough, and teenagers need freedom to grow. Many of these same young people were advised by their counselors to better conceal their drug use from parents to avoid overreaction. Others were advised to moderate use. Some "did" drugs with counselors who saw no harm in such practice, but viewed it instead as a way to establish rapport. All ended up progressing in use and dependency.

It is easy to find explanation for behavior problems in children. School and family problems can easily lead to low self-image, which has a high correlation with drug dependency. Learning disability may indeed predispose a child to chemical dependency but once trapped, the chemical dependency must be dealt with before learning remediation can hope to succeed. Chemical dependency is primary, and missing that point will doom all other therapy attempts to failure.

Concept of "Soft" or "Recreational" Drugs

Lack of knowledge of the dangers of marijuana has caused some physicians to discount or ignore its use. A further problem has been an artificial and dangerous classification of drugs into "soft" and "hard" categories. This classification flies in the face of the reality of the clinical deterioration observed in teenagers hooked only on so-called soft drugs. There is ample evidence that the syndrome described here can be seen in adolescents whose only drug is pot. Any drug that can produce euphoria has great potential for abuse. The fact that the euphoria of a drug like cocaine may be so overwhelming as to trap even the strongest of experimenters in no way alters the fact that cannabis dependency does occur.

Ambivalence

Many physicians and parents, aware of the widespread use of marijuana and alcohol by teenagers, have come to accept such use as a part of growing up. Their hope is that children will not abuse the drugs, but experiment wisely. Many parents, acknowledging their children's sexuality, have come to believe that most children will dabble some with sexual intercourse. Not knowing how to prevent such indulgence, parents may grudgingly accept it as inevitable.

Accepting drug use as normal obviously makes diagnosis of abuse difficult, if not impossible. When admission of occasional intoxication is seen as acceptable, early diagnosis of dependency will most often be missed. If physicians forget their knowledge of the developmental differences between adolescents and adults, they may have trouble dealing with the question of double standards. How, they may ask, can one accept drinking in adults and not accept it in children?

Ambivalence also exists in physician attitudes about adolescent abusers and about the value and appropriateness of treatment.[169] It is not difficult to get angry with teenage "con artists." Such anger may impair a physician's ability to deal with abusers, and if there is angry confrontation, parents will usually side with the child. Physicians must deal with their own discomfort. The question has been asked, "How does one move unflinchingly into an arena, where he is made to feel unwanted, incompetent and even malevolent?"[170] Physicians who are unaware of successful treatment programs are less likely to exert efforts to establish a painful diagnosis for which they believe there is no hope.

Relating Drug Use to the Physician's Recollection of Adolescence

Many of us see normalcy in terms of our own recalled behavior. The recollection many physicians have of their own adolescence includes episodes of alcohol use and intoxication. On this basis these same physicians may accept drug use in their patients as a normal part of growing up. Unfortunately, their recollection does not always jibe with the situation adolescents face today.

Adolescent drug use has changed. In previous times alcohol, which may have been an occasional drug for some, was generally consumed less often, in smaller quantities, and closer to maturity. With the average initial drinking age now at 12.6 years and over one quarter of high school senior boys intoxicated three or more times every two weeks,[3] it is time to reassess the relevance of previous experience. It has been estimated that 19% of youth are experiencing problems with alcohol.[171] Add marijuana, which was just a word to most physicians in their adolescence, to this picture, and serious misconceptions can occur.

It is also worth noting that even with the more moderate and delayed use adults remember, many did not escape. The current estimate that over 10,000,000 adults may be chemically impaired makes one wonder about the innocuousness of even this milder and later adolescent experimentation. To establish rapport with a teenager by swapping drinking stories is not likely to facilitate making the diagnosis of chemical dependency.

Overdependence on Physical, Laboratory, and Other "Hard" Data

Cough, sore throat, red eyes, and fatigue can all be symptoms of drug use, but none need be present to make the diagnosis. Teenagers, especially those with early drug problems, are excellent at cover-up. They know about mouth sprays to mask alcohol breath and eye drops to remove redness.

Detection of cannabinoids in the urine is a helpful tool, but not essential. Evidence of drugs in urine or elevated blood alcohol levels, while helpful, is not a part of establishing the diagnosis in most cases. As more emergency rooms order such tests for people involved in accidents, this may change.

The diagnosis of drug abuse is no trivial matter, and an attempt to establish definite confirmation is understandable. Because the diagnosis is often seen by the family as an accusation rather than a medical diagnosis, the physician obviously wants to have as much confirming data as possible. On the other hand, when a strong case can be made on clinical grounds, the physician has no choice but to proceed.

SIGNS AND SYMPTOMS

The same techniques regularly used in all medical diagnosis are used to clinically diagnose chemical dependency. These include a thorough history, a complete physical examination, and appropriate utilization of available laboratory and other testing procedures. When the diagnosis is entertained but not confirmed, a carefully monitored therapeutic trial or period of closely supervised observation may be prescribed to further establish the possibility.

There is no one laboratory test, physical finding, or incident on which the diagnosis may be pinned with absolute certainty. The pediatrician has precedents on which to make decisions based on a variable combination of soft and hard findings. The Jones criteria for making the diagnosis of rheumatic fever have been helpful for that disease in which no one single finding is diagnostic. Diagnosis requires establishment of an arbitrary combination of major and minor findings. Adolescent chemical dependency is very analogous, and it may be useful to adopt a similar concept of major and minor diagnostic criteria.

Major Criteria

The diagnosis of drug abuse is most easily established when it is known that the child is a regular user. In reality the diagnosis is made more often on the basis of suspicious behavior or physical changes that point to the need to investigate abuse possibility. Major criteria may be either (1) two occasions of acute drug abuse or (2) regular drug use. When drug use is known, the minor (behavioral and physical) criteria may be applied for the purpose of staging the disease to decide on an appropriate treatment response.

Acute Drug Abuse

Drug abuse may appear as an acute (and possibly isolated) incident resulting in an overdose detected by parents, police, or an alert emergency room physician looking for drugs as the cause of trauma in adolescents. Suicide attempts should also arouse suspicion, especially if they involve chemical ingestions. The more minor criteria that are positive, the more likely the acute episode is not an isolated event, but instead a helpful indicator of chronic use.

Regular Drug Use

A child who continues to drink or use drugs after a firm no-drug stand has been taken by his family and physician may be chemically dependent. His inability to discontinue use in spite of negative consequences identifies him as having a problem. When behavior changes in a child are noted, progressive disease must be suspected and drug abuse diagnosed. The laboratory can be most helpful in diagnosing marijuana use.

Minor Criteria

Any of these criteria, alone or with others, may indicate drug use. Use of a questionnaire may provide further diagnostic assistance. Standardized tests for adults such as the Michigan Alcoholism Screening Test (MAST) have high reliability and validity and are easily administered and scored.[172] Questionnaires for adolescents may also be helpful (see Appendix B). A combination of one major and three minor criteria should make chemical dependency the primary diagnosis. As the number of positive minor criteria grows, the likelihood of chemical dependency rises:
1. Deterioration in school performance.
2. Deterioration in family relationships, including such things as avoidance of family activity and refusal to do chores.
3. Negative personality changes such as amotivation, unpredictable mood swings, depression, or "conning" behavior.
4. Physical changes that might include frequent sore throat, cough, red eyes, and lack of affect. The physical assessment should also note hair length, dress style, and signs that the adolescent is getting his messages from the drug or alcohol culture.

5. Legal problems, including missing money at home, shop-lifting, vandalism, and traffic problems.
6. Change in peer group, especially if it includes young people the parents feel uncomfortable about or have never met.

HISTORY

As is true with much medical illness, the history often provides the most helpful diagnostic hints. The diagnosis of adolescent chemical dependency is most often made on the basis of the characteristic clinical picture described in Chapter 2. A typical picture will often unfold as the teenager and his parents are carefully questioned. To fill in the picture, it will be necessary to ask about school performance, peer group, attitude at home, and, of course, about drugs.

The child and parent(s) may be seen together in the examination room. Much can be learned by observing who answers which questions, whether interrupting occurs, and by noting the general relationship of parent and child. Body language and facial expressions may give clues to family strife. It is often helpful to ask the parent how she (he) is doing. This general question may provoke responses varying from very negative to very positive. Voice quality and presence or absence of eye contact may give more information than the verbal response itself. Parental discomfort is a good indicator of a child with problems.

In this session general questions are asked about school performance, participation in chores and home activities, and about general health concerns such as eating and sleeping. An effort is made to determine the stated purpose of the visit or the chief complaint. Depending on the purpose of the physical examination and the age and wishes of the child, the parent is either excused or encouraged to remain present. Whether the parent remains for the examination or not, time is set aside to talk alone with the teenager and with his parent(s).

When these interviews arouse real concern or uncomfortable suspicion, parent and child should again be called together. At this meeting, further questions may be posed followed by some explanation of the physician's concern and recommendations. This latter visit may be scheduled at a later time to allow an absent parent to be present or at a time when the physician is not under pressure from a packed office and tight schedule. Attempts to rush history, diagnosis, and recommendations are most unwise. On the other hand, suggesting a follow-up visit will frequently create anxiety. For this reason rescheduling should be for a time as soon as convenient for all.

You do not have to be a physician to diagnose drug abuse or chemical dependency, but it helps. People are used to doctors making diagnoses and subsequently prescribing treatment. The pediatrician or family physician who has known the child and his family for a number of years has an additional advantage. He knows the cast of characters, the background, and something about the way the child and his family relate to him and to each other. A physician may have problems believing drug abuse is a possibility in a family he has been close to, or he may have difficulty asking seemingly confrontive questions of "friends." It is helpful to gain experience in asking questions about behavior and feelings and to be open to social and emotional concerns. With a little practice, the physician should soon become comfortable with confronting drug issues head-on.

Children are good at judging how adults feel about them. A pediatrician who comes across as caring will have an easier job in interviewing. A relationship that has been warm over a period of time is a real plus for an examiner. Honesty and a track record of openness are most helpful. Trust is given slowly by teenagers. When given, however, its value may be tremendous.

The physician's attitude towards drugs may determine the responses he gets in taking the history. A physician who believes moderation is acceptable is more apt to get an admission of drug use. Physicians such as myself who believe that all nonmedical psychoactive drug use by adolescents is unacceptable may be less likely to receive admissions of use. The teenagers' tendency to conceal use may be partially overcome by the physician's style of questioning. If perceived as honestly concerned about the teenager's health instead of punitively legalistic or moralistic, physicians are more apt to have success.

The very important issue of confidentiality is discussed in Chapter 11. Honesty with the child about this issue is also important. Promises to keep all disclosures in confidence may help elicit a more reliable drug history, but may compromise the child in the long run. When a child's behavior becomes unacceptable, he may no longer be considered fully responsible. Announcing this belief in advance precludes breaking anticipated confidentiality.

Adolescent Interview

History of Drug Use

The most obvious indicator of a current drug problem is a history of use. On the other hand, beginning an interview with direct questions about drug use may be counterproductive. A preferable method is to set the adolescent at ease with less-threatening inquiries about school performance, recreational interests, future plans, jobs and, when appropriate, dating. Knowing what a child likes to do with his free time aids the physician in drawing a picture of how a child operates.

Sooner or later the child must be asked about his drug/alcohol experience. By stage 4, use is usually openly admitted and fairly obvious. In earlier stages there may be more difficulty in obtaining a positive history. Direct confrontation poorly handled may lead only to anger, denial, and refusal to cooperate. These negative reactions may occur even in the hands of well-trained physicians. Nevertheless, it is still important to at least ask about drug and alcohol use, especially when suspicion is present. The physician who regularly asks adolescents about such use will grow more comfortable with the questions and be less likely to provoke a negative reaction in the user.

Negative reaction is not all bad. Although it does little for rapport, it is often very helpful in diagnosis. The teen who explodes violently when asked about marijuana use is strongly suspect. Marijuana especially seems to be associated with such a paranoid reaction. It is interesting that tobacco smokers admit smoking is a "dumb" habit and announce their intention to quit (but not today).

Drinkers admit alcohol consumption has its risks and swear never to drive when drunk. Marijuana smokers, however, may become very argumentative about the harmlessness of marijuana and especially about suggestions that it may be affecting their behavior.

Where a positive history of current use is not obtained, questioning about previous use may be helpful: "Have you ever tasted beer?" "Where?" "Have you ever tried marijuana?" "When?" "Have you ever been high?" "How many times?" "How did it feel?" "Did you ever have problems related to alcohol or drugs, such as car accidents?" "Have you ever been sick on alcohol?" "Other drugs?"

Indirect questions are often more revealing than direct questions. Because there is such a high degree of correlation between tobacco and drug use, questions relating to tobacco smoking by patient and peers very often provide a clue. The patient is asked whether his friends drink. He or she is particularly questioned about dating and whether the girlfriend/boyfriend drinks or uses drugs. A child should be asked about drug and alcohol use in his family. A history of alcoholism or drug problems in parents or siblings should raise one's index of suspicion.

Questions About School, Peers, Family, and Attitudes

Be specific. Ask about grades for the last marking period. When a bad evaluation is revealed, ask about previous performance and inquire what action is being taken. A drop in grades may be a sign of inadequate study time, learning disability, or disinterest in curriculum, all of which deserve attention. It may also be a sign of drug use. If low grades continue, a child's feelings about himself may suffer. If drug use was not the initial cause of school problems, school failure may lead to drug use as the child looks for identity and good feelings elsewhere.

Another helpful question is inquiry about the child's plans for after school years. This may not have as much significance for the middle-school child, but a high schooler who has no ideas for the future is at risk. Worry about children who have no goals or only the goal of making money. Worry also about the child who expresses grandiose future plans that are completely inconsistent with the reality of his performance. None of these historic items are diagnostic of drug abuse or chemical dependency, but they all provide clues to how the child feels about himself.

Asking a child about his closest friend may provide additional helpful information. Inquiry about his friend's age, interests, school performance, dating patterns, and drug use may give considerable insight.

The relationship of the child to his family is also very important. This history may be obtained from other family members, but the teenager should be asked how he feels about his parents, their rules and attitudes, and how much he does with and for his family.

Parent Interview

The parent is asked the same questions the child is asked. Much may be learned from the way in which the parent answers the very general question, "How do you 'feel' your child is doing?" When problems are suspected, it may be helpful to inquire more specifically. A child with problems is not good for a parent's sleep, marriage, or general outlook on life.

Indications of poor school performance should be followed with questions about efforts at diagnosis and remediation. Attempts to excuse poor performance by blaming teachers or curriculum should be considered carefully. Whether the performance is drug-related or not, the pediatrician has a responsibility to direct the parent of a failing child to appropriate community resources for help. This, of course, implies a working knowledge of such resources.

Questions about drug use should be specific. Does or has the child smoked cigarettes, drunk alcohol, or used marijuana? Do his friends? Does the family? Has the child been intoxicated? Has he had problems related to intoxication, such as dented fenders? Has the family talked about drugs, and what has been the family and adolescent response to any drug incidents?

Have drugs been found at home or in the teenager's car? Questions about finding drugs and paraphernalia are not meant to imply searching the child's possessions, but relate to casual discovery. The discovery of paraphernalia is as important as the discovery of drugs. Eyedrops in a child's purse or medicine chest deserve explanation, as does excessive aspirin use. Throat sprays or lozenges to cover breath odor may be normal, imply dental decay, or be used to hide alcohol or tobacco smell. The parent should ask the child about these possibilities.

Questions about searching a child's room, listening to his phone calls, and reading his diary are most important. As a diagnostic tool, these activities can be most helpful, but all imply a lack of trust. Under what circumstances and in what fashion search might be recommended is discussed later in Chapter 11.

Parents should be asked about a child's friends and how they feel about these friends. If the friends are older, never brought home, or only known as voices on the telephone, suspicion should be raised.

Particularly important in the parent interview is evidence of excusing a child's negative behavior. Such defensive phrases as "Don't all children fight with their siblings?" or "He always has the bad luck of being caught" should be red flags. Blaming his troubles on laziness implies a punitive parental response and inadequate evaluation of the child. Explaining bad behavior on the basis of divorce, death, and changing neighborhoods may all be accurate assessments of the cause of difficulty, but should not be excuses leading to toleration of negative behavior.

Separation of a child from his family is a necessary and important part of the maturation process. However, when this separation means refusal to do chores, complete disregard for family rules, failure to participate in any family activity, and disrespect for parents and siblings, beware. Acceptance of such behavior by a family is enabling. Acceptance means permitting, and permitting turns control of the house over to the one least able to make responsible judgment, the troubled adolescent.

PHYSICAL EXAMINATION

Too much reliance on the physical examination in making a diagnosis is a mistake. The more obvious and severe medical complications tend to occur later in the disease and most often after the child has left the pediatric age range. The most common physical findings relating to drug use in adolescence are a characteristic appearance, signs of upper respiratory irritation, and evidence of trauma.

The general appearance of most drug users begins to change in stage 2 of the disease. Dress becomes less traditional. The picture of the mid 1960s hippie or of the 1980s rock star may be copied. Increasing fascination for T-shirts with drug or alcohol messages may be a sign. Cocaine spoons on necklaces, marijuana belt buckles, pierced ears in boys, and suggestive decals on books or purses should be noted. Girls may give the appearance of sexual promiscuity with tight-fitting, well-worn jeans, halter tops, see-through blouses, and overly made-up faces. A useful hint in boys has been center-parted, overly long hair.

Eye signs are especially helpful. The pupillary constriction seen with marijuana is so slight as to be of little value in diagnosis. Red eyes may be a clue, but the savvy adolescent usually uses eyedrops to cover this sign. The main eye signs to look for are avoidance of eye contact, especially when drugs and alcohol are being discussed, and sadness. This sadness or emptiness is often best appreciated by noting its disappearance when a child has been off drugs for 3 to 4 days. Seeing children in drug treatment, one often notes the sparkle that returns to the eyes after a short period of abstinence. Once aware of this eye sign, it is useful to note the discrepancy in the spoken "Everything's cool" and the obvious pain or sadness in the expression.

LABORATORY

Proper use of the laboratory can assist in diagnosis and management of drug use. As with any other test procedure, laboratory results must be interpreted in the light of the history and physical findings. At the present time, laboratory procedures for detection of drug use are vastly underutilized. Physicians tend to order drug screens most often in instances of acute life-threatening intoxication, less often in evaluation of trauma, and only occasionally in evaluation of children with nonacute behavior change.

The most widely used test is the measure of alcohol level, which is more often a police than a medical procedure. Blood alcohol testing and the less-invasive breath test for alcohol correlate well with the patient's state of intoxication at the time of testing. They will not remain positive the day after drinking. A standard urine drug screen will detect trace amounts of such chemicals as opiates, cocaine, Quaaludes, barbiturates, nicotine, and a number of tranquilizers. It does not reveal the level of intoxication nor relate to the amount ingested. Like alcohol, these drugs are rapidly metabolized, and urine testing is usually negative the day after ingestion.

Screening for marijuana products in the urine has different significance than screening for other drugs. The presence of these products does not mean that a person is intoxicated in the way elevated blood alcohol does, nor does it confirm recent exposure as other drug screens do. Cannabinoids in the urine only mean that the patient has smoked or eaten marijuana sometime in the recent past. This information may be of great value where a no-drug policy exists or where probation is based on nonsmoking.

Urinary excretion of marijuana metabolites varies greatly with individual differences in drug absorption, drug distribution, method of ingestion, and urine volume. Delta-9-THC, probably because of its lipid solubility, is slowly metabolized and passes from the body over a long time period. To demonstrate the long period over which cannabinoids are excreted, healthy young adult volunteers were asked to abstain from marijuana use for 30 days and then were tested for urinary excretion of cannabinoids. Each volunteer was then asked to smoke two marijuana cigarettes, each of which contained 9 mg of THC. Nine days later all were still putting out urine positive for cannabinoids. Significantly one of the women had a negative urine on day 6, but subsequently put out positive urines without further ingestion of the drug.[173]

The urine screen is sensitive, reliable, and requires only a small quantity of urine. Samples may be stored without difficulty for long periods of time. The literature accompanying the test kits suggests that urine, when frozen, may be tested for up to 1 month without loss of cannabinoids.[174] Practical experience in the California prison system[175] and elsewhere suggests that this statement is overly cautious, that cannabinoids are highly stable in urine for much longer periods of time, and that urine need not be frozen to achieve this stability. Laboratories may easily perform screening assays using equipment marketed by SYVA Laboratories of Palo Alto, Calif.[175] Hospitals that do not have this highly sophisticated laboratory instrument might be induced to purchase it if made to understand that the equipment has other medical uses, among which are checking blood levels on a variety of widely used drugs such as phenytoin (Dilantin), theophylline, and aspirin.

The United States military establishment now does extensive urine screening for cannabinoids on their personnel, using a modified SYVA system that requires little technical skill or training on the part of the tester. All methods for urine screening require some caution to be sure that the person being screened does not substitute someone else's urine or a nonurine sample for his own. Checking for warmth, pH, and specific gravity are helpful. Watching while the specimen is obtained may on occasion be indicated.

Urine testing for THC or 9-carboxy-THC, one of its metabolites, was not economically feasible until fairly recently. Prior to that, cannabinoid assays were done by gas chromatography or mass spectrometry which, though highly accurate, were cost-prohibitive as screening techniques.[176]

Unlike gas chromatography, the SYVA test does not give specific levels of 9-carboxy-THC. SYVA sought and found a reagent that would identify the presence of cannabinoids most of the time they were present. They wanted to set a level of detection that would pick up most positive urines, but not be so sensitive that it might report some negative urines as positive. They have done well at achieving these goals. Over 95% of urines that contain 50 ng or more of 9-carboxy-THC or THC will be reported as positive. A cautious claim is made by SYVA that less than 5% of drug-free urines will be positive. In my experience false-positives do not occur with this test, and any positive is strong indication of drug use. False negatives may occur. A negative urine does not rule out recent marijuana use. If the results do not fit the history, SYVA wisely recommends repeating positive tests. Gas chromatography may be ordered where repeat testing yields positive results that do not fit clinically. In practice, this may be overly cautious. The author has used the test many times with many positives and has yet to order gas chromatography.

Breath analysis for marijuana use has been described and may offer hope for future screening. Agar diffusion techniques are being studied by Hoffmann-LaRoche Inc. and perhaps offer the most hope for a simple, inexpensive screening tool for the small medical office.

A most valuable aspect of marijuana testing is the long period the urine remains positive. A child seen with fatigue on Friday may still have a positive urine from weekend smoking to support a diagnosis of drug use. If adolescents admit drug use, there is little purpose in diagnostic testing. In these adolescents, testing may be useful in monitoring a contract to remain drug-free.

Because of the epidemic use of marijuana and the devastating effects it may have on adolescents, a strong case can be made for routine screening of all adolescents. No treatment program has 100% success rates, and most adolescents who need it never receive treatment anyway. The answer has to lie in prevention or, where experimentation has already begun, in early detection. Detection of a user before he becomes chemically dependent has considerable value. Compared to routine urinalysis and tuberculin testing, which is regularly performed in health maintenance exams, screening for marijuana use may be considerably more cost-effective.

EMERGENCY ROOM AND HOSPITAL DRUG SCREENS

Adolescents admitted to the hospital with trauma should have an alcohol and/or drug etiology ruled out. When upon admission there is a clinical diagnosis of alcohol intoxication, a drug screen for other drugs may help identify the child with more advanced problems. Such alcohol or drug abuse should be identified not for legal purpose, but because of major health concern for the patient.

The physician who knows that accidents are the leading cause of death in the age group between 15 and 24 years has an additional responsibility. The fracture and its treatment are minor business compared to protection of pedestrians, passengers, and the patient himself, for whom the possibility of a next time must be considered. Isolated incidents of abuse do occur, but most often chemically related trauma reveals only a small part of the problem. To miss this tip when it appears is poor medical practice.

TEST RELIABILITY

Inaccurate urine test results, especially false positives, may be worse than not testing at all. Measures must be taken to prevent tampering with specimens and breaks in chain of custody of specimens, and ensure laboratory quality. All methods for urine screening require caution to be sure that the person being screened does not substitute someone else's urine or a nonurine sample for his own. Checking for warmth, pH, and specific gravity are helpful. Observation while the specimen is obtained may be indicated on occasion.

The U.S. military does extensive urine testing for cannabinoids and cocaine cut-off levels low enough to pick up most positive urines but not so low that they falsely report negative urines as positives. All positive screening results are confirmed by gas chromatography/ mass spectrometry (GC/MS). The military screening program costs less than $15 per urine, which includes confirmation when needed. To control quality, since 1984 each of the 12 laboratories used by the military receives 100 blind samples per month with no drug present and 100 blind samples which have been spiked with a known amount of a drug. In the first 50,000 samples, there were no false positives. The laboratory guidelines announced by the U.S. Department of Health and Human Services in April of 1988 should ensure similar high quality standards for all laboratories.

The most widely used test is the measure of alcohol level, which is more often part of a police procedure rather than a medical test. Both the blood alcohol testing and the less-invasive breath test for alcohol effectively measure the patient's level of intoxication at the time of testing. Standard urine drug screens can detect trace amounts of many psychoactive substances, but like alcohol, most of these drugs are rapidly metabolized, and urine testing is often negative the day after ingestion.

The urine screen is sensitive, reliable, and requires only a small quantity of urine to effectively detect even very small amounts of psychoactive substances. Laboratories most commonly use immunoassay methods such as enzyme-linked immunoassay (EMIT, TDX[175]), radio-immunoassay (Abusscreen*) and fluorescence polarized immunoassay (TDX†). Such tests do not, however, reveal the level of intoxication nor the amount of drug ingested.

Samples may be stored without difficulty for long periods of time. The literature accompanying the test kits suggests that urine, when frozen, may be tested for up to one month without loss of cannabinoids.[174] Practical experience in the California prison system[175] and elsewhere suggests that this statement is overly cautious, that cannabinoids are highly stable in urine for much longer periods of time, and that urine need not be frozen to achieve this stability.

Marijuana is notably different from the other illicit drugs because of the much longer period its metabolites can be detected in the urine after consumption. Delta-9-THC, probably because of its lipid solubility, is slowly metabolized and passes from the body over a long time period. Urinary excretion of marijuana metabolites varies greatly with individual differences in drug absorption, drug distribution, method of ingestion, and urine volume. In the casual user, we can expect to find levels of THC metabolites above the threshold level of tests for 2 to 5 days. In chronic users of higher concentrations, urines will be positive for much longer. To demonstrate the long period over which cannabinoids can be excreted, healthy young adult

*Abusscreen: Roche Diagnostic Systems, Inc., One Sunset Ave., Montclair, New Jersey 07042-5199.

†TDX: Abbott Labs, Abbott Park, Illinois 60064.

volunteers were asked to abstain from marijuana use for 30 days and then were tested for urinary excretion of cannabinoids. Each volunteer was then asked to smoke two marijuana cigarettes, each of which contained 9 mg of THC. Nine days later all were still putting out urine positive for cannabinoids. Significantly, one of the women had a negative urine on day 6, but subsequently put out positive urines without further ingestion of the drug.[173]

The length of time the urine remains positive may be of value when testing for marijuana. A child seen with fatigue on Friday may still have a positive urine from weekend smoking to support a diagnosis of drug use. If adolescents admit drug use, there is little purpose in diagnostic testing. With these adolescents, however, testing may be useful in monitoring a contract to remain drug-free.

The widespread use of marijuana and the devastating effects it may have on adolescents can make a strong case for the routine screening of all adolescents. No treatment program has a 100 percent success rate, and most adolescents who need treatment never receive it. Therefore, the solutions have to lie in prevention or, where experimentation has already begun, in early detection. Compared to routine urinalysis and tuberculin testing, which is regularly performed in health maintenance exams, screening for marijuana use may be considerably more cost-effective. Most important, detection of a user before he or she becomes chemically dependent has great value. Early detection of a user may help save the adolescent—and family—from the many human tragedies associated with drug use.

LEGAL IMPLICATIONS OF DRUG TESTING

The physician who orders drug screens in the diagnostic evaluation of his patients should not fear legal repercussion.[177] There is ample precedent for dealing with diseases that may have social and moral implications. It has become so routine to check for syphilis that some have forgotten that diagnosing venereal disease (VD) may also be a sensitive issue. The way in which positive tests are utilized relates less to law than to issues of confidentiality.

The legal connotations of testing children in schools are different from those of testing in a medical office or hospital. Although routine medical screening is performed increasingly in schools, marijuana use bears such strong legal and disciplinary implications that routine testing will not be allowed in the immediate future.[177] Similar obstacles exist to testing airline personnel, professional athletes, and others. The whole subject of routine testing for nonmedical purposes is a very thorny and controversial matter.

INTERVENTION: PRESENTING THE DIAGNOSIS

When the diagnosis of drug use is established or reasonable suspicion of the possibility exists, the child's family must be informed and then guided in suggested approaches to management.

The pediatrician who accepts experimentation as a phase not worthy of discussion with parents or who believes that adolescents can safely drink or take drugs in moderation faces a real dilemma. For the physician committed to drug-free adolescence, there is reason to be concerned about even a single episode of drug or alcohol use. Discovery without response may be viewed by the teenager as acceptance of the episode. More often, episodes thought to be isolated are but the first visible indicator of more advanced drug use. Carelessness, that leads to discovery, may indicate progression to a stage where the habit is firmly established.

The value of staging the disease is particularly obvious at this point. For those young people believed to be in stage 1 or early stage 2, parental education and counsel are most important. If parents and child are made aware of the progressive nature of use and of the mortality and morbidity associated with continued use, the process may be halted before disaster strikes. A single episode of intoxication or a change in behavior consistent with drug/alcohol use is reason for a family conference.

Care must be taken in presenting the diagnosis of drug abuse. There may be intellectual satisfaction in making a diagnosis, but little is gained by the patient or family if the diagnosis is not accepted or if no change occurs. Making the diagnosis stick and seeing to appropriate parental intervention is no easy task. No one wants this diagnosis.

Any major diagnosis may produce a grief reaction. The diagnosis of a disease such as leukemia is devastating. As a straight medical diagnosis, chemical dependency might be equally devastating, but an additional obstacle is involved. Parents who are told that their child has a drug problem often feel that an accusation rather than a diagnosis has been made. These parents are apt to feel strong moral or judgmental overtones directed at them.

There are several components to this grief reaction that should be known to the physician responsible for talking with the family. Perhaps the first is the shock that the family will feel. This shock may make them numb to everything else but the diagnosis and their interpretation of what it means. This factor makes it most important to schedule a follow-up visit after the initial numbness subsides.

A mother told me she could relate well to this explanation of the shock of diagnosis. The week before, her child was diagnosed as having aseptic meningitis, a serious illness, but one where complete recovery could be expected. She remembers hearing the dreaded word "meningitis" and little else. When she talked with her husband on the telephone, she told him the doctor believed the child would die. The next day she and her husband were able to talk with the physician and better understand what the prognosis and course of aseptic meningitis really were.

This point cannot be stressed too much. The physician who tries to accomplish too much at the visit where the diagnosis is presented may come to wonder why his recommendations are so often ignored. Careful discussion of the disease of chemical dependency and talking about treatment possibilities may be appropriate if decisions are not forced on parents in this hour of shock. These preliminary discussions may provide excellent groundwork for a later conference where more concrete action is planned.

A second component of the grief reaction is denial, which will lead the parents to reject the diagnosis. Because this denial is so easy to anticipate, the physician must be careful not to overstate his case. He needs to come across as caring, concerned, and well informed about the disease he diagnoses. The use of contracts with the child and trials of monitored abstinence discussed in the next chapter for children in stages 1 and 2 may help the family come to accept the reality of their child's problem.

Denial by the teenager is fairly routine. By nature and experience, teenagers argue well. Those who have had hidden drug and alcohol activity from their family may be excellent con artists. Parents, none of whom want to believe their child is involved, may be convinced relatively easily by their teenager that the doctor is all wrong. In the weeks following the office visit, the child may exhibit model behavior to convince his folks the doctor was in error. His denial may be complete, or he may admit to use but promise to quit. Further along he may admit use but angrily deny that it causes him any problem. Still further along he may claim the "right" to use. The physician must be prepared for these possibilities and have a plan for dealing with them.

The instinct for denial may be so strong that parents who come for consultation suspecting the diagnosis reject it when offered. Because of my local reputation as a "drug doctor," I consult frequently with families who set up appointments to discuss their children. These families, who have sought such consultation and who present strong histories of stage 3 drug use, frequently reject my assessment that indeed they do have a problem. These conferences often become very legalistic, with the physician being pushed to prove beyond reasonable doubt that their child's behavior and drug use are related. This reminds one of the pediatric task of convincing parents that their child's headache or stomachache is functional. They always want one more test or suggest one more possible cause that needs to be ruled out. It is often tempting to ask why they sought the "drug doctor" for consultation if they believed there was no problem.

The physician who has been involved with the family over an extended period of time has a real advantage. His credibility and concern for the child as a person and for the family are real assets in dealing with denial. The family who seeks consultation and denies its message may be in the process of shopping for a physician who will tell them they do not have a drug problem. They would often much rather accept the diagnosis of mental illness. Hopefully, they will eventually stop shopping and settle in with the diagnosis of this treatable disease.

Understanding that chemical dependency is a family disease may help. At least one of the parents has established a pattern of enabling that puts him or her in the position of "protector" of the child. They may have had much experience at shielding their child from what they perceive as "slurs" made by friends, neighbors, teachers, police, and now doctors. Great effort and skill may be necessary to break through this enabling process if it is well established.

Guilt is another part of grief and must be dealt with carefully. It contributes to enabling behavior and closes off the way to understanding that the child has a problem of his own making. When the parent is helped to understand that it is the child who is taking drugs on his own volition and that these drugs are causing him to change, guilt may be lessened. Environmental and home factors that may be associated with a child's increased susceptibility do not change the fact that he has a primary disease.

Anger, especially when directed at the physician, may be the most destructive part of the grief reaction. Care must be taken in the use of perjurious words such as "alcoholic," "pothead," and "druggie." Rest assured that more than ample shock value will be delivered by the subject matter discussed. The family will use these words themselves without prodding.

The patient is a child whom the family has loved and nurtured. He is not a drug addict, but a child who has a problem related to drug use. It is tempting to deal with the shock of the initial interview or with later denial by wanting to grab parents who refuse to listen and rub their noses in the diagnosis. A physician is well advised to control the anger he may feel towards parents who do not seem to be hearing what he is saying. His anger may be returned by parents, all too willing to see the physician as the one with the problem. They may have already rationalized their child's problem by calling it a normal phase of adolescence compounded by teachers or neighbors who do not understand kids.

Another direction anger may take is to divide the family. Each parent may blame the other for what has happened to their child. This anger may prevent them from working together to solve the problem. This very real component of the process must be dealt with firmly, but with understanding. Either parent may feel that he or she alone has the answer and that only by separating from the other parent can the child be helped.

SETTING UP A CONFERENCE

It is most important that both parents be present for the conference in which drug use is presented. Where only one parent is present at such consultation, the success rate may be close to zero. The denial or anger in the second parent may be so strong as to keep him away and must be dealt with.

I saw Shirley, a high school sophomore, for a routine checkup, and her responses to questioning suggested that she was chemically dependent. Unfortunately I was new at making this diagnosis and mentioned this possibility to her mother with no more care than if dandruff had been diagnosed. It was 19 months before her next pediatric visit.

Shirley's mother did call after the long interval, and when she asked for help, a conference was suggested for her and her husband. I was informed that the parents were divorced, but I persisted and eventually met with them both. Interim history revealed that Shirley had run up a $1,200 psychologist bill and attended two different schools since her last visit. The parents had fought about her management, and their divorce was in many ways related to the progression of her disease.

This conference went better, and both parents accepted the diagnosis. Shirley entered treatment, as did her younger sister, at a later date. She advanced to a staff position in the treatment program, performed well in junior college, and is now a marvelous young lady with a real future. Her parents, though still divorced, have a better understanding of what happened in their lives and are both proud and supportive of their daughters.

Each physician should establish a technique for family conference with which he is comfortable, understanding that his comfort may come only with practice and success. One approach is to inform the child and parent that because there is sufficient reason for concern, a meeting should be set up to discuss the concerns. This relatively vague approach braces the family for trouble, but is not specific enough for them to respond with denial.

When pushed for further explanation about a conference, the physician may mention those specific items that concern him, such as fatigue, school failure, a history of intoxication, or rebellion at home. It is best not to announce the diagnosis of drug abuse or chemical dependency at this point. If asked specifically regarding drug abuse, the physician may state that the possibility needs to be considered. Further probing may be forestalled by saying that it would be unfair to cheat them of adequate time for discussion. The follow-up meeting should be scheduled at a time when there is ample opportunity for questions. The importance of the father being present should again be stressed.

An all-too-frequent occurrence is for the designated time to arrive with only the mother showing up. When asked about the father, she may give one of a variety of fairly predictable responses. These most often fit the general pattern of "He really wanted to be here, but he got called away on business at the last minute." After acknowledging her statement, the physician should again point out the importance of the father's presence and arrange to reschedule the meeting. The parent may be informed that the physician has loads of things to do with his time and is not upset that rescheduling is necessary. The mother may persist by saying that both parents agree that it is all right to go ahead without the father. If at all possible, the physician should decline the bait.

Single-parent families may be exceptions to the above rule that both parents be present, but even here the absent parent should be considered. A manipulative child has on more than one occasion successfully used the absent parent to support his efforts to resist treatment. The absent parent, already angry at the parent who has won legal custody, may be quick to blame the custodial parent for the child's problems and reenter the legal arena. The only winners in such a battle will be the attorneys involved.

Another issue is who, besides the parents, should be present at the consultation. Where either or both parents have remarried, it is a good idea to include the new spouses. Where siblings or grand-parents are concerned, they may make good allies. When these parties are not made aware of the nature of chemical dependency, they may be apt to undermine the recommendations. By involving them this latter possibility may be avoided. Whether they are brought in for the first consultation, at later consultations, or not at all will depend on the judgment of the physician. Failure to even consider them may doom any plan to noncompliance, sabotage, and failure.

Most importantly, should the child be involved in the consul-tation? This is another matter requiring judgment, but the tendency should be towards involvement in at least some of the proceedings. When a child admits drug use or is in the early stages, his participation should be encouraged. Where the child is hostile or angrily denying that he has a problem in the face of strong evidence to the contrary, time alone with the parents has value.

Even in the early stages, some parents find it difficult to discuss their child's problems with the child present. An example of this that has always amazed me is how many parents do not want their child present when subjects such as bed-wetting are discussed. The parents may meet the physician in the hall outside the exam room and whisper something about the condition or spell the words when the child is present. It would seem obvious that the parents have already communicated their anxiety about the situation, and one wonders why they try to hide something the child already knows. Most often, some combination approach works best, where time is spent alone with the parents, some time alone with the child, and some time with parents and child together.

For the physician well-trained in physical disease, holding family conferences about problem behavior may seem foreign at first, but with practice can become routine. The rewards for learning are many, particularly in terms of personal satisfaction for a job well-done. Such techniques may be applied to anticipatory guidance and to a variety of nondrug-related pediatric problems. Plunging right in is often the best way to learn, but for the more cautious, courses that teach interviewing technique are available.

In the first conference, the physician should be direct about his findings and his suspicions. Having a copy of the material in Table 2 – 1 for the parents to hold is often helpful. As the physician reviews the history and findings with this chart as a reference, parents often come to place their child in one of the stages. The behavioral facts most often form the basis for staging the disease. A drug history or laboratory evidence of drug use may be very helpful, but often the full drug use story is not uncovered until the child is in treatment. Parents who place their child in stage 3 on the basis of his behavior may attempt denial by pointing out that his grades are still passing or his appearance is conservative.

Once the diagnosis is given to the parents, the physician must proceed cautiously. Very few are ready to consider treatment away from home at this time. The possibility of such being necessary should be mentioned if the physician believes the child is in late stage 2 or in stage 3. Most often the parents need time to recover from their shock, but during this time their education should begin. A variety of material such as *Gone Way Down,*[18] *Parents, Peers and Pot,*[165] *How to Get Your Child Off Marijuana,*[178] or *"How I Got My Daughter to Stop Smoking Pot"*[179] may be given as reading assignments before the next conference. In some cases a visit to a local treatment program or to an open AA meeting may be suggested.

No matter what course of action is selected, follow-up is essential. A definite appointment in the near future should be made. Failure to do so may make all of the earlier efforts a waste. At the follow-up visit, a definite plan of action should be agreed on as outlined in the next chapter. For those parents who still deny the diagnosis, a specific period of monitored trial may be prescribed.

SUMMARY

The diagnosis of adolescent drug and alcohol abuse is made on the basis of history, physical findings, and laboratory testing. A strong index of suspicion coupled with an understanding of the nature of chemical dependency and an awareness of the epidemic of use will avoid most of the difficulties in diagnosis. The pediatrician who has had a long period of rapport with families is well suited to make the diagnosis, present it to the families, and suggest a course of action.

9

Treatment

Adolescent drug abuse should be viewed as a preventable and treatable pediatric disease. Physicians cannot ignore the phenomenon of adolescent drug use and should make conscious efforts to assess all of their adolescent patients to estimate their stage of drug involvement. It is to be hoped that most younger patients will be in stage 0, the stage of nonuse. Young people and their families should be given anticipatory guidance about the risks of adolescence in an effort to minimize problems with alcohol, drugs, sex, and delinquency. Because of the statistics cited in Chapter 1 and the pervasive "do-drug" messages in our society, no child should be considered immune.

The aim of all treatment should be a return to and maintenance of health. Health means more than absence of disease. It is not sufficient merely to prevent drug or alcohol use or to remove a child from such use. Health care means assisting a child to establish a pattern of living in which he can feel good about himself, live up to his potential, find enjoyment in success, have a spiritual awareness, and care about his fellow man. Good adult health includes an ability to develop satisfying relationships and find satisfying work.

The management suggested for each child depends on his stage of drug use. It is a fairly common error to perceive a child as less involved than he actually is. The reverse may also occur, in which a child appears to be more involved than he actually is, but this is considerably less common than the former. No great harm should come from making an error of overconcern. As with any disease, careful follow-up of all users is necessary to adjust inaccurate earlier assessments. Follow-up will also detect children who have not responded to intervention efforts and whose diseases have worsened.

Beneficial effects may exist for all types of intervention. Often simply setting up an appointment brings about a change in parents. This act of acknowledging that a problem may exist is frequently accompanied by a new parental attitude and perception. Children sense change quickly. Awareness of increased attention given to them may cause them consciously or subconsciously to adjust their behavior. This possible effect should be mentioned to parents, who often gain support for their natural inclination to underestimate a child's degree of involvement because of sudden behavior improvement. The basis of such improvement may be either the fact that the child appreciates the attention or that he fears his secret may be uncovered. Such changes in the dependent child's behavior are apt to be superficial and transient. The modified behavior will not persist when parents, reassured by temporary improvement, return to their old attitudes and manners or when life deals additional stress to the affected child.

The best time to deal with drug use is before it begins. If this is not possible, next best is when the child has begun experimentation, but has not yet become dependent. In this stage he is learning how to feel good chemically and may be excited about his membership in a society where partying means being high. Some children may stop drug use spontaneously at this stage and return to abstinence voluntarily, but because parents or physicians have no really effective way of determining which child will progress or at what rate progression will occur, intervention seems appropriate for all. In addition to potential benefits to the child, intervention may benefit families and society generally.

Pediatricians are familiar with the concept of "herd immunity" and frequently base decisions on it. Rubella vaccination is given to children not so much to protect them from a relatively minor illness of childhood, but to protect others such as their unborn siblings and those of other families from the very destructive process of antenatal infection. When a high percentage of children are protected from mumps, other children are also protected, because the reservoir of potential carriers is decreased.

Some children perhaps may be able to "handle" drinking and marijuana use. Such use may nevertheless cause problems. If these youngsters support or encourage use as acceptable adolescent activity, they may lead others more susceptible than themselves to great harm. If these same strong children instead were to involve themselves in drug-free activities, their leadership might go a long way in establishing new standards for their peer group. By turning these leaders away from drug and alcohol use by education, parental action, and provision of attractive alternative activities, many lives other than their own may be saved.

TREATMENT BASED ON STAGING

For each stage of drug use, there are recommended courses of action. There is no one program that will work for all children or all families. Less invasive programs are generally more desirable, but may not be as effective as a progression in use occurs.

Stage 0

Anticipatory Guidance

Techniques of parenting should address the related issues of rights vs. responsibilities and needs vs. wants within a framework that moves toward an eventual goal of independence. Efforts aimed at helping the child bond to his family and building his self-esteem should be seen as parental duty. Clear family guidelines should be established on drug use and other issues to provide the child with additional support in his effort to resist drugs[180] (see Chapter 6).

Sobriety

Sobriety may be encouraged by provision of alternatives for young people not wanting to appear square, but not really wanting to do drugs either (see Chapter 6).

Parents, Peers, and Pot

The "Parents, Peers, and Pot"[165] approach is discussed more fully in Chapter 7. Unfortunately, in many instances parent groups are not initiated until stage 1 or 2 by parents already aware that drug use has begun. Attention to "do-drug" messages (Chapter 5), efforts to decrease supply (Chapter 10), and education of the child and family to the health consequences of drug use may be part of such parental efforts. Also included are parenting mandates and alternatives to drug use (1 and 2 above). Parents who are committed to drug-free adolescence for their children may work in cooperation with schools, police, church, legislature, and physicians to increase the child's chances. Self-education, time, and a willingness to work toward the common goal of drug-free youth must precede action. There should be a minimum amount of time spent blaming other people and agencies for the sorry state of current affairs. Where tested, this parent group approach has proven effective and may serve as a model for other parents and communities.

Parent group efforts, however, do not always succeed. The time and effort required for attainment of the goal of drug-free adolescence may be too much for most people and agencies. Making change is uncomfortable. Sometimes it fails because of denial that a problem exists or conversely that anything can be done about a generally pervasive societal change. Some children and families are too far along in their chemical dependency for such a relatively noninvasive treatment approach to succeed. Other groups start with every good intention, but eventually give up to the inertia of community and friends. When there is success and drug use ceases, parent groups are great. When drug use continues, parents had best consider the next step in intervention. They need to decide first whether an occasional drink for teenagers is permissible. Where there is a clear family understanding that any use will lead to negative consequences, persistent use implies dependency.

Negative consequences may not in themselves be good teachers. When such consequences are paired with positive reward and time spent in responsive communication with adults concerned about a child's personal worth and well-being, the results may be very rewarding. Harmful habits can be changed. The three As—acceptance, attention, and affection—can do a lot. Add to this a measure of environmental control over his peer group, and a child not too deeply involved will often show change in his drug-use pattern. When he does not, it is time to reassess the situation and place him in stage 2 or 3 drug use, where more extreme measures are needed.

Stage 1

Parents, Peers, and Pot

Some parents taking responsibility for their children emphasize education.[179] Others aim their efforts at separating the child from his source of supply while educating him and building a better relationship with him.[178] Parents have shown great ingenuity in the methods they have employed to set things right for their children.

Alternative Programs

These may stress the fact that fun and chemical "partying" are not synonymous. They may be church groups, school groups, Channel One programs (see Chapter 6), or programs specifically aimed at eliminating drug use such as the Palmer Drug Abuse Program (PDAP) (later this chapter).[181]

Stage 2

Parents, Peers, and Pot

Parental intervention may still work, but as dependency intervenes, outside help becomes increasingly more appropriate.

Classic Psychological Counseling and Psychotherapy

The results achieved with traditional therapeutic approaches such as individual psychotherapy have been discouraging.[182] The great cost of such methods has been poorly correlated with the rewards obtained. Where the focus is on the child with little or no emphasis given to providing help for parents or finding drug-free alternatives for the child in aftercare, recidivism rates will be high.[183] The major cost of programs that fail may be the loss of critical time during the important adolescent years. For a variety of reasons, but primarily because of failure of the traditional medical model, self-help groups have begun to develop outside the medical umbrella. These groups were preceded by the most successful self-help group of all, AA. These groups have flourished because they work.

Two intelligent men who banded together to deal with their mutual problem founded AA in 1935. These organizers, an alcoholic physician (Dr. Bob) and an alcoholic stockbroker, were at the end of their ropes. They had failed to gain control of their lives with a variety of medical, religious, and other approaches. In each other they found understanding and acceptance, through which they were able to give up alcohol and assist each other through times of crisis. Implicit in their success was an admission that they were powerless over alcohol and that only a power greater than themselves could restore them to sanity. From these humble beginnings sprang an organization gaining millions of members in towns and cities around the world. The organization's name reveals the stigma placed on alcoholism, and only in recent years have a few alcoholics admitted publicly that they were undergoing treatment and recovering.[184]

From "alcoholics helping alcoholics" came "alcoholic families helping alcoholic families" (Al-Anon), "teenagers with alcoholic parents helping other children with alcoholic parents" (Alateen), "narcotics addicts helping narcotic addicts" (Narcotics Anonymous or NA), "parents with problem children helping families with problem children" (Families Anonymous), Nar'anon Family Groups, and more. These groups grew and survived because they met a need. Physicians would do well to be aware of them and of the great benefit they can be as community resources. It is not difficult to obtain a list of local chapters, meeting places, and meeting times. The yellow pages of most telephone books will provide much information. National addresses that may be helpful are as follows:

Al-Anon Family Groups
1 Park Ave.
New York, NY 10016
(212) 481-6565

Alcoholics Anonymous
General Service Office
468 Park Ave. S.
New York, NY 10016
(212) 686-1100

Families Anonymous
P. O. Box 344
Torrence, CA 90401
(213) 774-3211

Nar'anon Family Groups
P.O. Box 2562
Palos Verdes Peninsula, CA 90274
(213) 547-5800

Narcotics Anonymous
World Service Office
P.O. Box 622
Sun Valley, CA 91352
(213) 768-6203

Intensive Drug-Free Programs

These are discussed below under stages 3 and 4. Many young people in late stage 2 will require intensive treatment.

Stages 3 and 4

Inpatient or Foster Care Programs

Outpatient management of chemically dependent children is likely to fail. By stage 3, the compulsion to use drugs is so strong that recovery may require an enforced period of drug-free living.

As the pattern of drug use began changing in the 1960s to involve younger and younger people in chemical experimentation, the numbers of dependent children rose. A search for recovery began, and a variety of programs with very different approaches began to report success using principles common to AA. Groups such as Synanon, Daytop Village, Phoenix House, PDAP, and Straight, Inc., all seemed to have success in the rehabilitation of compulsive drug users. Why they worked is open to some question, but a number of factors have been cited. These programs reduced the user's feeling of isolation and gratified his unmet need to belong. They provided successful role models. They had former drug users as staff who were able to convey empathetic understanding and concern. Because costs were often considerably lower than in medical facilities, they could retain clients for considerably longer periods.

In drug treatment, level of improvement seems directly related to length of stay, up to 18 months.[185] The treatment recommended at this level of disease may seem excessive to many families. Drug and alcohol dependency in teenagers is a very difficult illness to treat, and therapeutic results may relate directly to intensity of treatment. Families should be informed that complete drug treatment may take full family involvement for months, if not years. Early improvement is not cure. The most obvious changes that occur in a child tend to occur early in the course of his treatment. The most lasting changes come later.

Many of the most successful adolescent drug programs use innovative and scientifically unproven techniques. There have been few, if any, reports about them in the medical literature. Some of them have been shunned by the medical establishment and seen as cultish or at least involved in brainwashing. On the other hand, program directors, often former drug users with little formal training in psychology or counseling, have tended to see physicians as uncaring and/or ignorant about drugs or alcohol. Hopefully this situation is changing. More and more physicians are becoming aware of the effectiveness of the newer programs. Program directors, on the other hand, are learning that physicians do care and can be an important part of their team.

Five Adolescent Drug Programs

Described briefly here are five programs for treatment of adolescent drug users. These programs have little in common except that they all seem to work. All have powerful supporters who believe their program is "the best." All have detractors. All insist on absolute abstinence from drugs and alcohol. Only two come close to the mainstream of traditional care for troubled adolescents. They represent but five of thousands of new programs. Their inclusion here is not meant as an endorsement, but to give the reader some flavor of what is currently available. A referring physician may use these larger programs for comparison to programs in his area, using the outline for program evaluation found later in this chapter.

A search for treatment programs may begin in the yellow pages of most telephone books under "Drug and Alcohol Treatment." Another source of information may be AA. A third is a listing that can usually be obtained from the state agency responsible for drug and alcohol programs. Program evaluation may begin over the telephone, talking with people who work in and refer to various programs.

Drug Abuse Programs of America (DAPA).[186] This program, based in Pasadena, Tex., opened its doors in 1975 as a free-standing (nonhospital) residential drug treatment program. Its director sought to provide intensive and fairly traditional psychiatric care to clients over a short period of time and return them to community-based aftercare programs. The highly intensive treatment generally lasts 6 to 8 weeks and rarely over 8 to 10 weeks.

Upon entry the client enters an evaluation period where thorough examination occurs. Included are medical history as well as physical and psychiatric evaluations by the house physician and psychiatrists. A nurse performs an intake evaluation and a detailed psychosocial history. From this information a treatment plan is formulated. Therapy lasts 5 hours daily, 5 days per week, and includes daily individual therapy, psychiatric group therapy, psychological group therapy, and drug abuse counseling. There are 3-hour group sessions on Saturday and Sunday to decrease the likelihood of getting high while on weekend pass.

A variety of treatment modalities are available at DAPA, including biofeedback, remedial education, physical medicine, and activity therapy. Assertiveness training is taken by all.

The staff at DAPA is highly trained in drug abuse, from the psychiatrists to the primary therapists, who have at least master's degrees. Affiliated school teachers have had extra training to understand drug use. Individual drug counselors are often former users who have been through the program. Upon completion of therapy, clients are often referred to PDAP for aftercare. They may also be referred to AA, NA, local drug abuse programs, and private out-patient therapists, depending on the wishes of the child and his family and the resources available in his community. Following discharge from the inpatient program, 18 months of aftercare are recommended.[186]

The DAPA programs have become increasingly comprehensive and now address prevention, intervention, treatment (outpatient and inpatient), and extensive aftercare. Their community program, which provides many of these services, utilizes donated services of psychiatrists, psychologists, masters-level therapists, and certified substance abuse counselors. These DAPA outpatient programs offer 45 hours per week of individual and group meetings, all free of charge.

Palmer Drug Abuse Program (PDAP).[181] The founders of DAPA and PDAP both came to their programs having had previous experience at the very unsuccessful federal drug abuse hospital in Lexington, Ky. Jason Baron, M.D., medical director of DAPA, had been there as a staff psychiatrist. Bob Meehan's visit had been court-ordered for heroin addiction and alcoholism. Bob did not find help at Lexington and was unable to stay drug-free until he joined a group meeting at the Palmer Memorial Episcopal Church in Houston. The church's rector, Father Charles Wyatt-Brown, saw something in young Meehan and offered him a job as church custodian. Wyatt-Brown wondered what would happen if his drug-reformed custodian shared some of his experience with teenagers who came around. Before long it was obvious that the janitor had a "pied piper" personality for drawing young people to him and then leading them to drug-free lives. His approach to young people offered them an alternative to drug use. He called the sober teenager an endangered species and began meeting with those adolescents who wanted to spend time with straight people. He showed them that "straight" did not mean "square." They had fun, they rapped, they flirted, they giggled, and they made a commitment not to do drugs. Children got better, and the program grew. Approximately 6,000 young people in 14 states now attend PDAP meetings. A major advantage of this program is that it is free.

Parents who call PDAP for help are asked to come in for a visit with an adult staff member, who is most often a former user. The program is explained to them, and they are given help in understanding how they may best help their child. Whether or not their child elects to enter the program, they are encouraged to attend parent meetings to learn how other parents have coped with their difficult adolescents. They are encouraged to read "Fists and Hearts"[181] and "Tough Love"[187] to better understand themselves, their children, and PDAP. The 12 steps of PDAP are modeled after those of AA, as are its 12 traditions. When their child is active in the program, parents are encouraged to come in as often as they feel they need for individual counseling. At first this may be weekly.

At the child's first visit to the program, he is seen by a counselor who is close in age and is a former drug user. His message to the newcomer is, "I've tried it your way, and it didn't work for me. It doesn't look like it's working for you either. Here at PDAP I've found a new way that's changed my life, and I want you to give it a try." The counselor, formerly a con artist himself, cannot be easily conned by the newcomer who says he feels great. At the end of this session, the counselor hopes to extract a commitment from the user to abstain from drugs and alcohol for 30 days and attend as many meetings as he can.

The PDAP meetings are social gatherings, followed by 1 hour of serious discussion, followed by more fun time. At least once a month, major social functions are planned. These may include parents and involve camping, boating, or whatever interests the group. Groups are segregated by age. The younger participants are age 17 and under. There are also groups from ages 18 to 26 and for those age 26 and older. Some crossover from one group to another is permitted. The only rules at PDAP meetings and outings are that no one is to bring drugs, come high, have sex, or get violent.

Of 100 young people who entered the PDAP program in Midland, Tex., last year, 60 were able to earn their "monkey fist" for 30 days of abstinence. At 1 year, 25 were still clean. Many others improved, but had less than perfect records. Five were referred for inpatient treatment before returning to the program.[188] The PDAP program does not remove children from their homes and may have problems in separating the compulsive user from his drugs. Where this separation is impossible, PDAP may refer to inpatient facilities for the initial phase of recovery. The PDAP programs are relatively autonomous, much like AA programs, and success rates may vary greatly from one city to another. As excellent as PDAP may be, referring physicians are advised to become acquainted with the program in their area.

Impact.[189] Phoenix House, the country's oldest (founded in 1968) and largest adolescent inpatient drug treatment program, operates Impact as an intensive 24-week outpatient program. Based in New York City, Phoenix House has psychiatric leadership, and the Impact staff contains degreed professionals as well as former drug-user counselors.

Young people in the program meet twice weekly and are expected to remain drug-free. In the early weeks, they learn about drugs, chemical dependency, and themselves. Later they learn to work as a group and help each other with crises during the week. Group social activities are planned. Parents meet for 12 of the 24 weeks. In the early weeks parents are educated about drugs, chemical dependency, and their roles in the family disease. Later parents meet with their children in a group and work on communication skills. Finally they are taught parenting skills and how to apply them to their recovering child. Where compliance with the drug-free rule is maintained, success has been reasonably good.[189] As might be expected stage 2 users are more likely to comply with the rule of abstinence than the compulsive users of stage 3.

Teen Challenge.[190] This large, religiously oriented program has many centers around the country and 150 overseas chapters. David Wilkerson, a preacher who went to New York to convert a group of men on trial for senseless murder, saw a need, and Teen Challenge was born. Centered in Rehrersburg, PA., occupational skills are taught, and young people are offered an "alternative to selfish living." Teen Challenge boasts thousands of converts yearly. Not only a drug program, Teen Challenge opens its doors to people with a variety of behavior problems. The thrust of the program is that only through a spiritual awakening can these young people turn their lives around. Many drug programs, including AA, share this belief, but are not as strongly Christian as Teen Challenge. There is little medical input, and for this reason some physicians may have real difficulty in recommending Teen Challenge. For others it works very well. Like PDAP, individual programs may vary widely and an on-site visit is recommended before referral.[190]

Straight, Inc. This adolescent drug treatment program was founded by St. Petersburg, Fla., parents who had noted behavior deterioration in their pot-smoking adolescents. Unsatisfied with results of traditional counseling, they launched their own program modeled somewhat after an earlier treatment center. The success of Straight prompted parents elsewhere to want the same for their children, and Straight branches were organized in Atlanta, Cincinnati, and Washington, D.C.

Teenagers entering Straight begin an intensive five-phase program with an average treatment course of 13 months. The majority of daily face-to-face interaction is directed by closely supervised staff members still in their teens who have completed the program, received courses in counseling technique, and climbed up a ladder of staff advancement. Many of these young people are full-time students who put in their 40 hours a week at Straight in their "spare" time. Much of the day is spent in large group sessions, but there are also smaller groups and "one-on-ones" with adolescent and/or adult staff. Where indicated, family conferences are called.

There is no routine psychiatric or psychological evaluation of adolescents admitted to the program. On admission all clients show signs of emotional aberration. Later if these young people are drug-free and behaving in an unusual fashion, psychiatric consultation may be ordered. Despite lack of standard psychiatric supervision and inpatient therapy, psychiatrists who have visited the program have been impressed.

An unusual component of Straight is its use of foster care. On entering the building and agreeing to treatment, the adolescent enters Phase I, during which he will be in session from 9 AM to 9 PM, 6 days a week, and from 2 PM to 9 PM on Sunday. He will begin to feel the pressure of a large and loving group of peers working on living straight lives. He will be assigned to the care of an "oldcomer" further along in the program and will go at night to the home of this new companion. Little freedom will be permitted in the foster home.

Television, telephone, and reading material are privileges he will earn later on. His foster family will love him, support him, and learn about themselves from him.

When he has been in the program for 2 weeks, he may ask permission to enter Phase II and return home. His peers and staff will grant him this advancement when they feel he has taken an honest and serious look at himself and is working on self-improvement. He will know the seven steps of the program (patterned after the 12 steps of AA) and be writing a daily moral inventory. In this inventory he evaluates his day in terms of his feelings, accomplishments, and failures and sets his goals for the next day. He will have seen his parents only at the twice-weekly open meetings and then only across a crowded room. His family will have expressed their feelings to him in this large group. Closer contact with them will not occur until he has earned and requested the right for a short visit. During Phase I, parents meet in twice-weekly group sessions.

Daily activity in Phase II is much the same, but at night he will be in his own home under restrictions very similar to those of Phase I. His task is to work to build a healthy relationship with his family. After a fairly short period of time, he may request that a newcomer be assigned to him. His parents are often amazed at how much he has learned and how effective as a "big brother" he has become.

In Phase III he returns to school (or work), but returns to the program after classes to complete his day. Tutoring is available to him in the program, with full-time teachers assigned by the public school system. During Phase IV he begins to have days off, which he is expected to utilize for growth and the development of healthy friendships and activities. Additional free time is awarded in Phase IV. By Phase V he has learned the program and should be applying its lessons and using them to assist others less far along. Upon "graduation" he enters an aftercare program that meets two evenings weekly.

The great strengths of Straight are also its weakness. No program has a more effective peer component, but this has created some problems. Their ability to deal effectively with young users does not always translate into an ability to interface with parents and adults in the community. Adequate adult supervision should minimize this objection. Another great feature at Straight is the foster care component of the program, which keeps costs down and provides many opportunities for family education and growth. Problems have been created when foster families have been overzealous or lax in their standards. This risk also may be minimized with adequate supervision of foster homes.

Program Evaluation

The physician who cares for adolescents should be able to guide parents to inpatient or foster care treatment when a need for such exists. He should be able to help them evaluate local programs and be aware of effective programs outside the family's immediate area. The largest national adolescent treatment programs differ greatly in structure, but all share certain features that seem important in the treatment of youthful abusers.

Literally thousands of programs have opened their doors for the treatment of adolescents with drug and alcohol programs. There is no accrediting body that looks at these programs and sets standards for care. Some are run by hospitals, others by churches, and still others by parents. Some are free-standing drug and alcohol units, while others are parts of more general psychiatric facilities. There is much variety. There are zealots with almost all groups, and the drug field is no exception. Many excellent programs are still working on methods to provide internal checks and balances to insure successful continuation. The future is hard to predict, but there is great need for systematically comparing and evaluating the "apples and oranges" in the drug rehabilitation field as it now exists. Until accreditation is standardized, parents and physicians need to perform their own evaluations.

The final responsibility for selection of therapeutic modality should rest with parents. Even for parents who have recovered from the shock of realizing that their child has a drug problem, such decision making may seem an overwhelming task. The pediatrician, unable to treat stage 3 drug use by himself, may offer great service to families by giving them guidelines for program evaluation. There are programs that work and programs that do not work. By nature people are tempted to select the treatment modality that requires the least time, money, and parental involvement. These are indeed important considerations, but precious time may be lost if the family selects an approach likely to be ineffective.

Efforts to evaluate the effectiveness of drug treatment programs are tempered by the same problems encountered in the evaluation of other social programs. Among these factors are ages of the children treated, their underlying strengths and weaknesses, socioeconomic status, and the duration, degree, and type of drug involvement. The science of evaluation of adult drug programs is still in its infancy.[191] Adolescent drug programs are newer and have different variables. Further muddying the waters is the fact that evaluation of drug treatment programs has focused on those programs that proliferated in the early 1970s and dealt primarily with the "traditional" drug treatment client. In the years 1970 to 1973, federal expenditures and associated evaluations for drug treatment increased by nearly 13 times.[14] Unfortunately there is little evidence that the millions of dollars spent on hard-headed evaluations by federal, state, and local governments have greatly helped drug-dependent people, their families, or their physicians find better treatment programs. These expensive and sophisticated evaluations yielded little information that could not have been obtained subjectively. Because of the many variables, there is not, and probably never will be, a numeric evaluation that rates programs from best to worst.[192] Almost all of the money went for heroin programs. Little has been written about evaluation of programs dealing with adolescent marijuana and alcohol abusers.

This section will discuss the issues I look at when evaluating programs. More weight is given to some points than others. Points to be evaluated are listed in the order that I consider most important. Others may place their priorities in different order. In many ways the final evaluation is largely subjective, like selecting a personal physician. After all of the available data has been collected, the final choice is often made on intangibles. The physician meeting with parents should discuss his evaluation, but not be surprised if they assign weights different than his own. No program works for all, and no program appeals to all.

Physicians who are optimistic about treatment possibilities are more likely to be effective in their referrals[193] and more likely to see successful treatment outcomes.[194] The attitude that the physician has towards a treatment program does influence which program is selected.[195,196]

1. Does the Program Work? The bottom line in evaluating any therapy is its effectiveness measured against its costs and risks. A program that turns out drug-free youth should be measured on its percentage of success and rate of recidivism. Effectiveness of drug treatment however, must be evaluated by more than just numbers. Tangible guides for assessment of quality of recovery are not easy to come by, but are at least as important as the quantitative measure. Measuring quality may involve getting a feel for what is happening and how well "graduates" return to full health, pursuing lifestyles consistent with continued growth.

One good way to judge a program is to talk with young people in treatment and with others who have completed the program. Their families should also be interviewed. Programs should be able to provide you with names of such people who are willing to meet with you. Even when distance is a problem, such visits are worthwhile.

In effective programs one usually senses a feeling of love and caring. Alert, smiling faces and positive attitudes about life should be observed. Abstinence from drugs should not be seen as a program's only goal. Children should be developing attitudes and skills that make them able to live up to their potential, to feel good about themselves, and to learn the joy of personal accomplishment. It is helpful when the physician is able to perform such an evaluation, but families about to enroll a child should also visit and be satisfied with what they see, hear, and feel.

Several of the larger and more effective drug programs that were established almost overnight have not kept good records of program results. This puts the evaluator at a great disadvantage. Hopefully as these relatively new programs become more refined and sophisticated, they will be able to give accurate and current numbers relative to their operation. In keeping records it is important not to over-evaluate or to replace hands-on care with computers. The evaluator would like to know as a minimum how many children of each age are in the program, how long it takes the average child to complete the program, and what is the follow-up on children 1 and 2 years after "graduation."

A look at the demographics of noncompleters may also be helpful. An evaluator might like to know how long noncompleters remain in the program before they quit or are pulled out by their parents. A 1- and 2-year follow-up on these young people, though perhaps difficult to obtain, would be useful information. Benefits should accrue at all stages of any effective program, and it would be hoped that many of those adolescents and their families who did not complete the program might still have gained enough insight to modify their patterns of living. No program works for all children. Sometimes a combination does. There may be children doing well in program A who did not complete program B and vice versa. Because the changes the child and his family need to make may be so difficult for them, a certain amount of program-shopping occurs.

Adolescent drug abuse and treatment is a new field. Therapy is sure to change, and it is difficult to fully predict the direction such change will take. The effectiveness of newer programs may be hard to judge. They will have little, if any, data on program success and failure. Those patterned after successful models may be comparable to the models. Those that use new and varied approaches are not necessarily good or bad, but they are more difficult to recommend.

2. Is the Program Drug-Free?   Because chemical dependency is a primary disease, abstinence from psychoactive chemicals is a must. The controversy surrounding methadone substitution and maintenance for the opiate-dependent is not discussed in this book, as these users are generally not adolescents.

Cindy, age 16, was in treatment for problem drinking. She expressed anxiety to her counselor about her weekend social life. Her counselor, who knew Cindy could not handle alcohol, suggested that she might smoke an occasional joint to help her relax at those times when her anxiety was running high. Cindy accepted the advice, and it was 2 years and two suicide attempts later before she entered drug-free treatment and began her recovery.

The use of tranquilizers has become so accepted and commonplace that many hospital programs forget to realize that taking Valium to deal with withdrawal from alcohol is just a substitution of dependencies. In psychiatric units where no drugs are prescribed for the chemically dependent, care must be taken that other potential drug sources are monitored. Other psychiatric patients may give (or sell) their prescriptions to the abuser. Orderlies and other personnel, convinced that marijuana is harmless, may sell it (often for a profit) to patients.

3. Is There a Strong Family Component?   The family commitment to recovery from drugs and achievement of recovery go hand in hand. Many parents who reluctantly accept the fact that their child has a drug problem would prefer to drop him off for treatment and return later to pick him up cured. Such an approach is unlikely to work. The more a family comes to understand chemical dependency and supports their child's progress and program, the better their child will do. A family willing to make personal changes in support of drug-free adolescence will do even better. Programs aiming for high success rates must educate families, provide support for hurting parents, and give assistance in adjusting the dynamics of family interaction. In evaluating a program's family component, look for what is provided for and expected of the family before intake, while the child is in treatment, and in the aftercare period.

PREINTAKE.   Programs can do much to help parents deal with their child's need for treatment. Classes offered to confused and stunned parents coming to decide on treatment can greatly assist their acceptance of the diagnosis and need for treatment. Leaders of such classes should be caring individuals with adequate training in drug use, dependency, and treatment. Compassionate parents of children in treatment and/or recovery may be helpful in such groups if able to relate to the experiences of the newcomer.

Preadmission groups may meet on a regular basis, with newcomers entering and leaving as their needs demand. Where such groups do not exist in a community, Al-Anon, open AA, or Families Anonymous meetings may be substituted. At these meetings parents may hear stories remarkably like their own. Visitors are encouraged to consult with members about disease and treatment. One risk of counseling groups is that some emphasize how the parents may adjust to their grief and put less emphasis on the need to enter the child in treatment. There comes a time when education must give way to therapy for a disease that is progressive and potentially fatal. The physician who schedules follow-up visits with his patients should deal with procrastination if the parents have not. Such follow-up visits are not essential if the child has entered treatment, but may still be useful for families working through their feelings. The physician should leave the door open for such possibility.

IN TREATMENT. Programs vary greatly in the demands they make on parents and on the services they offer after admission. In addition to formal presentations and group sessions, programs may offer counseling sessions for the individual parent, both parents, or the whole family. While their child is in treatment, parents may become aware of problems that have previously been ignored. It is not unusual for parents to discover, for instance, that they themselves are chemically dependent and need to practice the steps of the program in which their child is enrolled. Some enter AA. Some uncover psychiatric difficulties that require referral and treatment outside the program. Psychiatrists in university treatment centers point out that a high percentage of the children they see with alcohol and drug abuse come from families with major degrees of psychopathology.[50]

The complicated interrelationship of family problems to adolescent drug abuse has been discussed in Chapter 3. A family approach to treatment makes sense even where the family dysfunction is believed to be only secondary to the teenager's use of drugs. Where drug use is believed to be secondary to family dysfunction, family therapy becomes mandatory.

As the child advances through a program, increasing attention should be given to teaching effective parenting techniques. Issues such as dating, curfews, effective use of leisure time, homework, chores, trust, and responsibility should be discussed. Communication skills should be emphasized, and families should learn to deal with problems and negative feelings before they are blown out of proportion.

Siblings should not be forgotten. Drug use among siblings is relatively common and must be dealt with for the sake of the child in treatment as well as for the affected sibling. A number of reasons for such sibling involvement seem obvious. Whatever the cause of sibling drug use, whether environmental, social, or even genetic, allowing a child in treatment to be continually exposed to a drug user under the same roof compromises treatment success.

Sibling programs should deal with more than just drugs. Living in a family with a chemically dependent person brings about protective adaptation in all family members. Recovery is most likely to occur when all family members adjust their lives to a new definition of family health. Siblings should have opportunity to participate in the treatment process, understand what is happening, and share their feelings with others. Sibling meetings or attendance at open meetings may be helpful. Counseling sessions for siblings may be appropriate. Programs that have strong sibling components should be given plusses in their rating.

FAMILY AFTERCARE.   Aftercare support for families is also desirable. Techniques with which the family has become familiar during the active phase of the program may be used. These may include rap sessions, family conferences, or social events with other parents or families where time is allowed for some sharing of postprogram progress. In addition there may be personal calls on a routine periodic basis by designated program representatives to chat about the status of the program "graduate" and family. Where programs have reason to feel concerned about a child's posttreatment course, visitation may be indicated.

A program that believes that adolescent drug treatment is best accomplished with the support and assistance of involved and committed parents and works to strengthen and modify parental attitudes and behavior is likely to have a good track record of success. A family that is healthy, bonded, and communicating offers the best chance for long-term recovery.

4. Is There a Peer Component?   Using the force of positive peer pressure to turn a teenager around can be a very powerful therapeutic tool. If a teenager can identify with others in treatment who are striving to put drugs behind them, he will have a stronger inclination to work for his own recovery.

Programs made up of older people or people of different socioeconomic cultures are less likely to work for the adolescent than programs where he sees and raps with kids of his own age and background. Being able to confess the shame, guilt, depression, frustration, and anger he has felt with his life to young people who have known the same feelings aids his recovery. Hearing others tell of their crimes, misdeeds, lies, and sexual problems, which may match his own, help him with group identity. Belonging to a peer group that cares for him and where drug use is not considered "cool" may open a new world to him.

5. Are There Aftercare Provisions?   It is a real tragedy to see a child and family go through the difficult process of drug rehabilitation only to return to drug use. A very critical period for a child leaving the active support of a therapeutic community is the time immediately following his "graduation." Unless some support is provided to assist him through this risky separation period, recidivism rates are likely to be high.

Some programs have aftercare groups that meet regularly, provide support, and deal with pressures of the "do-drug" environment. By providing peer friendship and companionship, they help the adjusting adolescent build his new life in ways that are healthy and productive. Where such organizations do not exist or when a teenager moves to a new town or goes to college, other options may be suggested. National organizations such as AA and NA often have groups that welcome teenagers and make them feel comfortable. Groups including other adolescents are often best. A child should be taught to keep searching until he finds "his" group with which he can be comfortable. Conservative religious organizations with strong drug and alcohol prohibitions such as the Mormons and Southern Baptists may suit the wishes of some teenagers for peer companionship. As important as families are, teenagers grow and survive most effectively in the support system of a healthy peer group.

6. What Are the Costs and Risks?   The cost of treatment may vary widely, and physicians should have some idea of how best to match family need with family resources. Medical insurance coverage of drug treatment also varies greatly from company to company and from program to program. Some programs offer scholarships.

The personal cost to family members also needs to be considered. Family involvement is essential, but demands on parents may be excessive and at times artificial. Parents frequently need to make adjustments in their lifestyle to facilitate recovery, but those adjustments that require job change or moving the family should be considered carefully.

7. What Beliefs Are Instilled? Returning a drug-free child to an unchanged environment with an unchanged belief system dooms him to failure. All good programs aim in some way to strengthen his belief in himself. A return to the mainstream of traditional cultural values that honor God, country, and family is a desirable goal. Some programs require commitment to specific ideology ranging from belief in the cult of Scientology to acceptance of Christ as savior. Parents and referring physician should be aware of the beliefs a program espouses.

How seriously a program is committed to reacculturation of its clients may be judged by how much attention it pays to "do-drug" messages and other components of the drug culture. Tobacco use by minors is illegal and should be questioned. T-shirts and clothing with drug and alcohol messages are suspect. Attention to such things as reading material, television, movies, and music with strong counterculture emphasis should be noted. Suspect the child who says he is straight, but continues to exhibit an attraction to the trappings of the drug culture. Be wary if he tells you he knows he cannot handle drugs, but still shows preference for his old drug-using friends, their music, and their hangouts.

8. What Are the Staff Credentials? The success of AA (alcoholics helping alcoholics) led to changes in the credentialing of treatment staffs. Formal training in psychiatry and psychology did not lead to the therapy success rates seen in AA. In similar fashion Overeaters Anonymous and Weight Watchers followed the AA model and success story by realizing that only people with weight problems truly understand how it feels to be fat.

The "chemistry" that may exist between a former alcoholic or drug user and a current one is almost magical to watch. It is more than just a shared awareness of the alcohol or drug scene. I was made keenly aware of this magic in a meeting that occurred as I involved myself in intervention with an adult alcoholic friend. The day prior to the meeting, I had visited my friend and found him drunk. I did not refer to his condition until he began to cry and tell me he was having trouble controlling his drinking. I spoke with him and with his wife and suggested that he enter treatment. I told them I would make necessary arrangements for the next day.

The following morning I returned with my wife and a neighbor who had recently completed treatment at the facility to which we hoped to send Ralph. Ralph's wife acted surprised that we really meant business, and Ralph seemed to have little recall of the previous day. At that point Richard, our neighbor, began to talk. Ralph and Richard had not previously met. Prior to this I had never heard Richard say more than three sentences at a time and would have described him as a nice, quiet guy. Two hours later Richard was still talking, and Ralph had not taken his eyes off of him. It was as if the other three of us at the table were not even there. Ralph agreed that he needed help and entered the program that afternoon. I had witnessed magic.

It is very difficult for a client in treatment to lie to a former user on staff without the staff member sensing the dishonesty. There is a saying in drug treatment centers that "you can't con a con." You can, of course, but not as easily as you can fool someone who has not been there. More and more programs employ former users effectively. An added plus exists when these former users are young and can relate to clients on that additional basis. Where such young users are not on staff, a talented group leader may accomplish much of the same effect by utilizing the talents of group members who are further along in their treatment.

Confrontation is a widely used and highly effective technique in the treatment of teenage drug abuse. Effectiveness is increased when the confronter is a peer with whom the client in treatment can relate. Teenagers are natural confronters who use the technique regularly in dealing with parents and authority. They may not like confrontation about their own problems, but overall they come to accept the method. As with any therapy, confrontation can be overdone and carry risk. Professional supervision is important.

Medical degrees are not essential. A number of the more successful programs are led by people with little in the way of formal counseling credentials. The physician who refers patients may feel some discomfort related to this, but when success rates and other factors are considered, his discomfort may give way to relief at finding hope for his patients.

Most desirable is an approach that utilizes the passionate strength of young former users tempered with the judgment, experience, and learning of age. A balance of subjective feelings and professional skill provides strong therapeutic potential. Peer counselors require close supervision, but with a minimum of training can become highly effective at reaching teenagers.

9. What Are the Ancillary Services?

MEDICAL. Is medical referral or examination on intake required? Who is responsible for the issues of contagion and diet? Who sees the children when sick, and who decides when a child should see a physician? Who oversees a child's medication needs?

A plan for emergencies should be in place to care for drug withdrawal reactions and other emergencies. Drug withdrawal reactions are fortunately rare in adolescent treatment programs. In the population covered by this book, heroin and barbiturate addiction are uncommon problems. Alcohol addiction is not, but the DTs of alcohol withdrawal are rare. This severe and potentially fatal condition, seen after years of drinking, is very seldom a part of adolescent alcoholism.

Adolescents with psychiatric problems are at least as likely to have drug problems as the relatively normal adolescent whose problems are primarily related to drug use. Any program that deals with a number of adolescent drug users is bound to have clients who will need psychiatric help. Even these should benefit from a drug-free program, but they will be less likely to recover if attention is not given to their underlying problem. How these young people are identified, referred, and managed should be a concern of the referring physician and parents.

Requiring psychiatric evaluation on intake may miss the point that almost all drug abusers have distorted thinking with elements of depression, paranoia, denial, and sociopathic behavior. Their underlying personalities may be mixed with their chemical personality and show up only when they are drug-free. Deviant personality characteristics of drug users may disappear with removal of drugs. Other psychological aberrations secondary to drug use should be managed in the course of the drug program itself.

EDUCATIONAL RESOURCES.   Children with a preexisting learning disability and subsequent low self-esteem are susceptible to drug
involvement. However, children with no preexisting learning disability who begin to cut classes, fall asleep in class, or arrive stoned
at class will develop a "learning disability" of drug use. Marijuana,
with its effect on short-term memory and attention span, may further
add to school problems.

George, age 15, was doing well in drug treatment and feeling
good about himself and his family relationship. He returned to school
ready to take on the world, but was stunned to find he still could
not do algebra. His frustration eventually led to resumption of drug
use. Programs that consider this very real situation may provide
educational evaluation and remediation for students like George in
hopes of forestalling such relapse.

GUIDANCE COUNSELING.   The younger adolescent leaving treatment returns to school, but the older child may be faced with a major
career decision. The anxiety produced by trying to decide between
job and college (and which job and which college) can be strong.
Adolescents often react by postponing decisions that will not get
easier with time. Recidivism rates are apt to be lower where teenagers
leave the program with fairly definite and realistic short-range goals.

Guidance counseling, educational assistance, and psychiatric/
psychological services need not be part of any drug program, but
must be recognized as needs for many children. Programs should be
able to work well with those community resources available to them.

Programs should provide feedback to referring physicians and
make it known how they wish referrals to be made. Physicians are
most apt to entrust their patients to the care of consultants who keep
them informed as to the progress of therapy and those plans for
aftercare with which the physician may need to involve himself.
Mutual respect between program and referring physician is most
desirable. The informed and involved primary care physician can
add much support to the family and client.

10. Is There Community Outreach?   Successful programs often reach out to the community and involve themselves with community efforts at education and prevention. They may make themselves available as resources to schools, churches, and civic groups.
Their mission in such roles should not be primarily to talk about

treatment, but to share insights they have gained about the reasons behind and patterns of adolescent drug use with an emphasis on prevention.

How well a program is received in a community and asked to assist in community efforts is a sign of its effectiveness. Most towns would like to deny that drug problems exist for their children. Areas in proximity to drug programs may express initial fear at having "addicts" close at hand. With time these objections should fade as the program serves its function of returning healthy young people to a society that had previously ignored them or seen them as incorrigible.

11. What Are the Intangible Factors? Look for optimism and positive attitudes on the part of staff members. Drug treatment is difficult. Rules often need to be very strict and rigid, especially in dealing with young people who have compulsive drug use problems and who have paid little attention to rules in their past. Feeling loved is equally as important as learning to obey rules. All effective behavior modification techniques employ negative and positive consequences. The balance of negative vs. positive varies greatly from one program to another and from staff member to staff member. Fear and discipline may more closely correlate with short-range improvement, but love and encouragement will correlate better with long-range change. Where either seems out of balance, success rates may suffer. Evaluation of the balance between the "tough" and the "love" components of "tough love" may come from talking with staff, parents, and young people. Look for smiling faces.

12. Does the Program Evaluate Itself? The whole business of adolescent drug and alcohol abuse as it now exists is new and changing. Treatment plans exist that seem effective, but are often widely at variance with older and more accepted methods. Even the effective programs continue to change in attempts to improve. Drug treatment is such a personal business that even those programs that appear stable may in reality be changing as their staffs, clients, and families change.

There is a saying in political campaigning that only 5% of the effort pays off—the problem is, no one knows for sure which 5% that is. Much of what goes on in therapy may be unnecessary, some may be harmful, and the really successful ingredients may be unknown. Clinical trials indicate that when two or more treatment modalities are used in combination, treatment outcome improves considerably.[197] As programs change, some method of evaluation is valuable to judge if things are getting better or worse. Objective criteria for evaluation may be difficult, especially for those emotionally involved in day-to-day operations. At a minimum there should be numeric figures for average duration of treatment, percentage completion rate, and numbers maintaining recovery one year after graduation.

RELAPSE

There may be relapse for even the best treatment programs. This does not necessarily mean the program has failed, but is often just being tested by a person not quite ready to accept the fact of his disease and the need to stay with his new direction. Short refreshers in the same program setting are often very effective. Some children will drift from program to program, sort of shopping for a different answer to their problem, before they settle in with who they are and what they must do.

SUMMARY

Robert L. DuPont, M.D., the founding director of NIDA and currently president of the ACDE, made the following comments regarding this chapter:

"In terms of thinking about treatment, there are several principles that underlie all successful approaches: (1) First is the use of *education*. They tell drug-dependent youth and their families what is wrong and what to do about the problem. This is in dramatic contrast to the traditional psychotherapy approach, which relies on such techniques as "Tell me what you think." (2) Successful programs insist on *drug-free living* without compromise. (3) They involve the *family* actively in the treatment, reinforcing the health of the family rather than focusing on its pathology. Often this is done in family groups. (4) They have substantial *duration* and *intensity*. They are not brief or casual. (5) They reinforce *prosocial, community-based values and lifestyles* (love, duty, hard work, caring for others, etc.). (6) They have *structure*—a beginning, a middle, and an end (or "steps" or "stages").[192]

Treatment of drug use will vary depending on stage of involvement, community resources, and desired goals of therapy. The bottom line in the evaluation of any treatment plan is its long-range effectiveness in reaching desired goals. What seems least conservative in therapy may, in fact, be the most conservative if less rigorous approaches lead to failure or delay of recovery.

10

Prevention Through Laws and Education

Should we aim our prevention efforts at decreasing the supply of drugs or at reducing the demand? There are some who believe that stronger laws and stronger law enforcement are the answer to our drug problem. There are others who believe the answer lies in education. Advocates of both these beliefs are guilty of proposing overly simplistic solutions to a problem of complex cause. There are many factors responsible for our drug use epidemic. Paying attention to each etiologic factor would seem the best avenue to effective treatment of the problem.

A look at a standard Venn diagram (Fig. 10–1) is helpful in understanding the multiple factors involved in causation of the drug problem. This diagram suggests in graphic form that trouble occurs only where there is an overlap of factors as represented by circles in the diagram.[198]

The three general areas involved in the cause of the drug epidemic are the strengths and maturity of the individual child, the messages and support systems of his environment, and the availability and attractiveness of drugs to him. It is obvious that if there were no drugs, there would be no drug problem and that if the individual were stronger, there would be less risk. Approaches to the drug problem that focus on just one part of the puzzle are less likely to be effective than an approach aimed at all three general

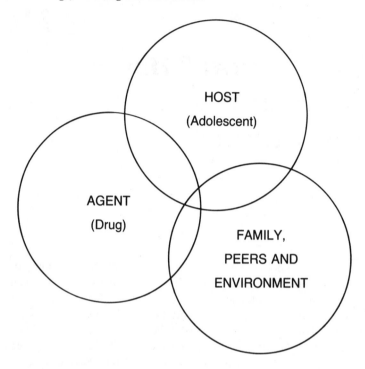

Fig 10–1.
Standard Venn diagram illustrates overlap of factors involved in adolescent drug abuse. (Adapted from MacKenzie R.G.: The adolescent as a drug abuser: A paradigm for intervention. *Pediatr. Ann.* 11:659-668, 1982.[198])

areas. In this chapter we will look at decreasing the attractiveness and availability of drugs by education and legislation.

A nonblaming approach is important. If one is tempted to use a simplistic approach to drugs, then one may also be tempted to assign blame for the problem to schools or the police. An approach that builds on mutual support and cooperation of schools, parents, police, students, and medical community will be most effective. Assignment of blame should be considered secondary to acknowledging that a problem exists and working together towards its alleviation.

THE ROLE OF THE SCHOOL
General

School administrators are generally fed up with those who would blame the drug problem on inadequate education and lack of controls in school. Many are frustrated and often angry at the assumption that it is their responsibility to set things right, because they believe this implies in a way that they are the cause of what has happened. Too much reliance on schools to right social wrongs is not new. They have been given major roles in racial integration, sex education, and a variety of other programs. They have seen mainstreaming of the retarded, exceptions made for pregnant students, teachers unions, budget deficits, and scoliosis-screening weeks, and they are now asked to solve the drug problem. Many school teachers entered the field because they liked children and enjoyed teaching. They can be very helpful in antidrug efforts, but they will be less likely to assist community efforts if they feel they are being held responsible for the current crisis.

Becoming More Aware

School administrators and teachers often deny drug problems exist in their schools. Students rarely do. Some of this denial may be based on an understandable reaction to a fear that they will be blamed for the problem and expected to correct it. Denial is just as often based on ignorance of what current drug and alcohol abuse are and how they may be recognized. Before teachers can teach, they must know the facts about drugs, alcohol, and adolescents. As long as they think experimentation is harmless and natural, they will be unable to deliver strong antidrug information. They should learn how to identify the drug user and know what to do for the child suspected of problem use. They should not be expected to preach.

Presentation of up-to-date and factual material should be adequate.

Teaching the Facts

Schools must join parents in educating children about the dangers of drugs. When armed with facts, people can and do change behavior. Adults demonstrated this in the decade from 1970 to 1980 with a 25% reduction in death rates from the two major killers, heart disease and stroke.[7] Although no one knows exactly why these improvements occurred, we do know that in the same time period there was a decrease in use of tobacco, saturated fats, and salt coupled with an increase in regular exercise.

Adolescents also have modified their health behavior. When daily use of marijuana by high school seniors reached its peak in 1978, there was a widespread belief in its harmlessness, with only 35% of seniors believing daily use was dangerous (see Table 1–1, Chapter 1). By 1982 when 60% believed daily use was risky, the number of daily users tumbled to 6.3%, a 41% reduction in 3 years. Tobacco smoking also decreased markedly over these same years and was associated with a rise in the number of students who believed that daily smoking was dangerous. With additional education about the harmful effects of drugs, further improvements may be anticipated.

Identifying and Helping Drug-Using Students

Each school must have a plan for intervention with the child suspected of drug use. Teachers who see children asleep in class or acting strangely should know how to respond. Help for the child must be the key word. Punitive measures may be dictated by law or be useful to push the child into treatment, but the focus should be on returning the child to the classroom in a condition receptive to learning. Teachers must teach, but they cannot do this when children sleep, disregard assignments, or disrupt other children in class. One plan for intervention involving six steps is outlined here.[199] This plan, which is being used at Cleveland's University School, may have more relevance for private schools, but parts may be applicable also to public schools.

1. Select a number of faculty members to receive intensive training in identification and understanding of the child who is chemically dependent. This training should include age-appropriate techniques of confrontation and intervention.

2. Communicate to the rest of the school staff and students the need to channel drug concerns to those trained to respond to them.

3. Acquaint the faculty with the signs and symptoms of drug use (Chapter 2), and establish clear procedures for referral of students with suspicious behavior such as truancy, falling grades, tardiness, or sleeping in class. Students so identified should be confronted by the trained faculty about their behavior and asked specifically about drug use.

4. Parents should be notified of problem behavior and told that such behavior may be a sign of drug use. Teachers may feel reluctant to report suspected drug abuse use to parents for fear of legal repercussions. Oklahoma and Maryland have recently adopted model ordinances to protect school personnel from such reaction. In those areas where school attorneys advise against notification of parents, alternate options should be spelled out by the school administration. Even where legal protection seems adequate, great care should be taken to insure that this meeting does not get out of control with emotional outbursts or angry denial by parents. It is best if the trained staff have a plan of action and designated leader. Having both parents present is a good idea. At the meeting specific items of concern should be pointed out. These might be to the effect that the child has been tardy for class five times in one week, has slept in class once, has changed in appearance, and is falling behind in homework. If drugs or cigarettes have been found in the child's possession, the finding should be mentioned. The parents should be asked about drug use.

The team should be prepared for angry response and denial. Some parents will blame their children's school difficulties on the school and teachers. Although such blame may be warranted on occasion, it is more often a sign of parental denial of the fact that their child is slipping. The team should be trained in dealing with this anger. The more factual and less accusing the better. There is always the risk that the meeting will result in abuse to the child when he gets home. This possibility may be lessened if it is discussed. The meeting should end with a specific plan of action and a contract relating to the child's behavior. It is best if the child can be involved in the terms of the contract. The message parents and child receive from the school should be that the behavior must improve.

5. If the problem behavior continues after such a conference, the school may suggest professional evaluation by someone skilled in adolescent chemical dependency. Private schools may insist on such evaluation. Public schools may also insist where behavior infringes on the rights of other students.

6. If the diagnosis of chemical dependency is established, the school may assist in the transfer of the child to an appropriate treatment facility. Parents may need much support at this time.

Treatment

School systems across the country are adopting alternative education and "time-out" programs for drug users. They are to be saluted, because they have acknowledged the existence of drug use among their students. Unfortunately, though, few of these programs are likely to be successful, because referral is rarely made before stage 3 of drug use. These programs may fail because most do not address the issues of family disease, alternative peer groups, and aftercare. Even more important, few insist on or can enforce absolute abstinence from drugs and alcohol.

Those schools that identify and report drug users are to be commended. The responsibility for providing drug therapy, however, is not a school function. The role of the school is to teach. Retaining a chemically dependent child in school ignores the fact that such a child is not working up to his full potential. Bad grades may be a late sign of problems. Good grades may continue for a while in chemically dependent children because of superior intelligence or an ability to cheat. Experience at Straight, Inc., is interesting in that students who returned to school after treatment were often so highly motivated that they not only made up for months lost, but frequently went on to their best academic years ever.

Schools should *treat drug abuse as a contagious disease*. Not only is the drug-using student in trouble, but so are those around him. In his need to find acceptance, he will try to convince his peers that drug use is all right. As his use progresses, he will increasingly need money, and selling drugs to classmates becomes more and more likely. In addition to these obvious, direct messages from users, students note when schools turn their backs on drug use, and such nonresponse may be seen as approval. If marijuana were associated with aggressive behavior, it would be much harder to ignore the users. It is easier to overlook lethargy.

Setting Good Examples

Teachers who have drinking problems or who use drugs need to be seen as poor role models. They should be offered help for their problems or removed from contact with students, especially if their attitudes and lifestyles seem to condone the use of drugs. Teachers who believe that alcohol and drug experimentation are a normal and acceptable part of growing up need to do some rethinking.

Enforcing Existing Rules[200]

Bill Rudolph, principal of Atlanta's Northside High School, has gained national recognition for changes in drug-related behavior among students at his school. Rudolph, who does not consider himself an expert on drugs, was assigned to Northside in 1977 and set as his goal improvement of the school's educational position. He attacked an existing drug abuse problem by restating existing rules and strictly enforcing them. He was encouraged and supported in his efforts by a strong and active parent movement.

The five rules for Northside are (1) anything illegal out of school is illegal in school, (2) the law requires children under 16 years of age to attend school, (3) it is a student's responsibility to get where he is going on time, (4) no one may interfere with anybody's right to be at school (or in educational jargon, "obstruct a student's access to education"), and (5) rules 1 through 4 will be obeyed. Where illegal drugs are involved, police (not parents or counselors) are called. Truancy is taken seriously and reported. Tardiness is punished.

The results have been outstanding. The school's SAT and achievement test scores have increased yearly. Drug-use incidents on campus have declined from three to four per week to three to four per year. Student involvement in extracurricular activities has quadrupled, and the quality of participation has improved. Girls soccer and other new sports have been added. The track team is nationally ranked. In 1977, 20% of students opted for courses above the required state minimum. In 1982, 80% chose courses above these minimum requirements. As Rudolph is fond of saying, "Northside has been lifted out of the quagmire of mediocrity."[200]

Supporting the Parent Movement

Parent groups do better with school support and approval. They have much to offer the school in terms of volunteer help, assisting with such problems as truancy calls, and chaperoning of school functions. In Naples, Fla., truancy rates dropped markedly after parents began calling other parents notifying them that their child was missing from classes. Peer groups that want to provide alternative activities for students and approach new students about such things as drug-free parties also benefit from school support.

THE ROLE OF THE LAW
General

Police, judges, and legislatures cannot do it alone either, but they can help. Their cooperation with community efforts is also more readily obtained when a nonblaming approach is used. The frustration of police concerning drug issues and their refusal to accept blame for the problem is not difficult to understand.

Legal loopholes have been particularly frustrating. Officers tell of risky operations leading to little or no action. For every drug arrest, too few come to trial, too few of these lead to conviction, too few convictions are appropriately sentenced, and too few complete their sentences. Policemen do not like being called "pigs" by vandalistic youth or the parents who come to their rescue. They are unhappy with media portrayal such as "The Dukes of Hazzard," of law officers as morons. Most will admit there are bad police officers, but would remind others there are also bad doctors, parents, and teachers.

Being Aware

Police are more apt to be aware of the prevalence of drug use than other adults. They need also to be made aware of the health risks. Marijuana and alcohol dangers should be known to them. They are often aware of the relationship of alcohol to highway accidents. They need to know that marijuana, Quaaludes, and other drugs can also be involved with a decrease in driving ability. The relationship of vandalism, shoplifting, breaking and entering, and violent crime to drug use should be known. Caring for youngsters in trouble is better given with knowledge that these young people may be suffering from the disease of chemical dependency.

Dealing With Youthful Offenders

Each community must establish clear procedures for dealing with the child who violates drinking and drug statutes. To do otherwise is to sacrifice not only the involved child, but also his peers, family, and eventually his community.

It is in children's best interests if drug hangouts and bars that attract juveniles are identified and closed or well patrolled. Children in schools across the country know the more common spots near their schools for drug sale and consumption and will willingly impart such information when asked. Among the locations frequently mentioned are school parking lots, vacant woods near their schools, convenience stores, game rooms, and certain school bathrooms. To ignore this readily attainable information is to accept drug use.

When apprehended, school children must be dealt with fairly, evenly, and firmly. A gentle warning with confiscation of drugs is not helpful to the child and on more then one occasion has been interpreted by young people as a way for policemen to obtain drugs. These children must be booked and their parents notified. Overreaction may be equally dangerous. Hopefully, the days of jailing youthful offenders for first offenses are a thing of the past.

Fear of overreaction has led to widespread underreaction. Some punishment for illegal activity is warranted, and arrest for possession or use should not be excepted from this rule. A community plan for dealing with first offenders might sentence them to attend a class on drugs and to perform a weekend of civic work. A second offense might lead to after-school work for a week plus two weekends of civic activity. Subsequent offenders would receive harder sentences.

Judges who understand chemical dependency will be better able to deal with youngsters. Before assessing a penalty, they might refer offenders to professionals skilled in evaluation of this disease. Certainly offenders who have received probation for a first offense and are again found guilty deserve such referral. To send a chemically dependent person to jail and later release him untreated will usually assure a return to crime.

The primary emphasis should be concern for the child. The father who hires the best attorney available to defend a son obviously guilty of driving while intoxicated is doing his son no favor. The child would be better served by an attorney who argues for probation. Such probation should be contingent on attendance in a program that deals with chemical dependency and/or the dangers of drunken driving. If other facets of the child's behavior indicate drug problems or if there are repeated driving violations, evaluation directed towards treatment should be mandatory.

Decreasing Drug Traffic

Most children in stage 3 drug use sell drugs occasionally or frequently to support their habit. These troubled young people must be dealt with, but for many the major concern is those who reap huge drug profits.

Huge profits may be made in the drug business, and as long as profits outweigh risks, criminals will surface. As long as people are dependent on drugs, profiteers will rise to serve them. Addressing the issue of decreasing supply are six areas of fairly recent government involvement. There has been increased international cooperation, return to the use of paraquat, partial repeal of the posse comitatus statute, outlawing of drug paraphernalia, confiscation of property from drug dealers, and a federal task force on drugs.

International Cooperation

Over 90% of the illicit drugs consumed in this country are produced elsewhere. A top federal priority is crop control of the opium poppy, the coca bush, and the marijuana plant at their source. Key strategy objectives are to (1) assist foreign countries in this effort, (2) develop intergovernmental mutual assistance treaties aimed at facilitating judicial action, (3) encourage other nations to support international narcotics control programs, (4) encourage international development banks to prohibit loans that might enhance growing crops for illicit drugs, (5) curtail diversion from legitimate international channels of chemicals and pharmaceuticals necessary for manufacture of illicit drugs, and (6) increase effectiveness of international organizations involved in drug control.[119] The billions of dollars involved in the drug industry have helped to support government officials in many areas and on occasion have made cooperation most difficult.

Posse Comitatus

Until partial repeal of this statute in 1980, federal law enforcement agencies and military forces were severely limited in being able to assist local law enforcement efforts. The posse comitatus statute, passed in 1878 by Southerners newly elected to Congress, outlawed the use of federal forces to deal with civil problems. Drug dealers in Florida often had more modern and sophisticated equipment than the local sheriffs in the counties where they brought the smuggled goods. The partial repeal of the posse comitatus statute did much to change this with stepped-up Coast Guard involvement and use of such sophisticated equipment as AWACS planes. It also made possible cooperative efforts of federal agencies such as that of the FBI and the Drug Enforcement Agency with local law enforcement forces.

Drug Paraphernalia

An early target of angry parent groups was the paraphernalia industry, which sprang up almost overnight selling drug wares in malls across the country. These neighborhood stores with their "how-to" literature, rolling papers, bongs, roach clips, and look-alike drugs have now been legislated almost completely out of existence.

Paraquat

Though never illegal, paraquat spraying of marijuana crops fell victim to a National Organization of Marijuana Laws campaign aimed at producing hysteria about its toxicity. People tended to lose sight of the fact that the "dreaded" paraquat is the herbicide most widely used in the world today. Four million pounds are used annually in the United States. This information has been largely ignored in press reports of marijuana spraying and paraquat. When 1 qt of paraquat was diluted in 100 gals of water and sprayed on an 80-acre field of cannabis in Red Bay, Fla. (1982),[201] press coverage was extensive and coupled with reports of human toxicity.

All agree that paraquat is highly effective. Safety is the concern. Pharmacologists at Exxon have extensively reviewed the literature and believe their product is safe for controlled use. Those who worry point to the risk of smoking marijuana that may contain residue of the highly corrosive agent, even though no human case of such poisoning has been verified. Among the reasons given for this safety record is the fact that paraquat is biodegradable and does not persist long on the sprayed plant. The active material that remains is largely pyrolyzed, with only 0.02% of the smoked material reaching the lips.[202] That which does is highly water soluble, which may mean that little if any escapes the mouth and upper airway. What does pass is widely dispersed and is believed by many to be a negligible hazard.

When paraquat was first widely used in Mexico, marijuana growers quickly realized that if paraquat-sprayed plants were harvested before exposure to sunlight, desiccation would not occur. Paraquat destruction is also facilitated by sunlight, and marijuana that was picked early to avoid plant breakdown would be expected to have higher levels of the active chemical. In 1978, the last year the U.S. government assisted Mexico in paraquat spraying, 13% of the samples of marijuana confiscated in this country were found to be contaminated with paraquat.[201]

The coughing reported after inhalation of paraquat-treated marijuana smoke is believed to be due to the presence of 4,4′-dipyridyl, a product of paraquat pyrolysis. This compound is a pulmonary irritant, but apparently not an agent of permanent change.[73] The clinical significance of low levels of residual toxic chemicals on marijuana is not known, but because toxicity is a function of both dose and duration of use, it is expected that the paraquat controversy will continue. The potential risk of paraquat toxicity must be weighed against the known risks of a marijuana epidemic.

Forfeiture of Property

Risks of doing business have been considerably increased by the recent imposition of much higher limits of bail bond more in keeping with the profit figures involved for the drug trafficker. Of even more economic import has been the passage in several states of laws that allow civil forfeiture of the property of drug dealers. The legal requirements for civil cases are considerably easier to make than those for criminal action. Criminal cases assume the suspect innocent until proven guilty beyond a reasonable doubt and often involve lengthy court appeal procedures. Civil forfeiture of cars, planes, homes, and other possessions in Texas and Florida may be strong deterrents.

Task Force on Drugs

President Reagan's appointment of a task force on drugs and the assignment of a large strike force to the Miami area had immediate and significant results in decreasing that city's drug-smuggling industry. The cooperation of several federal agencies with local law enforcement agencies was made possible by this presidential commitment and the partial repeal of the posse comitatus statute. Such major drug busts as that involving automobile manufacturer John DeLorean would not have been possible without these new legal initiatives.

Legalization of Marijuana

There are seven common reasons given for legalization of marijuana, none of which hold up well to close scrutiny:

1. *Marijuana users are guilty of a "victimless" crime.* The argument is that the mature individual who likes to smoke, knowing the risks involved, has the right to make this free choice. However, when the rights of others are involved, this "victimless" crime claims victims. Those who may be affected are the family, friends, and employers of the chemically dependent. Society is affected by his highway performance, his military performance, and in the long run by his school performance. When members of society perform at less than their potential, society is the victim.

2. *Tax revenue or "sin" taxes may be provided by legalization.* In the balance this might prove a very bad deal. In 1975 the estimated cost to society of alcohol abuse in this country was $43 billion.[203] This $43 billion includes the cost of treatment, accidents, and lost productivity, but does not include the suffering of family abuse, suicide, and depression. There is little reason to think marijuana legalization would do otherwise.

3. *Legalization would promote responsible use.* It is believed by some that the guilt of using an illegal substance contributes to an increased need for chemical relief. Others believe that by legalizing marijuana we would be better able to keep children uninvolved. Neither of these arguments hold up well if we realize that there are 3 million American children between the ages of 14 and 17 who are problem drinkers or alcoholics in a society[1] where alcohol is legal. Cirrhosis of the liver, now the no. 7 leading cause of death in adults, did not appear on the charts during prohibition. The evidence does not speak for moderate or responsible use.

4. *We would save money fighting crime, and the Mafia would be better controlled if we legalized marijuana.* Following this line of reasoning, we might next legalize heroin and prostitution. It does cost money to control crime, but with forfeiture laws as outlined above, this government enterprise may eventually more than pay for itself. Just as repeal of prohibition did not stop the rise of organized crime, neither should we believe legalization of marijuana would. Even if marijuana were legalized, a market would remain for stronger and stronger varieties of cannabis, and illegal industry in cocaine, Quaaludes, and heroin would continue.

5. *Marijuana laws are generally unenforceable and, because they are so widely broken, seem to give the dangerous impression that it is permissible to break certain laws.* Even this argument warrants further scrutiny. Most adults admit to having broken the 55 mph speed law on occasion. Despite this, there is no denying that highway deaths have declined markedly since the imposition of 55 mph as the legal limit. The illegality of marijuana does serve to deter some from use and subsequent dependency and is of value for this if for no other reason.

6. *You can't legislate morality.* This well-worn expression may or may not be true, but there is evidence to show that you can legislate behavior. The only consistently favorable effects on drug epidemics have occurred in societies that decided to put an end to them using measures aimed at stamping

them out. The rates of opium addiction in the United States, for example, were reduced by 90% between the years of 1923 and 1939[204] with neither treatment or research. The instrument was a firm, restrictive, and consistent drug policy.

An epidemic of amphetamine use occurred in Japan after World War II. By 1954, 2 million Japanese were abusing amphetamine tablets, and over half a million took IV injections. A dramatic change in drug policy introduced sentences of 3 to 6 months for possession, 1 to 3 years for pushing, and 5 years for illicit manufacture of drugs. In 1954, 55,600 persons were arrested in Japan for amphetamine offenses. By 1958 only 271 persons were arrested, and the epidemic was over.

The Japanese had learned from the Chinese, who between the years 1951 and 1953 put a stop to a 300-year-old epidemic of opium smoking. At the time there were 20 million active opium smokers in China, 10% of whom were sentenced to labor camps. The other 90% quit on their own with neither treatment or psychotherapy.[204]

7. *Marijuana use cannot be stopped anyway.* Nils Bejerot, director of Sweden's Carnegie Institute, agrees with those who believe that the legal measures outlined here will only nibble at the edges of the drug epidemic, which he calls the present-day equivalent of earlier plagues. In an extensive study of drug epidemics,[204] Dr. Bejerot has found there is only one irreplaceable factor in the drug equation, and until we come to grips with that factor, the epidemic will continue. He believes elimination of the supply is not possible: As long as there are people willing to buy drugs, there will be pushers willing to profit from their needs. Complete eradication of the opium poppy and the cannabis bush, plants which are so easily propagated, is also not possible. It is the opinion of this noted psychiatrist that efforts aimed at decreasing the susceptibility of the child through education and improved parenting techniques will also largely fail. Only when the irreplaceable factor, the user, is given adequate reason to quit, will epidemics cease.

Initiation to drug use, as described in Chapter 2, typically occurs when a neophyte is introduced to a pleasure-producing chemical by a friend or older sibling. The initiator is usually still in the honeymoon phase of his own drug use in which he has had few if any social, legal, physical, or educational consequences to offset the euphoria he wishes to share. By the time he reaches the stage where such consequences occur, the person he initiated may still be in the honeymoon phase and initiating others to the "wonders" of drugs. Dr. Bejerot sees this early stage of drug use as the one that must be stopped if the epidemic is to be halted. Bejerot believes that only when a society makes it very uncomfortable to use drugs (as the Japanese did with amphetamines in 1954) can epidemics such as current marijuana use be halted. He does not favor a return to the harsh sentences that were meted out in this country in the 1930s. In Sweden he has recommended that drug users spend a month clearing the forests for their first offense, 2 months for the second, and so on. In a country that has accepted one drug responsible for 25,000 automobile-related deaths a year, another that when smoked kills over 200,000 people each year, and that speaks of "moderation" in drug use, it seems unlikely that the measures Professor Bejerot suggests will be soon employed. Until the time when national outrage reaches a point where such action is taken, efforts must be aimed at reducing somewhat the risks of a disease that will claim millions. Legalizing or decriminalizing marijuana would further fuel the epidemic.

SUMMARY

Neither laws or education can do it all, but both are greatly needed if we are to see a reversal of the drug use epidemic in progress. A cooperative, nonblaming, community-wide approach to the problem involving schools, law enforcement agencies, judges, and lawmakers could do much to augment the efforts of parents, children, and physicians.

Two very effective methods have been mentioned for dealing with drug abuse epidemics. These do not treat drug abuse as a disease, but rather as a contagious violation of existing rules and regulations. An understanding of chemical dependency is important for treating the individual abuser, but drug epidemics are most effectively terminated when experimentation is reduced or eliminated by legal action. One high school in Atlanta has been turned around by an administration that employed logical and inexpensive techniques to improve the quality of student education. Drug epidemics have been reversed in two countries that took a serious approach to discouraging drug use. There is much the government can do.

11

Areas of Controversy

There are considerable differences of opinion in many areas related to drugs, drinking, and adolescence. Particularly important are the issues discussed here, which affect profoundly the way one deals with drug education, prevention, diagnosis, and treatment. Hard data for this chapter are not readily available, and the discussion of each issue is obviously slanted by my own personal viewpoints. Each physician who deals with adolescents must resolve these sensitive questions for himself. How he resolves them may determine to a large extent the success he has in dealing with the spectrum of adolescent drug abuse.

Three major factors have helped shape my opinion. First was a heightened awareness of the prevalence of the adolescent drug and drinking problem. Second came an understanding of the progressive and serious nature of the disease process, and third was my knowledge of how successful treatment can be. Now I push hard for prevention, early intervention, and, where necessary, treatment. Those physicians who do not believe adolescent abstinence is a realistic option or who are unaware of successful treatment models may feel differently about the issues presented here. Those who believe that drug abuse is a sign of underlying problems and almost never the direct cause of problems will almost surely reach conclusions different than mine. Each physician and parent must weigh the facts for himself and decide what is just and appropriate for the child, the family, and the society in which we live.

The major questions covered here are: (1) Can we teach teenagers to use chemicals responsibly and moderately? (2) How seriously should we treat a teenager's right to confidentiality? (3) Is it ever permissible to force a child into treatment against his will (the issue of consent)? (4) A fourth emotionally charged issue relating to the question of trust is, is it ever permissible to search a child's room, read his mail, or eavesdrop on his phone calls?

MODERATION AND RESPONSIBLE USE

Responsible adults, in seeming acceptance of or resignation to the new phenomenon of widespread adolescent drug use, have added to our vocabulary such phrases as "moderate use" and "responsible use." Those who have suggested attitudes and practices aimed at nonuse by adolescents have been frequently branded as unrealistic or as not responsive to the rights and realities of adolescence.

Cigarette, alcohol, and drug use by adolescents is illegal. Indulging in illegal activity should never be considered responsible.

Even assuming that some adolescent drinking and drug use will not progress past stage 1, there is concern that what may be moderate use for an individual may not be moderate use for his peer group. Those teenagers who are "moderate" drinkers may set examples of "acceptable" drug use that will lead more susceptible young people to dependency.

Moderation is a word with many definitions that can be used to cover all of stage 1 and much of stage 2 drug use. By the time moderate drinking has become "immoderate," as it frequently does, a child may be lost. There are some who would speak of occasional bouts of immoderation as being responsible if the young person is wise enough not to drive at such times. Unfortunately one of the properties of intoxication is an alteration of judgment that often makes the otherwise sensible adolescent believe he can still drive when he obviously should not.

Another group of adults believe that "practice drinking," or controlled drinking at home, prepares a child for his later exposure to American social life. To my knowledge there are no studies to indicate that students who have learned to drink moderately in high school fare better with college drinking than do those who have abstained. I have heard numerous stories that lead me to believe the reverse may be true. Even if one assumes (which I do not) that social acceptance at college requires the ability to drink, I would trade 4 years of sober developmental maturation in high school for 4 years of drinking practice.

Adults have as much right and responsibility to insist on abstinence among our developing adolescents as they do to insist that younger children are transported in car seats. With time the irresponsibility of the "responsible use" approach may become more obvious.

CONFIDENTIALITY

The right of a patient to confidentiality is a key issue in dealing with children who drink and use drugs. As a child reaches maturity, it is proper to expect that he will assume more and more control over his medical care. Physician, parent, and child should work toward the goal of having the child reach independence in this area. As a child matures, he should eventually schedule his own appointments, give a good medical history, understand and consent to treatment, and eventually pay for medical services and prescriptions. With the acquisition of these skills and abilities, he should be granted increasing confidentiality of care.

With the demonstration of increasing medical maturity will also come an increasing right of consent to care. When 3-year-olds are judged by their parents and physicians to require medication, such medication should be given. Hopefully, they will consent to open their mouths to the proffered prescription and thereby participate in care. If they do not, other ways requiring less cooperation will be found. Where the child demonstrates little or no ability to participate in his medical care, little or no confidentiality should be expected. Where he shows higher levels of understanding about his medical situation, increasing degrees of confidentiality and rights to consent should be granted. As long as he is dependent on his parents, his parents rights and responsibilities must also be considered. Individuals concerned with their child's care cannot be glibly excluded. Between the extremes of a complete right of adolescents, expecting total confidentiality, to consent to treatment and the lack of such rights given newborns, there are many levels of what should be expected and granted.

The issues of children's rights, parents' rights and responsibilities, and consent to treatment are strongly involved in the issue of confidentiality. In some cases the serious nature of confidential information may be so obvious as to make health concern override other issues. An example might be the child who confesses serious thoughts of suicide. Most would agree that admission of suicidal intent by an adolescent mandates disclosure to parents. Determination of drug use is next in line. The question in this chapter is, should a physician inform the parents of an adolescent that their child is using drugs?

A number of factors must be considered. For some doctors the overriding factors in breaking confidentiality are a refusal of the user to accept the harmfulness of drug use, the inability of a chemically dependent child to stop use, the progressive nature of the disease, and the fact that drug use affects the health of more people than the user himself. The rights of his family and society must also be considered.

The report of the American Academy of Pediatrics Conference on Consent and Confidentiality in Adolescent Health Care[205] examined the thorny areas of controversy related to these issues. They concluded that adolescents generally should be entitled to confidentiality in their own health care and that presumption should be overridden only by good reason. Where drugs are involved, there would appear to be more than ample good reason. The report also commented on "an enduring need to balance delicately the relative rights and needs of minors to confidential health services with the relative rights and responsibilities of parents toward offspring."

The ability of adolescents to make mature health judgments varies from child to child and situation to situation. The seriousness of the problem is a factor as is "how the adolescent's decision affects the rights and interests of other persons." The developmental (not chronologic) age of the child should be taken into account. To be considered in this determination of maturity are (1) "satisfactory progress in school and moving towards reasonable goals for adulthood, (2) holding down a job, (3) managing day to day affairs in an independent and effective manner, (4) personal stability and apparent levelheadedness (omitting occasional impulsive lapses), (5) a sense of altruism and consideration of the rights, privileges and needs of others.''[205] Problems in many of these areas begin to show up in stage 2 drug use.

In the past, one of the main reasons for encouraging confidentiality with teenagers was related to concern about VD transmission. It was argued that more adolescents would seek treatment if their problem was not revealed to parents, and this seemed like a good idea. Whether granting such confidentiality has indeed had any important effect on the VD epidemic in progress has not been proven. Those who opposed confidentiality even in this area pointed out that VD might be the only indicator of a child with adolescent adjustment problems. Such a child may need increased parental support.

The child who himself seeks medical care because of a drug or alcohol problem may be a different story. This child demonstrates a degree of maturity by his admission of problem behavior. In seeking medical attention, he acknowledges that a health problem exists. In my practice only one young person has come for help in this manner. He was no longer a teenager, but at the upper end of the pediatric age range.

John, age 21, scheduled a consultation to discuss his concern about his drinking. He asked about options for help. His parents were not notified by the physician, but such was hardly necessary, as John had already spoken to them about his concerns and the scheduling of a consultation. John entered a treatment program and while there discovered that his marijuana use was also a problem for him. He did well in treatment, recovered quickly from one relapse, and is presently working, back in school, buying a house, planning his wedding, and attending at least two AA meetings a week. His parents were actively involved in his treatment and have come to understand their roles in his chemical dependency. They are very supportive of their recovering son.

For every John there are many, many others who deny use or lie about what they use and how often. There is no real point in checking a child's urine for cannabinoids if he admits use. Where checking does reveal the presence of these compounds, it is questionable whether the child has earned the right to confidentiality.

Some physicians lean towards protecting the rights of confidentiality even in those situations where the child has been less than honest. When they have made their diagnosis, which may have included a positive urine test, they confront the teenager. Time may be spent expressing concern about continued use and their strong belief that use must cease. The child is provided with literature and an opportunity to have his questions answered. An agreement is made to keep his secret with the understanding that the child agrees to give up use. A plan of follow-up is arranged to offer support while closely monitoring abstinence by urine screening. Changes in behavior are expected, and specific limits of performance are set. The child is made to understand the deep concern of the physician and the fact that the parents must be notified if the child is unable to quit on his own. For the adolescent in late stage 2, this method is most unlikely to work.

Consideration must be given to who the parents are. Where there is apt to be severe punishment as a parental response to a child's drug use, the physician must exercise caution. By presenting his findings in family conference and discussing the possibility of appropriate punishment, he may somewhat control the possibility of harsh parental overreaction.

Extreme caution must be used where parental alcoholism, child abuse, or incest are suspected. When these serious possibilities are considered, they should not be ignored even in the child who has no obvious drug problem. Where severely abusive conditions do indeed exist, the physician is mandated by law to intervene. Parents who deny their own drinking problems may still come to accept problems in their children. Realization of their own alcoholism often comes only after their child enters treatment and the parents come to understand the nature of his disease.

I practice in an attractive middle-class community where patients are generally brought in by their parents. Although divorce, alcoholism, and abuse exist as they do everywhere, the practitioner generally has a family to work with. Usually, these families care about their children, although in later stages of drug use, some are about to give up on them. Those physicians who practice in inner-city areas may have to face the problem of confidentiality and parental support systems from a different perspective. Children who do not have good family structure and daily adult support have a very poor prognosis once they begin drug use.

Each physician must decide for himself how to handle the issue of confidentiality with each child in each situation, understanding that protection of health is a central duty and obligation of health care providers.

SEARCHING A CHILD'S ROOM

The question of whether or not to search a child's room, read his diary and mail, and listen in on his phone calls touches an emotional and controversial area. I was once asked if a parent should ever read a child's mail. My reply of "no" was countered by the mother's reply that, because she was concerned, she had and in so doing had discovered her daughter was planning to commit suicide.

A lack of trust is implied when a parent searches a child's room, and this makes it difficult for physicians to suggest or for parents to perform such a search. Many teenagers have learned how to use the word "trust" to suit their own purposes. The parent who expresses discomfort about some phase of their adolescent's activities may often be stopped in his tracks by the child who says, "You don't trust me." Parents have somewhere gotten the idea that a lack of love is shown when trust is not given carte blanche. The parent's response may be along the lines of "It's not that I don't trust you, it's just that I worry" when they really mean that they do not trust their child in the situation at hand.

Trust should be given where there is reason to believe that it is justified. Children who are 3 years old should not be trusted to cross interstates. Children who are 9 years old should not be trusted to drive cars, and pediatricians should not be allowed to do brain surgery. Trust is granted on the basis of competence and performance. Parents want to trust their children and children want to be trusted, but there must be limits. The child who is trusted to drive a car and returns with alcohol on his breath and dented fenders needs to be trusted at a different level on his next outing.

James, age 16, had developed an explosive temper at home. His mother had set up a consultation to ask for guidance. She reported that this once-bright student had dropped out of school and had been discharged from several jobs because of poor performance and absence. She denied any knowledge of drug or alcohol use. When I asked whether she had searched his room for evidence of drugs, she seemed stunned that a physician who had cared for James since birth would ask such a question.

If I had suggested lumbar puncture, liver biopsy, or any number of similar invasive procedures, she might have been less shocked. It was not easy to convince her that James might be suffering from a disease that could kill him or others. Strong diagnostic efforts seemed indicated.

I pointed out that his behavior warranted such search, and any lack of trust that it implied was well earned. I also pointed out that although the room was her son's to use, it was paid, furnished, electrified, and cooled by his parents. The child's contribution to the family was indeed a negative one, with his refusal to participate made worse by his violent outbursts.

The mother agreed reluctantly to such a search and I then told her of the places in which teenagers hide their stuff. I gave her a brief introduction to stash cans, those look-alikes with removable tops that resemble soft drink or deodorant cans. I told her to look in the back of stereo speaker cabinets, in the hems of drapes, underneath dresser drawers, inside toilet tanks, and behind pictures— in short, to use her imagination in an attempt to outthink a bright child who had the advantage of help from peers and the paraphernalia industry. I told her to look for seeds, roach clips, bongs, rolling papers, *High Times* magazine, and other unusual possessions.

Children's ingenuity may be truly fantastic. One child who knew his father well knew that the expensive suit his father owned and loved would never fit him again. He knew that his father would not throw such expensive clothing away, so he stashed his pot in the inside pocket of the suit, which hung in his father's closet.

Privacy is a related issue. Where a child has earned trust by his performance and behavior, he may be granted a fair degree of latitude with his privacy. Indiscretions, behavior problems, and signs of rebellion that are isolated incidents need not be indications for searching a child's room, but such a possibility should be discussed with the child. The purpose is not to hang threats over the child's head, but to make it clear that his rights and privileges have limits and must be measured against family rights and the responsibility of his parents to protect him. Where there are strong indicators of drug use, search may become mandatory.

Drug use is serious business, and parents have a right and a responsibility to protect their children. Children do not have rights that allow them to destroy themselves. Rights of privacy are given in return for acceptable behavior. Like trust they must be earned. It may be no more a violation of a 16-year-old's rights to read his mail when adequate suspicion exists of dangerous drug use than it is to insist that a 3-year-old not cross the street unassisted. There is ample precedent for physicians refusing trust to adolescents with health behavior problems. A useful analogy may be drawn with the conditions anorexia nervosa and bulimia, in which denial (lying) and deceit should be expected. When dealing with these conditions, search for hidden discarded food or accompanying the teenager to the bathroom to forestall vomiting of ingested food may be indicated. The whole controversial area of search must be examined by each physician in the light of knowledge of the epidemic of drug and alcohol use, the rising adolescent mortality, and the nature of chemical dependency. Only when these things are considered should a risk-vs.-benefit judgment be made.

THE CHILD WHO DOES NOT WANT TREATMENT

Children with drug problems rarely, if ever, request treatment. This should come as no surprise. Likewise, virtually all alcoholic patients come into treatment as a consequence of some form of coercion.[197] Adolescents most often show a strong resistance to therapy and employ their best "conning" behavior to convince their parents that their family or environment is the source of their problems.[169] Many will have temper tantrums when informed that they need to embark on a program aimed at making them drug-free. These children may have become accustomed to setting their own rules and defying parental requests. Parents usually need help.

The physician or drug counselor who convinces the family that their child has a drug problem will have wasted the effort if the family does not follow through and enter the child in a treatment program. To make a diagnosis may be intellectually satisfying, but the real joy comes in seeing a child in recovery. There are difficult ethical and legal considerations involved, but it is my opinion that the rights of the child are best served when he is firmly pushed into treatment. Physicians who are unaware of the great record of success in some treatment programs, who are ambivalent about the treatment programs in their area, or who do not believe that chemical dependency is a primary disease are less likely to share this opinion and less likely to see their patients enter effective therapeutic programs. Few physicians ask a child whether he would "like" to have his hot appendix removed.

According to AA a person has to hit bottom before he can be motivated sufficiently to seek recovery. If we are willing to wait for children to hit bottom and voluntarily accept treatment, we should be aware of some unpleasant possibilities. Death by suicide, accidents, or homicide is a real one. Another is entrance into the ranks of the "new drifters" (see Chapter 2), where therapy is more strenuously avoided and where success is much less likely to mean return to full function. When a child reaches age 18, he will have increased legal rights to refuse treatment even if his developmental and dependency ages are much younger. Adolescence is an important developmental stage, and physicians should strongly encourage parents to take action without undue delay. If a child must hit bottom before he is motivated to enter treatment, the parents can be given techniques to "raise the bottom."

Programs that provide preintake counseling for parents can do much to help parents in this often difficult time. Parents of children in the program who have passed this hurdle may offer much support, encouragement, and specific suggestions that were helpful for them.

Most children must be pushed into treatment by a firm decision, made known to the child, that the child has run out of options. No longer is he to consider himself entitled to free food, lodging, and telephone in a home where he contributes nothing, shows disrespect for the other tenants, and refuses to comply with house rules, most specifically those related to drugs and alcohol. The only options offered to the child who has refused (or been unable) to clean up his act are treatment or flight. To the old "shape up or ship out" has been added "We love you, we know you hurt inside, and we're going to make you take the medicine you need." If suicide is threatened, stronger and more immediate steps aimed at incarceration may be required.

Teenagers will usually employ their best "conning" behavior to test the firmness of the parental ultimatum. The "enabling" parent must receive strong support to prevent a weakening of their resolve to enter the child in therapy. Some parents will accept their youngster back on any terms he wishes rather than let him face the dangers of "the street." The adolescent may run away and test both his parents and his chances of making it without them. He is likely to find that his skills and habits have ill prepared him for survival. When he runs out of friends who are willing to support him and put up with his behavior, he may increasingly come to appreciate the comforts of the home he fled. Upon return he should be immediately entered in treatment.

Parents whose children remain on the street engaged in profitable enterprises such as drug dealing and prostitution may wish to act more directly. Police and judges can be most helpful at this time by arresting these children, finding them guilty of the crimes in which they are engaged, and sentencing them to treatment. Some children may even then revolt and need a time to experience the "logical consequences" of their lifestyle, including a period of detention within the penal system.

In taking a child to a program such as PDAP, the child may be told that he only needs to go for an interview. It then becomes the job of the program to convince him of his need to enter treatment. Successful programs do this so well that many parents rely heavily on these skilled intervenors. I do not recommend lying to a child to get him in for program intake, but am not overly critical of those parents who bend the truth some to get their child to the center. Many drug-affected children have so overwhelmed their parents that the parents are unable to make them even comply with a request that they visit a counselor one time. Others, understandably, do not wish to offer the option of flight to children who have a previous history of leaving home and being returned only under duress.

Real dilemmas exist. Successful drug treatment requires motivation on the part of the user. Unfortunately drug use may have taken away all motivation except the drive to instant euphoria. Prolonged THC retention may further complicate the problem by exerting a long-term effect on the user's brain that delays his return to full rationality.

The goal of commitment to a straight life is not one that should be expected in the pretreatment phase of the child's life. His motivation to visit the program should come from a family that gives him little or no choice to refuse the initial interview. Physician support in this "tough love" decision can be most helpful to a family who has had little previous success in setting limits for their teenager. This support is more likely to be helpful when it comes from a physician who has a positive attitude about the treatment programs, does not see the child as a rotten person, and who believes treatment can work wonders. At the program, motivation should come from counselors who help the child look at his repressed bad feelings and offer a better way of living. You cannot force a child to be motivated any more than you can lead a horse to water and force him to drink. You do, however, increase the likelihood of success when you bring a horse to water or a child to a place for treatment.

Following his resignation to the fact that his family stands united in insisting he accept treatment, the child enters a new drug-free world. The blur of intoxication begins to wear off. His initial anger should be replaced by acceptance of his need for help and reliance on the program to make him better. Later he will come to know that the program is only a vehicle and that he himself will have to work on change. If the program is fully successful, there will eventually be a commitment to a new drug-free lifestyle.

SUMMARY

Before one can deal with adolescents and drug use, he must make decisions on the important issues of responsible use, moderate use, confidentiality, consent to treatment, and the use of invasive procedures that imply a lack of trust. I believe teenagers should not use psychoactive chemicals except when medically indicated and supervised. In my opinion use in any other fashion is irresponsible and immoderate.

Confidentiality and consent to treatment are not absolute rights, but privileges granted on the basis of a number of factors, among which are competence, trust, and maturational and chronologic age. Particularly relevant to these issues in the case of drug use is an understanding of the serious and progressive nature of chemical dependency and of its effects not only on the individual, but on his family and his society.

12

The Role of the Physician

Health implies more than just the absence of disease. To healing, the traditional role of the physician, have been added the tasks of disease prevention and health promotion. Lifestyles consistent with long and satisfactory life should be encouraged. In our stress-filled society, the physician must assume a major role in the prevention and management of stress-related health problems.

Pediatricians must reappraise their practices in light of what is happening to today's children. In 1940 the majority of deaths came from traditional organic agents such as infections. In 1980 approximately 75% of deaths resulted from organic disease related to styles of living. It seems inappropriate to spend such great effort on such relatively minor problems as phenylketonuria testing and screening for urinary tract disease and so little on prevention of the major killers. Reflecting this medical attitude, mothers who will bring a child for pediatric care at the first sign of a cold may not come in for help with temper tantrums and other stress-producing behavior problems, which they may see as normal phases of development.

PRIMUM NON NOCERE

The old medical rule "above all do no harm" may be applied to potentially dangerous prescribing practices and to the current medical ambivalence regarding adolescents and drugs. Not knowing about drugs and chemical dependency is one thing. Thinking one does, when one does not, and giving advice and making judgments on the basis of such ignorance is worse.

Prescribing psychoactive medication to adolescents may be hazardous even if done for good purpose. A study of 1,000 randomly selected New Haven, Conn., students in grades 10 through 12 looked at this possibility. Those students who had received three or more recommendations for a psychoactive medication by their physicians were 8.6 to 11 times more likely to be involved in nonmedicinal use than those who had received no such prescriptions.[206] The prescription drugs given were diet pills, sleeping pills, and tranquilizers. There is some question whether such prescriptions are the cause of problems or a sign of such problems. Whether they were prescribed for drug-seeking "con" artists or "disturbed" children who might otherwise have been at increased risk is not known, but enough question is raised to urge caution.

Inappropriate use of psychoactive drugs for minor complaints includes overly frequent use of elixirs with their high alcohol content, opiate-containing drugs such as paregoric, and numerous cough preparations.

The AMA has taken a serious look at the diversion of psychoactive prescription drugs into the illegal market and is spearheading a national project to coordinate the efforts of concerned agencies and organizations. The AMA effort is directed at identifying and sealing off the leakage of drugs from ethical to unethical uses. Physicians who contribute to the drug problem by overprescribing may do so with a variety of motives. These overprescribing physicians have been divided into four categories[207]: (1) the duped physician, who is conned by the drug seeker; (2) the dated physician, who has not kept up on the abuse situation; (3) the disabled physician, who may prescribe drugs for himself; and (4) the dishonest physician, who overprescribes for profit. To this AMA list should be added the careless physician, who neglects to safeguard his prescription pads from theft.

The whole issue of medicines given for placebo effect or symptomatic relief may need reexamination. Physicians are often pushed heavily by families to prescribe for conditions they know to be minor and self-limited. Not only does this practice increase the cost of care, but the child may be given the distinct impression that there is a drug for whatever ails him, and the way to feel good is to take something. The fact that all drugs have risk needs to be continually stressed.

Ambivalence on the part of the physician can also be harmful. Preaching moderation in drugs and alcohol use (rather than abstinence) and "expecting" teenagers to experiment as a part of growing up may give signals that are harmfully permissive. A spectrum of ambivalence exists, ranging from the position that drugs are immoral and should never be used, to varying degrees of resignation to the likelihood that teenagers will drink and experiment with drugs, to those who see nothing wrong with drinking or drugs in "moderation." There is enough evidence of the harmful health consequences of alcohol, tobacco, and marijuana to make strong statements about adolescent use without involving moral judgment. The Surgeon General, the AMA Council on Scientific Affairs, and the American Academy of Pediatrics all have made statements about marijuana and its health consequences.[92-94] Despite the fact that most physicians regard tobacco smoking as dangerous, there are differences of opinion about how strongly a teenager should be urged not to experiment or how strongly encouraged to quit once hooked.

Some physicians, well aware of the risks of alcohol and drug use by adolescents, believe that there is little that can be done to prevent such use. With this perspective, their efforts are aimed at stressing moderate use. Unfortunately, moderate use may not be possible for the child most susceptible to chemical dependency, and in suggesting it as a reasonable course of action, the physician may become guilty of contributing to progressive use. Other physicians, while understanding that many "normal" children will experiment, will continue to do everything they can reasonably do to discourage such use.

DIAGNOSIS

Awareness of prevalence of use and a high index of suspicion must usually precede the diagnosis of chemical dependency. In acute drug abuse (overdose) resulting in trauma or unconsciousness, the diagnosis should be fairly easy. Assuming the incident is an isolated finding rather than a symptom of dependency may be a mistake. Over 50% of all serious accidents are drug- or alcohol-related. Treating the injuries of such accidents without investigating the possibility of drug use is inadequate medical practice. A fair number of adolescents who are chemically dependent began their use by overdose on their first exposure to alcohol. An understanding pat on the back and gentle admonition to be more careful next time may be an insufficient physician response to such "marker" incidents.

Chronic abuse and dependency are not rare conditions, and diagnosis should be made regularly by the alert pediatrician. A knowledge of the stages of such use (Chapter 2) and of the characteristics of the user may frequently lead to an explanation for a child's changing behavior and/or physical symptoms.

INTERVENTION AND TREATMENT

The physician's rapport with the child and his parents makes him particularly well suited for the task of intervention. His training and experience in crisis management are valuable tools in presenting a diagnosis that is often seen as an accusation. Anger, denial, and guilt should be anticipated in child and parent and responded to in firm but gentle fashion. If the family is provoked to anger leading to a breakdown in rapport, nothing will be accomplished for the patient. Where the parents are unable or unwilling to accept a diagnosis, lines of communication must be kept open for further consultation. Unfortunately, some families will be unable to accept the diagnosis and the need for treatment. Hopefully some of them will eventually return to the physician who has not completely alienated them.

The physician should familiarize himself with treatment resources available to his patients and be able to provide parents with an evaluation of such resources. In some cases the physician must learn to work with programs that are suspicious or jealous of physicians, but are highly effective programs. Using the material in Chapter 2 to determine the degree of the child's involvement will assist in recommending a course of action. Where a child is believed to be in stage 1, families may be directed to approaches similar to those of stage 0, which involve preventive techniques. Knowing the progressive nature of the disease, the wise physician will establish follow-up techniques to monitor the effectiveness of suggested therapy.

PREVENTION

The pediatrician should talk to adolescents and their parents about the dangers of drug abuse and freely provide them with literature, but is this enough? The prophylactic approach, so well-outlined by Glenn[155] in his paper, "The Developmental Approach to Preventing Problem Dependencies," should speak directly to the pediatrician. Parents need specific help in teaching their children how to listen, communicate feelings, make rational decisions, defer gratification, and exert self-discipline. Children need to be made to feel they are responsible and useful members of their family and to be taught to identify with a higher power. The task is clear. The child's coping mechanisms must be built.

Anticipatory guidance begins with the prenatal visit. In this visit with the prospective parents, the pediatrician should establish himself as a listener who is available and willing to assist families in all aspects of child rearing. He should inquire about the parents' goals for their child, deal with bonding and bonding techniques, and comment on marriage as it relates to a child's self-esteem and development. Groundwork should be laid at this visit for subsequent family conferences at critical times in a child's development. Family meetings with the physician may be suggested at 6 weeks, in the second 6 months, around age 2, before school entry, before adolescence, before high school graduation, and after completion of high school. Whether these appointments are a part of the routine health maintenance visits recommended by the Academy of Pediatrics or whether they are free-standing consultation visits is up to the practitioner. Their value, in the eyes of the eminent child psychiatrist who recommended them, could be immense.[208]

How a physician proceeds with preventive counseling in his office will vary with his experience and with the time he makes available. Time spent alone with the teenager is recommended, but the long-term value of a brief discussion of drugs, sex, and depression has not been proven. The greatest value of such discussion may be to identify the physician as a person available and willing to openly discuss such subjects.

My preference in anticipatory counseling of adolescents is to allow for time alone with the teenager, but not at the expense of time with the teenager and parent together. When both are present I ask if there have been discussions about smoking, drinking, and drug use. I suggest that it is a parental responsibility to learn about these substances, and I offer reading material. Perhaps more important than factual data, I tell the parent, is establishment of a family position and policy on adolescent drug use. As an example of the latter, my 17-year-old son knows clearly that if he drives and arrives home in the family car with alcohol on his breath, we will talk about driving again when he is 19. The pediatrician will be most effective when he prods the family to discuss and deal with important issues on a regular basis. A single-shot discussion of sex or drugs with no follow-up at home is likely to be of limited value.

Anticipatory guidance should assist the family with their task of setting goals for their child that are consistent with good health. The aim should be eventual release of the child as an individual capable of mature and independent function. This does not imply that as an adult he need sever a family relationship of mutual support and respect. The all-too-frequent goal of perpetual happiness needs to be questioned.

The pediatrician has opportunities to discuss disappointment each time he is pushed to make an ill child well for a big event scheduled for the next day in the child's overly busy life. How a child learns to cope with illness and its restrictions will relate to how well he is building his self-image.[156]

Anticipatory guidance should help parents look at the issues of boredom, loneliness, rejection, frustration, defeat, pain, and death. For years many pediatricians and parents shared the belief that the role of the parent was to prevent all trauma from touching children. When a child was bored and upset, it was believed to be the parents' responsibility to act. Now when an infant cries at 5 days of age, his mother is faced with a difficult decision. She may have read a number of books saying that to let the child cry will be traumatic for him.

On the other hand, she may be getting signals from her mother-in-law that tell her if she always picks up the crying infant, she will spoil him. What should she do? An answer might be that she should do what she feels like doing based on her "gut" assessment of the cause of the crying. Sometimes she will want to pick up the infant, and at others she will not. The mother who is encouraged to develop her natural feel for her child will become increasingly able to deal appropriately with his signals. Some mothers try so hard to be perfect that they are afraid to attempt anything on their own for fear they will do something wrong. Mothers should be given permission to make mistakes and reassured that none of us are perfect.

The mother who shields her child from stress does little to prepare him for life. She should not put his fingers on the hot burner to teach about fire, but she should help him learn to deal with everyday problems. Sleeping and eating are both normal functions about which much stress may be generated. Pediatricians have great opportunity to help families develop approaches to preventing and dealing with problems in these areas.

Anticipatory guidance also involves knowing critical times in marriage and working to keep marriages healthy. It involves dealing with temper tantrums, toilet training, sibling rivalry, preparation for school, and normal phases of child development. It means anticipation of the problems of adolescence. The related issues of trust, rights, extension of privilege, and responsibility should be mentioned. Information and methods of discussing sex and drugs with children should be given. Help with career guidance and talk about moral and social development are important. In short there is much the pediatrician can do to help families make themselves and their children stronger and better able to deal with stress.

THE PHYSICIAN AS A COMMUNITY VOICE

Parents, students, schools, police, and others may turn to physicians for assistance in the war against drugs. The physician interested in community health should be prepared to help. He may be asked to give talks, serve on committees, or make statements about adolescent drug use. Once he has established for himself a position on such use, he may become a great community asset.

When talking to groups, each speaker should adopt a style with which he is comfortable and when possible use visual aids to assist him. How he presents himself and his material may be as important in reaching an audience as the material itself. In addition to the presentation of factual material, any message that the speaker wishes to impart should be identified by him before he begins. The more he knows about his audience, their interests, and their level of awareness, the more effective he is likely to be. If signs of restlessness and boredom are detected in the audience, a change of direction may be indicated, skipping over or speeding up what for them may be boring material. Allowing a stretch break and a time for questions may help. An excellent guide for speaking to audiences about drugs is available from the NFP.[209]

Speaking to Students

The toughest and most critical audiences can be students, but when a speaker reaches them, it is well worth his while. In high school assemblies, there are apt to be students in various stages of drug use, and the speaker who aims his message to all at the same time may have difficulty. Generally speaking, he is most likely to reach and be helpful to students in stage 0 or 1. He must remind himself that there are many in the audience who do not want to take drugs and are looking for reasons to say no. The message to them often makes more advanced drug users uncomfortable, and the speaker should be aware of their efforts to disrupt or discredit him. The speaker who is unprepared for such heckling is apt to lose his temper, which is exactly what some students would like him to do. If he does become angry, he may lose the respect of the nondrug using audience he seeks to reach. To prevent this, it is wise to limit the size of the group or insist on adequate faculty presence. Heckling may often take the form of talking to neighbors in the audience and drawing attention away from the speaker. Drug users can be funny, and if allowed to, will steal an audience, leaving the speaker frustrated and helpless. Attention given directly to the whispers and waiting for quiet can be effective methods of dealing with inattention. The speaker should come across as caring, informed, and strong. It is better still if he is entertaining and interesting. In truth a well-prepared speaker usually has no problems with students.

Students are most interested in material to which they can relate. Statistics bore them. Moral lectures turn them off. The speaker armed with good biomedical information can reach a teenage audience. He should be aware, however, that he may be bearing bad news for many and take care to couch such information appropriately. Lung cancer and other long-range consequences of drug use may concern adolescents less than being able to identify themselves or friends in one of the stages of drug use. Many students have seen people they cared about slide downward and been unable to understand what happened to them. Students should be cautioned about the risk of remaining socially close to drug-using friends for fear of joining them in a progressive disease. They may be advised that it is fine to tell someone you care for them and believe they may be destroying themselves. Campus leaders who think they can handle drinking and drugs should be reminded that, even if correct in their self-judgment, they may be responsible for leading others to destruction. Many students are looking for alternatives to drug use. With these they will need adult assistance. Presentations to students should be part of a planned program aimed also at parents and faculty.

Allowing time for questions is often the best way to reach young people, but the speaker should be prepared. Students generally like to be involved, and many speakers who present no formal material are very effective with audiences using a question and answer approach entirely. This may begin with the speaker asking questions of the audience and lead to questions in return. The speaker must be honest, avoid the use of put-downs, and stay in control. When he does not know the answer to questions, he should say so or ask if someone in the audience can help him. He may be tested with seemingly absurd questions such as "Can you get high on oregano?" or drug-related questions such as "Which is worse—smoking or chewing tobacco?" He should be prepared to answer honestly or parry questions such as "Have you ever been high?" and "How much do you drink?" Parrying questions might be "How do you feel about adults who drink?" or "How do you feel about the statement 'Don't knock it if you haven't tried it?'" which might also be applied to reckless driving and Russian roulette. If he is open and responsive, students will be more apt to open up with him. He should not attempt to be popular by compromising his views. I remember well the first young lady who came up to me after an assembly and said, "You're the first one who's ever told us it was okay to say no." After the session students may approach the speaker to talk about friends or family with problems or to seek more information for themselves. Those who express concern about their parents' drinking may be referred to Al-Anon, which usually is listed in the telephone book.

Speaking to Parents

Parents who attend drug talks are usually thirsty for information and usually are the easiest audience to address. These audiences often are skewed toward parents whose children are already in trouble and looking for specific management answers or clues to making the diagnosis at home. Preschool and elementary school parents are most interested in prevention or effective parenting techniques. Having a list of reading material or handouts can add to the long-range value of any presentation.

Speaking to Faculty

Most teachers are somewhat aware of the prevalence of drug use, if not of the dangers. Most are interested in clues helpful in identifying users. Many have seen drugged children in their classes, whom they have ignored for a variety of reasons. Most commonly the reason has been lack of a specific school policy dealing with such incidents. It should be pointed out that ignoring such occurrences is neither in the best interest of the affected student nor the best interests of other students, who may treat the teacher's non-response as acceptance of drug use. The teacher has a responsibility to report incidents for the purpose of helping the student. Neither rehabilitation nor punishment are the teacher's responsibility. A teacher's job is to teach, and stoned children cannot be taught.

The teacher can teach about drugs by example as well in the classroom. Those faculty members who would establish rapport by talking of their weekend social activities should rethink statements such as "Thank God it's Friday" if such means to them and students that "Happy Hour" is near. Faculty members should be encouraged and given techniques for assisting students interested in programs of drug-free activity. Faculty groups, like student and other groups, may be composed of members in various stages of personal drug or alcohol use. Those who would seek to justify their own use may make the speaker uncomfortable with their inattention or questions. For the sake of those teachers seeking information and assistance, the speaker should not overreact to leading questions and be drawn into making statements that are so polarized as to alienate a whole audience.

Relating to the Law

More than any other group, the police know that drugs are everywhere. Some lose sight, however, of the fact that much of the crime they see is drug- and alcohol-related and that approximately 60% of all those imprisoned may be chemically dependent. Many are frustrated by mixed messages from physicians and by a court system that seems to favor drug use. The physician should emphasize the importance of early intervention by the law and that "minor" incidents such as toking a joint or drinking under age should not be ignored. Many policemen who think they are doing young people a favor by letting them off with a warning would be better advised to make reports to their parents.

Judges must come to learn that drug use is not only a crime: it may also be an illness. The chemically dependent burglar who is sentenced to jail will probably return to burglary when released if his rehabilitation does not include drug treatment. With younger offenders and minor crimes, it may be helpful to couple probation with drug treatment as a way of service to the offender and his community.

SUMMARY

The current epidemic of teenage drug and alcohol abuse is wiping out parental and pediatric investment in early childhood care and protection. Pediatricians need to be aware of this epidemic, the clinical syndrome of such abuse, and the importance of its prevention or, where necessary, its early diagnosis and treatment.

APPENDIX A

Proposed Parent-Teen Guidelines

Social Life Outside of School

A. *Curfews* are necessary for safety and cooperation within each family and among families. The following are suggested:
   - School week: home after supper, except for specific event approved by parent.
   - Weekends: 9th grade—11:00 PM
                 10th grade—11:30 PM
                 11th grade—12 midnight
                 12th grade—12:30 AM
   - Holidays and vacations: 10:30 PM, except weekends as above, with reasonable exceptions.
B. *Parties* should be chaperoned by adults who are occasionally visible, and alcohol and drugs should not be available or served. In addition,
   - Small parties should be encouraged;
   - Anyone with alcohol or drugs should be told to leave the premises;
   - Parents should feel free to contact host parents and offer assistance;
   - Parents should have the telephone number and address of the

party and should expect a call from their teenager in case of any location change.

C. *Parent-teen cooperation* is vital, keeping in mind that parents can be held liable to civil and criminal charges if injury to a minor results from underage alcohol consumption or illegal drug use on their premises; moreover, a car can be impounded if it is stopped for any reason and ANYONE in the car is in possession of illegal drugs. In addition,

- Parents and teens should know where to reach each other by phone;
- Parents should be awake (or expect to be awakened) when a teenager comes in at night—this time is an opportunity for open communications;
- Parents should get to know the parents of their teen's friends.

(From Mannatt M.: *Parents, Peers and Pot*. Rockville, Md., U.S. Dept. of Health and Human Services, National Institute on Drug Abuse, 1979. Used by permission.)

Adolescent Failure Syndrome Test

An Aid to Parents Concerned About Children Who May Be Harmfully Involved With Drugs

	DOES NOT APPLY	POSSIBLY APPLIES	DEFINITELY APPLIES
1. A change in the family's communication with the adolescent. Refusal to take part in discussions concerning unacceptable behavior. Previous closeness may dissipate, and disciplinary talk is interrupted either by "he tunes me out" or angry outbursts.	0	1	2
2. Refusal of the adolescent to recognize the impact on the family of unacceptable behavior, e.g., arguments or intoxicated events or delinquent acts.	0	2	4

	DOES NOT APPLY	POSSIBLY APPLIES	DEFINITELY APPLIES
3. Concern expressed by others, i.e., siblings, classmates, teachers, other family members, or authority figures, concerning personality change, suspected drug usage, or traveling with the "wrong crowd."	0	2	4
4. Expressed concern for oneself, e.g., "I'm worried I might get involved with drugs or alcohol," or "My life is meaningless, and I want to die."	0	2	4
5. Involvement in hard rock music, preoccupation with rock stars, attendance at rock concerts.	0	1	2
6. "Rebellious" dress style, e.g., rockbeer commercial T-shirts, army jackets, worn jeans, long hair.	0	1	2
7. Poor choice of friends, choosing to be with kids known or suspected of being delinquent and/or involved with drugs and alcohol.	0	2	4
8. Mysterious comings and goings, frequent unexplained telephone calls and visits by unfamiliar youth.	0	2	4
9. Change in social group, grade school friends left behind for a more "down and out group."	0	2	4
10. Incidents of untrustworthiness, particularly incorrect explanations of absence from school or lies about location of parties or parental chaperoning.	0	2	4
11. Unexcused absences from school or missed classes.	0	1	2
12. Minor or major delinquent involvement, especially where participants were intoxicated or drugs were involved.	0	2	4

	DOES NOT APPLY	POSSIBLY APPLIES	DEFINITELY APPLIES
13. Any violence or threat of violence toward parents or siblings.	0	2	4
14. Any violent episode away from home, including injury to self or others.	0	2	4
15. Minor or major automobile accidents.	0	1	2
16. Vocal disrespect for parents, teachers, or other authorities.	0	1	2
17. Unhealthy relationships. This includes a variety of unfortunate social styles, e.g., isolation from any close friends, choice of older, perhaps delinquent friends, or choice of a single friend to the exclusion of all others. No healthy involvement or interest in the opposite sex.	0	1	2
18. Premature adult behaviors, e.g., seductive dress or behavior, pseudo-sophisticated "existential" concerns, unreasonable questioning, or rejection of family values, especially regarding "recreational" drug usage.	0	1	2
19. Early sexual involvement, e.g., concerns of pregnancy or discovery of birth control materials.	0	2	4
20. Mood swings, such as depression, irritability, or unexplained euphoria and talkativeness.	0	2	4
21. Sleep disturbances, particularly staying awake for long periods at night, or going to bed immediately after supper or returning home.	0	2	4
22. A drop in grade averages, perhaps accompanied by a stated loss of interest in academic pursuits.	0	1	2

	DOES NOT APPLY	POSSIBLY APPLIES	DEFINITELY APPLIES
23. Money problems: Missing money from purses or coin collections at home or babysitting jobs or homes of grandparents or holds a steady job but does not show money in savings.	0	2	4
24. Annoyance or tantrums occur when questioned, e.g., about possible drug involvement.	0	2	4
25. Cigarette smoking.	0	2	4
26. Discovery of marijuana, pills, or alcohol. Missing bottles of liquor or diluted liquor in the family supply.	0	2	4
27. Discovery of a diary recounting drug experiences or involvement with the drug scene or finding notes stating usage or drug exchange.	0	2	4
28. Episodes of intoxication, either marijuana or alcohol.	0	2	4

Parents should score their children on each item: 0 for not at all; the intermediate column for possible or single occurrence; and the "Definitely Applies" column where it applies without question or there has been more than one instance. The entire score on all items should then be added. A total of 8 should be viewed as suggestive, that is, worthy of gathering further information; a score of 12 or more is probable for harmful involvement with drugs worthy of further data gathering and an evaluation by a knowledgeable person. A score of 16 or more should be viewed as nearly diagnostic, a full evaluation should be carried out, and serious consideration should be given to seeking treatment.

REFERENCES

1. Donovan S.E., Jessor J.: *Problem Drinking Among Adolescents: A Social-Psychological Study of a National Sample*, Contract No. ADM 281075-0028. Report prepared for National Institute on Alcohol Abuse and Alcoholism, 1976.

2. Johnston L.D., Bachman J.G., O'Malley P.M.: *Student Drug Use, Attitudes, and Beliefs: National Trends 1975-1982*. Rockville, Md., National Institute on Drug Abuse, 1982 (available from National Institute on Drug Abuse, Division of Research, 5600 Fishers Lane, Rockville, MD 20857).

3. Bachman J.G., Johnston L.D., O'Malley D.M.: Smoking, drinking and drug use among American high school students: Correlates and trends, 1975-1979. *Am. J. Public Health* 71:1, 1981.

4. *Social and Economic Characteristics of Students*. U.S. Dept. of Health, Education and Welfare, Bureau of the Census, School Enrollment, U.S. Government Printing Office, various years.

5. School dropouts by state. *U.S. News and World Report*, May 30, 1983, p. 9.

6. Tuckfield B.S., Leary K.R., Waterhouse G.L.: *Multiple Drug Use Among Persons With Alcohol Related Problems*. Springfield, Va., National Technical Information Service, 1975.

7. Surgeon General: *Healthy People: The Surgeon General's Report on Health Promotion and Disease Prevention*. U.S. Dept. of Health and Human Services, 1979.

8. Alcohol-related highway fatalities among young drivers: United States. *Morbidity Mortality Weekly Rep.* 31:641-644, 1982.

9. RBI: Preliminary Results of 1988 Worldwide Survey of Substance Abuse and Health Behaviors Among Military Personnel; final report due 8/12/88. U.S. Department of Defense, 1988.

10. Louisell W.C., in Blasinsky M., Russell G.K. (eds.): *Urine Testing for Marijuana Use: Implications for a Variety of Settings*. Rockville, Md., American Council for Drug Education, 1981, pp. 45-47.

11. Korcok M.: Worksite anti-alcoholism saves jobs, money, medical news. *J.A.M.A.* 249:2427-2433, 1983.

12. Burnett J.: Safety Recommendations R-83-28 and 29. To W.H. Dempsey, President, Association of American Railroads, from National Transportation Safety Board, March 7, 1983.

13. Hastings J.: *The Hastings Report*. Tulsa, Okla., Oklahoma State Leg-

islature, 1979 (available from the Oklahoma State Legislature, 4148 E. 51st St. Tulsa, OK 74135).

14. *National Commission on Marijuana and Drug Abuse: Second Report*, stock No. 5266-00003., U.S. Government Printing Office, 1973.

15. Wilford B.B.: *Drug Abuse: A Guide For the Primary Care Physician.* Chicago, American Medical Association, 1981.

16. Nizama M.: Jerga utilizada por los consumidores de drogos. *Rev. Sanid.* 39:175-191, 1978.

17. Macdonald D.I., Newton M.: The clinical syndrome of adolescent drug abuse. *Adv. Pediatr.* 25:1-25, 1981.

18. Newton M.: *Gone Way Down: Teenage Drug Use Is a Disease.* Tampa, Fla., American Studies Press, Inc., 1981.

19. Johnson V.E.: *I'll Quit Tomorrow.* San Francisco, Harper & Row, 1980.

20. Hochman J.S., Brill N.O.: Chronic marijuana use and psychological adaptation. *Am. J. Psychiatry* 130:132-140, 1973.

21. McGlothin W.H., West L.J.: The marijuana problem: An overview. *Am. J. Psychiatry* 125:1126-1134, 1968.

22. Malcolm A.: The amotivational syndrome: An appraisal. *Addiction* 23:28, 1976.

23. Cohen S.: Cannabis: Effects on adolescent motivation, in *Marijuana and Youth: Clinical Observations on Motivation and Learning.* Rockville, Md., National Institute on Drug Abuse, 1982.

23a. National Center for Health Statistics, Advance Report of Final Mortality Statistics, 1985. Monthly Vital Statistics Report, Vol. 36, No. 5, August 28, 1985. Washington D.C., U.S. Department of Health.

24. Bachrach L.L.: Young adult chronic patients: An analytical review of the literature. *Hosp. Community Psychiatry* 33:189-197, 1982.

25. Pepper B., Kirshner M.C., Rygleqicz H.: The young adult chronic population: Overview of a population. *Hosp. Community Psychiatry* 32:436-439, 1981.

26. Sheets J.L., Prevost J.A., Reihman J.: Young adult chronic patients: Three hypothesized subgroups. *Hosp. Community Psychiatry* 33:197-201, 1982.

27. Gruenberg E.M.: The social breakdown syndrome and its prevention, in Caplan G. (ed.): *American Handbook of Psychiatry: Child and Adolescent Psychiatry, Sociocultural and Community Psychiatry, II,* ed. 2. New York, Basic Books Inc., 1974, pp. 697-710.

28. Lamb H.R.: Young adult chronic patients: The new drifters. *Hosp. Community Psychiatry* 33:465-468, 1982.

29. Schwartz S.R., Goldfinger S.M.: The new chronic patient: Clinical characteristics of an emerging subgroup. *Hosp. Community Psychiatry* 32:470-474, 1981.

30. *Statistical Abstracts of the United States, 1988,* ed 108. Washington D.C., U.S. Department of Commerce, 1987.

31. Talbott J.A.: The emergency crisis in chronic care. *Hosp. Community Psychiatry* 32:447, 1981.

32. Prevost J.A.: Youthful chronicity: A paradox for the 80's. *Hosp. Community Psychiatry* 33:173, 1982.

33. *DSM III: American Psychiatric Association Diagnostic and Statistical Manual,* ed. 3. Washington, D.C., American Psychiatric Association, 1980.

34. *WHO Expert Committee on Addiction Producing Drugs: 13th Report,* publication 273. World Health Organization Technical Report Series, Geneva, 1964.

35. Wegscheider S., Wegscheider D.: *Family Illness: Chemical Dependency.* Crystal, Minn., Nurturing Networks, 1976 (available from Nurturing Networks, 4857 Maryland Ave. N., Crystal, MN 55428).

36. Dependency and Age: A world survey. World Health Organization, 1980.

37. Criteria Committee, National Council on Alcoholism: Criteria for the diagnosis of alcoholism. *Ann. Intern. Med.* 77:249-258, 1972.

38. Goodwin, D.W.: Alcohol in suicide and homicide. *Q.J. Stud. Alcohol* 34:144-156, 1973.

39. Winokur G., Clayton P.J.: Family history studies: IV comparison of male and female alcoholics. *Q.J. Stud. Alcohol* 29:885, 1968.

40. Schuckit M.A., Goodwin D.W., Windkur G.: A half-sibling study of alcoholism. *Am. J. Psychiatry* 128:1132-1136, 1972.

41. Ewing J.A., Rouse B.A., Pellizar E.D.: Alcohol sensitivity and ethnic background. *Am. J. Psychiatry* 131:206-210, 1974.

42. Stamatoyannoupoulas G., Chen S.H., Fukui M.: Liver alcohol dehydrogenase in Japanese: High population frequency of atypical form and its possible role in alcohol sensitivity. *Am. J. Hum. Genet.* 27:789-796, 1975.

43. Jones B.M., Jones M.K.: Male and female intoxication levels for three alcohol doses or do women really get higher than men? *Alcohol Rep.* 5:11-24, 1976.

44. McGlothin W.H.: Drug use and abuse. *Annu. Rev. Psychol.* 26:45-64, 1975.

45. Pendergast T.J. Jr.: Family characteristics associated with marijuana use among adolescents. *Int. J. Addict.* 9:827-839.

46. Hunt D.G.: Parental permissiveness as perceived by the offspring and the degree of marijuana usage among offspring. *Hum. Relations* 27:267-285, 1974.

47. Streit F., Halsted D.L., Pascale P.J.: Differences among youthful users and non users of drugs based on their perceptions of parental behavior. *Int. J. Addict.* 9:749-755, 1974.

48. Brook J.S., Lukoff I.F., Whiteman M.: Family socialization and adolescent personality and their association with adolescent use of marijuana. *J. Gen. Psychol.* 133:261-272, 1978.

49. Brook J.S., Whiteman M., Gordon A.S.: The role of the father in the son's marijuana use. *J. Gen. Psychol.* 138:81-86, 1981.

50. Fishman H.C.: A family approach to marijuana use, in *Marijuana and Youth: Clinical Observations on Motivation and Learning.* Rockville, Md., National Institute on Drug Abuse, 1982.

51. Gay G.R., Way E.L.: Pharmacology of the opiate narcotics, in Smith, D.E., Gay G.R. (eds.): *It's So Good, Don't Even Try It Once.* Englewood Cliffs, N.J., Prentice-Hall, Inc., 1972.

52. *Drug Abuse Warning Network, 1979: DAWN Annual Report,* Contract No. DEA 79-15. Report prepared for Drug Enforcement Administration and National Institute on Drug Abuse, 1980.

53. Jaffe J.H.: Drug addiction and drug abuse, in Gilman A.G., Goodman L.S., Goodman A. (eds.): *The Pharmacologic Basis of Therapeutics,* ed. 6. New York, Macmillan Publishing Co., 1980, pp. 535-584.

54. *ICD-9: The International Classification of Diseases: Clinical Modification,* 9th revision, 1978 (available from the Commission on Professional and Hospital Activities, 1968 Green Rd., Ann Arbor, MI 48105).

55. Golum M.S., Sassenrath E.N., Chapman Z.F.: An analysis of altered attention in monkeys exposed to delta-9-tetrahydrocannabinol during development. *Neurobehav. Toxicol. Teratol.* 4:469-472, 1982.

56. Goldberg L.: Quantitative studies on alcohol tolerance in man: The influence of ethyl alcohol on sensory, motor and psychological functions related to blood alcohol in normal and habituated individuals. *Acta Physiol. Scand.* 5(suppl. 16):1-128, 1943.

57. Salium I.: Delerium tremens and certain other acute sequels of alcohol abuse: A comparative clinical, social and prognostic study. *Acta Psychiatr. Scand.* 235:15-145, 1972.

58. Jones R.T., Benowitz M., Bachman J.: Clinical studies of cannabis tolerance and dependence. *Ann. N.Y. Acad. Sci.* 282:221-239, 1976.

59. Holley J.H.: Analysis of THC concentration in marijuana, hashish, and hash oil. Personal communication, 1983 (available from Project Coordinator, NIDA Marijuana Project, Research Institute of Pharmaceutical Sciences, University of Mississippi, Oxford, MS 38677).

60. *Testimony of Coy W. Waller: Marijuana-Hashish Epidemic and Its Impact on United States Security: Hearings Before the Subcommittee to Investigate the Administration of the Internal Security Act and Other Internal Security Laws of the Committee of the Judiciary.* U.S. Senate, 94th Congress, first session, May 8, 1975.

61. Turner C.E.: *The Marijuana Controversy.* Rockville, Md., American Council for Drug Education, 1981 (see ref. 143).

62. Moskowitz H., Peterson R.: *Marijuana and Driving: A Review.* Rockville, Md., American Council for Drug Education, 1982 (see ref. 143).

63. Burns M., Moskowitz H.: Alcohol, marijuana and skills performed, in *Alcohol, Drugs and Traffic Safety.* Stockholm, Almqust and Wiksell International, 1981, vol. 3, pp. 954-968.

64. Moskowitz H., Sharma S., McGlothlin W.: The effects of marijuana upon peripheral vision as a function of the information processing demands upon central vision. *Percept. Mot. Skills* 35:875-882, 1972.

65. Sharma S., Moskowitz H.: Marijuana dose study of vigilance performance. *Proceedings of the 81st Annual Conference of the American Psychological Association,* Montreal, 1973, vol. 8, pt. 2, pp. 1031-1032 (available from The American Psychological Association, 1200 17th St. N.W., Washington, D.C. 20036).

66. Klonoff H.: Acute psychological effects of marijuana in man, including acute cognitive, psychomotor and perceptual effects on driving, in Fehr K.O., Kalante H. (eds.): *Adverse Health and Behavioral Consequences of Cannabis Use.* Presented at the Addiction Research Foundation/ World Health Organization Scientific Meeting, Addiction Research Foundation, Toronto, 1982.

67. Heath R.G.: Pleasure response of human subjects to direct stimulation of the brain: Psychologic and psychodynamic considerations, in Heath R.G. (ed.): *The Role of Pleasure in Behavior.* New York, Harper & Row, 1969, pp. 219-243.

68. Heath R.G., Fitzjarrell A.T., Fontana C.J., et al.: Cannabis sativa: Effects of brain function and ultrastructure in rhesus monkeys. *Biol. Psychiatry* 15:657-690, 1980.

69. Heath R.G.: *Marijuana and the Brain*. Rockville, Md., American Council for Drug Education (see ref. 143).

70. Chapman L.F., Sassenrath E.N., Goo G.P.: Social behavior of rhesus monkeys chronically exposed to moderate amounts of delta-9-tetra-hydrocannabinol, in Nahas G.G., Paton W.D.M. (eds.): *Marijuana: Biological Effects*. Advances in Biosciences, New York, Pergamon Press, 1979, vol. 22-23, pp. 693-710.

71. Sassenrath E.N., Chapman L.F.: Primate social behavior as a method of analysis of drug action: Studies with THC in monkeys. *Fed. Proc.* 35:2238-2243, 1976.

72. McGahan J.P., Dublin A.B., Sassenrath E.N.: *Computed tomography of the brains of rhesus monkeys after long term delta-9-tetrahydro-cannabinol treatment*. Presented at the 67th Scientific Assembly and Annual Meeting of the Radiological Society of North America, Chicago, November 1981.

73. Tashkin D.P., Cohen S.: *Marijuana Smoking and Its Effects on the Lungs*. Rockville, Md., American Council for Drug Education, 1981 (see ref. 143).

74. Mann P.: Marijuana alert II: More of the grim story. *Readers Digest*, November 1980.

75. Copeland K.C., Underwood L.E., VanWyk J.J.: Marijuana smoking and pubertal arrest. *N. Engl. J. Med.* 96:1079-1080, 1980.

76. Block E.: Effects of marijuana and cannabinoids on reproduction, endocrine function, development and chromosomes, in Fehr K.O., Kalant H. (eds.): *Adverse Health and Behavioral Consequences of Cannabis Use*. Presented at the Addiction Research Foundation/World Health Organization Scientific Meeting, Addiction Research Foundation, Toronto, 1982.

77. Hembree W.C. III, Zeidenberg P., Nahas G.G.: Marijuana's effect on human gonadal function, in Nahas G.G., Patton D.M. (eds.): *Marijuana, Biological Effects: Analysis, Metabolism, Cellular Responses, Reproduction, and Brain*. New York, Pergamon Press, 1979, p. 521.

78. Harmon J., Aliapouluis M.A.: Gynecomastia in marijuana users. *N. Engl. J. Med.* 287:936, 1972.

79. Wirth P.W., Murphy J.C., El-Feraly F.S., et al.: Constituents of cannabis sativa L. XXI: Estrogenic activity of a non-cannabinoid constituent. *Experientia* 37:1181, 1980.

80. Smith C.G., Asch R.H.: *Marijuana and Reproduction*. Rockville, Md., American Council for Drug Education, 1982 (see ref. 143).

81. Bauman J.: Effect of chronic marijuana use on endocrine function of the human female. Presented at the Second Annual Conference on Marijuana: Biomedical effect and social implications, New York University Post Graduate Medical School and American Council on Marijuana, New York, 1979.

82. Munson A.E., Levy J.A., Harris L.S., et al.: Effects of delta-9-tetrachydro-cannabinol on the immune system, in Braude M.C., Szara S. (eds.): *The Pharmacology of Marijuana*. New York, Raven Press, 1976.

83. Munson A.E., Fehr K.P.: Immunological effects of cannabis, in Fehr K.O., Kalant H. (eds.): *Adverse Health and Behavioral Consequences of Cannabis Use*. Presented at the Addiction Research Foundation/ World Health Organization Scientific Meeting, Addiction Research Foundation, Toronto, 1982.

84. Ader R., Grota L.J.: Immunosuppressive effect of tetrahydrocannabinol plus cyclophosphamide. *N. Engl. J. Med.* 305:463, 1981.

85. Fried P.A.: Marijuana use in pregnant women: Neuro behavioral effects in neonates. *Drug Alcohol Depend.* 6:415-424, 1980.

86. Landsman-Dwyer S., Keller L.S., Steissguth A.P.: Naturalistic observations of newborns: Effects of maternal alcohol intake. *Alcoholism* 2:171-177, 1978.

87. Hingson R., Alpert J.J., Day N., et al.: Effects of maternal drinking and marijuana use on fetal growth and development. *Pediatrics* 70:539-545, 1982.

88. Kagen S.L.: Aspergillus: An inhalable contaminant of marijuana. *N. Engl. J. Med.* 304:483-484, 1981.

89. *Morbidity Mortality Weekly Rep.* 30:77-79: Communicable Disease Center, Atlanta, 1981.

90. Cohen S., Andrysiak T.: *The Therapeutic Potential of Marijuana's Components*. Rockville, Md., American Council for Drug Education, 1982 (see ref. 143).

91. Clifford D.: The analogues may relieve some tremors. *J.A.M.A.* 248:2215, 1982.

92. AMA Council on Scientific Affairs: Marijuana: Its health hazards and therapeutic potentials. *J.A.M.A.* 246:1823-1827, 1981.

93. Committee on Drugs: What You Should Know About Marijuana. Evanston Ill., American Academy of Pediatrics, 1981.

94. Koop C.E.: Statement made in Public Health Service bulletin (ADM) 82-1216, August, 12, 1982, referring to the following article: *Marijuana and Health: Ninth Report to the U.S. Congress from the Sec-*

retary of Health and Human Services 1982. U.S. Dept. of Health and Human Services, Public Health Service, 1982.

95. Relman A. (ed.): *Marijuana and Health*. Washington, D.C., National Academy Press, 1982, (available from the Institute of Medicine, 2101 Constitution Ave., Washington, D.C. 20418).

96. Eckardt M.J., Harford T.C., Kaelber C.T., et al.: Health hazards associated with alcohol consumption. *J.A.M.A.* 246:648-666, 1981.

97. Franks H.M., Hensley V.R., Hensley W.J., et al.: The relationship between alcohol dosage and performance decrements in humans. *J. Stud. Alcohol* 37:284-297, 1976.

98. Parsons O.A.: Neuro psychologic deficits in alcoholics: Facts and fancies. *Alcoholism* 1:51-56, 1977.

99. Parker E.D., Noble E.P.: Alcohol consumption and cognitive functioning in social drinkers. *J. Stud. Alcohol* 38:1224-1232, 1977.

100. Lefebure-D'Amour M., Shahani B., Young R., et al.: Importance of studying sural conduction and late responses in evaluation of alcoholic subjects. *Neurology* 2:95-110, 1977.

101. Medhus A.: Mortality among female alcoholics. *Scand. J. Soc. Med.* 3:111-115, 1975.

102. Goodwin D.W.: Alcohol in suicide and homicide. *Q.J. Stud. Alcohol* 34:144-156, 1973.

103. Gordon G.G., Southern A.L.: Metabolic effects of alcohol on the endocrine system, in Liebea C.S. (ed.): *Metabolic Aspects of Alcoholism*. Baltimore, University Park Press, 1977, pp. 249-302.

104. Masters W.H., Johnson V.E.: *Human Sexual Inadequacy*. Boston, Little, Brown & Co., 1970.

105. Jenkins J.J., Connolly J.: Adrenocortical response to ethanol in man. *Br. Med. J.* 2:804-805, 1968.

106. Fuchs A.R., Wagner G.: Effect of alcohol on release of oxytocin. *Nature* 198:92-94, 1963.

107. Eggleton M.G.: Diuretic action of alcohol in man. *J. Physiol.* 101:172-191, 1942.

108. DeMakis J.G., Proskey A., Rohimtoola S.H., et al.: The natural course of alcoholic cardiomyopathy. *Ann. Intern. Med.* 80:293-297, 1974.

109. Lyons H.A., Saltzman A.: Diseases of the respiratory tract in alcoholics, in Kissin B., Belerter H. (eds.): *The Biology of Alcoholism: Clinical Pathology*. New York, Plenum Publishing Corp., 1974, pp. 403-434.

110. Edmundson H.A.: Pathology of alcoholism. *Am. J. Clin. Pathol.* 74:725-742, 1980.

111. U.S. Vital Statistics 1975. National Cancer Center for Health Statistics, U.S. Government Printing Office, 1975.

112. Reeve V.K.: *Incidents of Marijuana in California Impaired Driver Population.* Sacramento, Calif., California State Dept. of Justice, 1979.

113. Warner R.H., Rosett A.L.: The effects of drinking on offspring. *J. Stud. Alcohol* 36:1395-1420, 1975.

114. Rouguette J.: Thesis, Paris, 1957.

115. Lemoine P., Harrousseau H., Borteyru J.P., et al.: Les l'enfants de parents alcooliques: Anomalies observées à propos de 127 cas. *Oest. Med.* 21:476-482, 1968.

116. Jones K.L., Smith D.W., Streissguth A.P., et al.: Outcome in offspring in chronic alcoholic women. *Lancet* 1:1076, 1974.

117. Hanson J.W., Streissguth A.P., Smith D.W.: The effects of moderate alcohol consumption during pregnancy on fetal growth and morphogenesis. *J. Pediatr.* 92:457-460, 1978.

118. Streissguth A.P., Martin D.C., Barr H.M.: *Neonatal Brazelton Assessment and Relationship to Maternal Alcohol Intake,* International Congress Series No. 426. Fifth International Conference on Birth Defects, Montreal, 1977, p. 62.

119. Smith W.F.: *Drug Traffic Today: Challenge and Response,* Drug Enforcement vol. 9, No. 1. U.S. Department of Justice, Drug Enforcement Administration, 1982.

120. Abelson H.I., Fishburne P.M., Cirin I.H.: *National Survey on Drug Abuse, 1977: A Nationwide Survey. Youth, Young Adults and Older Adults, I: Main Findings,* publication No. (ADM) 78-618. U.S. Dept. of Health, Education and Welfare, U.S. Government Printing Office, 1977.

121. Anderson K., Cale B.W., Jackson D.S., et al.: Crashing on cocaine. *Time,* April 11, 1983, pp. 22-31.

122. Catanzaro R.J.: The Palm Beach Institute, West Palm Beach, Fla. Personal communication, 1982. (The Palm Beach Institute, 1014 N. Olive Ave., West Palm Beach, FL 33401.)

123. Thompson T., Pickens R.: Stimulant self-administration by animals: Some comparisons with opiate self-administration. *Fed. Proc.* 29:6-12, 1970.

124. DeLeon G.: An intervention model, in deSilva R., DuPont R.L., Russell G.K. (eds.): *Treating the Marijuana Dependent Person.* Rockville, Md., American Council for Drug Education, 1981, pp. 44-48 (see ref. 143).

125. Peterson R.C.: Cocaine: The lessons of history, in *Cocaine: A Second Look*. Rockville, Md., American Council for Drug Education, 1983, pp. 7-16 (see ref. 143).

126. Byck R. (ed.): *Cocaine Papers: Sigmund Freud*. New York, Stonehill Publishing Co., 1974.

127. Cohen S.: A cocaine primer, in *Cocaine: A Second Look*. Rockville, Md., American Council for Drug Education, 1983, (see ref. 143).

128. Jeri F.R., Sanchez C., Del Pozo T., et al.: The syndrome of coca paste. *J. Psychedelic Drugs* 10:361-370, 1978.

129. Paly D., VanDyke C., Jatlow P., et al.: Cocaine: Plasma levels after coca paste smoking, in *Cocaine 1980*. Lima, Peru, Pacific Press, 1980, pp. 106-110.

130. Jeri F.R.: The coca paste epidemic in South America, in *Cocaine: A Second Look*. Rockville, Md., American Council for Drug Education, 1983, pp. 23-31, (see ref. 143).

131. Coleman D.L., Ross T., Naughton J.: Myocardial ischemia and infarction related to recreational cocaine use. *West. J. Med.* 136:444-446, 1982.

132. National Institute of Drug Abuse: Data From the Drug Abuse Warning Network (DAWN), Semiannual Report, Trend Data, July–December, 1987. Series G, No. 21, Washington D.C., U.S. Department of Public Health, Drug Abuse and Health Administration.

133. Byck R., VanDyke C.: What are the effects of cocaine in man? *Cocaine 1977*. Rockville, Md., National Institute on Drug Abuse, 1977, pp. 97-117.

134. Post R.M.: Cocaine psychosis: A continuum model. *Am. J. Psychiatry* 132:225-231, 1975.

135. Fischman M.W., Schuster C.R., Rosnekov L., et al.: Cardio-vascular and subjective effects of intravenous cocaine administration in humans. *Arch. Gen. Psychiatry* 33:983-989, 1976.

136. Freedman D.X.: The use and abuse of LSD. *Arch. Gen. Psychiatry* 18:300-347, 1968.

137. Jacobs R.: Deaths, arrests related to use of PCP increasing. *Pediatr. News,* October 1981, p. 14.

138. Tenant F.: Heroin use booming in L.A. area. *Dallas Times Herald,* March 19, 1982, p. 12.

139. Robins L.: *The Vietnam Drug User Returns: Final Report, Sept. 1973.* U.S. Government Printing Office, Series A, No. 2. Special action office monograph, 1977.

140. Nahas G.G., Frick H.C. II: *Drug Abuse in the Modern World: A*

Perspective for the Eighties. New York, Pergamon Press, 1981.

141. Nahas G.G.: *Keep Off the Grass.* New York, Pergamon Press, 1979.

142. Russell G.K.: *Marijuana Today.* New York, The Myron Institute for Adult Education, 1982 (available from The Myron Institute for Adult Education, 136 E. 64th St., New York, NY 10021).

143. American Council for Drug Education, 6193 Executive Blvd., Rockville, MD 20852, (301) 984-5700.

144. Lindsey R., Harmetz A.: Hollywood's drug use reportedly at 'epidemic' level. *New York Times,* Nov. 2, 1982.

145. DeMott J.S., Ferenbaugh D., Mandelkorn P.: Puffing hard just to keep up. *Time,* July 18, 1983, pp. 40-41.

146. *Federal Strategy for Prevention of Drug Abuse and Drug Trafficking, 1982: The Drug Abuse Office and Treatment Act of 1972.* Office of Policy Development, Drug Abuse Policy Office, Washington, D.C.

147. *Statement of Mitchell Rosenthal before Subcommittee on Criminal Justice.* U.S. Senate, 96th Congress, 2nd Session, Jan. 17, 1980.

148. Kandel D., Kessler R., Margulies R.: Antecedents of adolescent initiation into stages of drug use: A developmental analysis. *J. Youth Adolescence* 7:13-48, 1978.

149. Jessor R.: A psychological perspective on adolescent substance use, in Litt I. (ed.): *Adolescent Substance Abuse.* Ross Roundtables on Critical Approaches to Common Pediatric Problems. Columbus, Ohio, Ross Laboratories, 1983.

150. Elkind D.: Developmental structuralism of Jean Piaget, in Kaplan H.I., Freedman A.M., Sadock B.J. (eds.): *Comprehensive Textbook of Psychiatry,* Baltimore, Williams & Wilkins Co., 1980, vol. 3, pp. 371-378.

151. Kaplan H.I., Sadock B.J.: Eric Erikson in theories of personality and psychopathology: Other schools, in Kaplan H.I., Freedman A.M., Sadock B.J. (eds.): *Comprehensive Textbook of Psychiatry.* Baltimore, Williams & Wilkins Co., 1980, vol. 3, pp. 798-805.

152. Milman D.H.: Effect on children and adolescents of mind-altering drugs with special reference to cannabis, in Nahas G.G., Frick H.C. (eds.): *Drug Abuse in The Modern World.* New York, Pergamon Press, pp. 47-56.

153. Jessor R., Jessor S.L.: Adolescent development and the onset of drinking. *J. Stud. Alcohol* 36:27-51, 1975.

154. Jessor R., Chase J.A., Donovan J.E.: Psychosocial correlates of marijuana use and problem drinking in a national sample of adolescents. *Am. J. Public Health* 70:604-613, 1980.

155. Glenn H.S.: *The Developmental Approach to Preventing Problem Dependencies*. Bethesda, Md., Family Development Institute, 1977.

156. Coopersmith S.: *The Antecedents of Self Esteem*. Palo Alto, Calif., Consulting Psychologists Press, Inc., 1981.

157. Pendergast T.J. Jr., Schaefer E.S.: Correlates of drinking and drunkenness among high school students. *Q. J. Stud. Alcohol.* 35:232-242, 1974.

158. Horney K.: *Neuroses and Human Growth*. New York, W.W. Norton & Co., Inc., 1950.

159. Adler A.: *The Practice and Theory of Individual Psychology*. Totowa, New Jersey, Littlefield, Adams & Co., 1968.

160. Misseldine H.: *Feelings and Their Medical Significance*. Columbus, Ohio, Ross Laboratories, 1970-1975 (various issues).

161. Varenhurst B.: The adolescent society, in *Adolescent Peer Pressure: Theory, Correlates and Program Implications for Drug Abuse Prevention* Rockville, Md., U.S. Department of Health and Human Services, National Institute on Drug Abuse, 1981.

162. Resnick H.S., Gibbs J.: Types of peer program approaches, in *Adolescent Peer Pressure: Theory, Correlates and Program Implications for Drug Abuse Prevention*. Rockville, Md., U.S. Department of Health and Human Services, National Institute on Drug Abuse, 1981.

163. Resnick H.S., Adams T.: *Channel One: A Government/Private Sector Partnership for Drug Abuse Prevention*. Rockville, Md., National Institute on Drug Abuse.

164. Westin J.: *The Coming Parent Revolution*. Chicago, Rand McNally & Co., 1981.

165. Manatt M.: *Parents, Peers and Pot*. Rockville, Md., U.S. Dept. of Health and Human Services, National Institute on Drug Abuse, 1979.

166. National Federation of Parents for Drug-Free Youth, 1820 Franwall Ave., Room 16, Silver Springs, MD 20902, (301) 649-7100.

167. Parent Resources for Drug Education, Robert W. Woodruff Building, Volunteer Service Center, Suite 1216, 100 Edgewood Ave. N.E., Atlanta, GA 30303, 1-800-241-9746.

168. Chappel J.N.: Physician attitudes and the treatment of alcohol and drug dependent patients. *J. Psychedelic Drugs* 10:27, 1978.

169. Chappel J.N.: Attitudinal barriers to physician involvement with drug abusers. *J.A.M.A.* 224:1011, 1973.

170. Cohen C.P., White E.H., Schoolar J.C.: Interpersonal patterns of personality for drug-abusing patients and their therapeutic implications. *Arch. Gen. Psychiatry* 24:353, 1971.

171. Rachel J.V., Maisto S.A., Guess L.L., et al.: *Alcohol Use Among Adolescents,* Contract No. ADM 281-70-0022. Report prepared for the National Institute on Alcohol Abuse and Alcoholism, 1980.

172. Selzer M.L.: The Michigan alcoholism screening test (MAST): The quest for a new diagnostic instrument. *Am. J. Psychiatry* 127:1653, 1971.

173. Clark S., Turner J., Bastiani R.: *Emit cannabinoid assay,* Clinical Study No. 74, Summary Report. Palo Alto, Calif. SYVA Co., 1980.

174. *New one-minute Emit-dou cannabinoid assay.* Palo Alto, Calif., SYVA Co., 1979.

175. Alcott H.: Urine testing for marijuana use: Implications in corrections, in Blasinsky M., Russell G.K. (eds.): *Urine Testing for Marijuana Use: Implications for a Variety of Settings.* Rockville, Md., American Council for Drug Education, 1981, pp. 28-30 (see ref. 143).

176. Blasinsky M., Russell G.K.: Methods of testing and analysis, in Blasinsky M., Russell G.K. (eds.): *Urine Testing for Marijuana Use: Implications for a Variety of Settings.* Rockville, Md., American Council for Drug Education, 1981, pp. 8-12 (see ref 143).

176a. H.H.S. Mandatory Guidelines for Federal Workplace Drug Testing Programs: Final Guidelines, April 11, 1988. Washington, D.C., Department of Health and Human Services.

177. Wynstra N.: Urinalysis screening for marijuana use: Legal and ethical considerations, in Blasinsky M., Russell G.K. (eds.): *Urine Testing for Marijuana Use: Implications for a Variety of Settings.* Rockville, Md., American Council for Drug Education, 1981, pp. 15-18 (see ref. 143).

178. Voth H.M.: How to Get Your Child Off Marijuana. Stamford, Conn., Citizens for Informed Choices on Marijuana, 1979 (available from the Parents' Resource Institute of Drug Education, see ref. 166).

179. Brownell S.: How I got my daughter to stop smoking pot. *Good Housekeeping,* March 1979, pp. 112-120 (available from the American Council for Drug Education, see ref. 143).

180. *Helping Your Child Resist the Marijuana Culture.* Austin, Tex., Citizens for Informed Choices on Marijuana, Drug Abuse Research and Education Foundation, Inc., 1979. (available from the Drug Abuse Research and Education Foundation, Inc., 7800 Shoal Creek Blvd., Suite 318 W., Austin, TX 78757).

181. Fists and Hearts: The Story of PDAP. Dallas, Palmer Drug Abuse Program, 1981 (available from Palmer Drug Abuse Program, 3966 McKinney, Dallas, TX 75204).

182. Edwards G., Orford J., Egert S., et al.: Alcoholism: A controlled trial of "treatment" and "advice." *J. Stud. Alcohol* 38:1004-1031, 1977.

183. Kanfer F.H., Goldstein A. (eds.): *Maximizing Treatment Gains*. New York, Academic Press, 1980.

184. *Alcoholism Anonymous World Services*. New York, Alcoholics Anonymous, 1955.

185. Sells S.B.: Treatment effectiveness, in DuPont R.L., Goldstein A., O'Donnell J. (eds.): *Handbook on Drug Abuse*. National Institute on Drug Abuse, U.S. Government Printing Office, 1979, pp. 105-118.

186. Baron J.D.: *The Parent Handbook of Drug Abuse: Prevention and Treatment* ed. 5. Pasadena, Tex., Drug Abuse Programs of America, 1981 (available from Drug Abuse Programs of America, P.O. Box 5487, Pasadena, TX 77505).

187. Neff P.: *Tough Love: How Parents Can Deal With Drug Abuse*. Nashville, Tenn., Abingdon Press, 1982.

188. Savage R.: Palmer Drug Abuse Program in Midland, Tex. Personal communication, 1983.

189. DeLeon G.: An intervention model, in deSilva R., DuPont R.L., Russell G.K. (eds.): *Treating the Marijuana Dependent Person*. Rockville, Md., American Council for Drug Education, 1981, pp. 44-48 (see ref. 143).

190. Manuel D., Wilkerson D., Yake R.: *The Jesus Factor*. Plainfield, N.J., Logos International, 1977.

191. Bray R.M., Hubbard R.L., Rachal J.V., et al.: *Client Characteristics, Behavior and Treatment Outcomes*. Triangle Park, N.C., Research Triangle Institute, 1981 (available from Research Triangle Institute, Box 12194, Research Triangle Park, NC 27709).

192. DuPont R.L.: Critique of chapter 9, this book. Personal communication, 1983.

193. Chafetz M.E., Blane H.T., Hill M.J.: The doctor's voice: Post-dictor of successful referral of alcoholic patients, in *Frontiers of Alcoholism*. New York, Science House, 1970.

194. Goldstein A.P. Therapist-patient expectancies, in *Psychotherapy*. New York, Macmillan Publishing Co., Inc., 1962.

195. Mendelson J.H., Wexler D., Kubansky P.E., et al.: Physician's attitudes towards alcoholic patients. *Arch. Gen. Psychiatry* 11:392, 1964.

196. Knox W.J.: Attitudes of psychiatrists and psychologists towards alcoholism. *Am. J. Psychiatry* 127:1675, 1971.

197. Selzer M.L.: Alcoholism and alcoholic psychoses, in Kaplan H.I., Freedman A.M., Sadock B.J. (eds.): *Comprehensive Textbook of Psy-*

chiatry. Baltimore, Williams & Wilkins, Co., 1980, vol. 3, p. 148.

198. Mackenzie R.G.: The adolescent as a drug abuser: A paradigm for intervention. *Pediatr. Ann.* 11:659-668, 1982.

199. Hawley R.A.: *The Purposes of Pleasure: A Reflection on Youth and Drugs.* Wellesley Hills, Mass., The Independent School Press, 1983.

200. Rudolph W.: The Northside High School Experience. Personal communication, 1983.

201. Landrigan P.J., Powell K.E., James L.M.,et al.: Paraquat and marijuana: Epidemiologic risk assessment. *Am. J. Public Health* 73:784-788, 1983.

202. Hawks R.L.: *Chemistry and Toxicology of Paraquat-Contaminated Marijuana.* Rockville, Md., National Institute on Drug Abuse, 1978.

203. Berry Jr., R.E., Boland J.P.: *The Economic Cost of Alcohol Abuse.* New York, Free Press, 1977.

204. Bejerot N.: *Prevention and Control of Drug Abuse Epidemics.* Presented at the 1983 Conference of the Parents' Research Institute of Drug Education, Atlanta, 1983.

205. Moore R.S., Hofmann A.D. (eds.): *American Academy of Pediatrics: Conference on Consent and Confidentiality in Adolescent Health Care.* Evanston, Ill., American Academy of Pediatrics, 1982.

206. Roush G.C., Thompson B.A., Berberian R.M.: Psychoactive medicinal and non-medicinal drug use among high school students. *Pediatrics* 66:709-715, 1980.

207. Skom J.H., Brill H., Cohen S., et al.: Drug Abuse Related to Prescribing Practices. Report of the A.M.A. Council on Scientific Affairs as adopted by the House of Delegates, June 1981.

208. Schulman J.L.: Reprise: Speak up for pediatricians. *J. Pediatr.* 102:5, 1983.

209. Barton P.: *NFP Educational Kit and Public Speaking Manual for Drug Education.* National Federation of Parents for Drug-Free Youth, 1982 (available from the Drug Abuse Research and Education Foundation, Inc., 7800 Shoal Creek Blvd. Suite 318 W., Austin, TX 78757).

Index